REBEL
FOOTPRINTS

REBEL
FOOTPRINTS

*A Guide to Uncovering
London's Radical History*

David Rosenberg

Foreword by Billy Bragg

PlutoPress
www.plutobooks.com

First published 2015 by Pluto Press
345 Archway Road, London N6 5AA

www.plutobooks.com

British Library Cataloguing in Publication Data
A catalogue record for this book is available from the British Library

ISBN 978 0 7453 3410 3 Hardback
ISBN 978 0 7453 3409 7 Paperback
ISBN 978 1 7837 1329 5 PDF eBook
ISBN 978 1 7837 1331 8 Kindle eBook
ISBN 978 1 7837 1330 1 EPUB eBook

10 9 8 7 6 5 4 3 2 1

Typeset and designed by Melanie Patrick
Maps by Chris Browne
Simultaneously printed by CPI Antony Rowe, Chippenham, UK
and
Edwards Bros in the United States of America

For Julia, Jacob and Reuben,
and in memory of a ground-breaking London historian,
Bill Fishman (1921-2014)

CONTENTS

ACKNOWLEDGEMENTS

I would like to thank the staff at Pluto Press, who have been consistently encouraging and helpful. Thanks to the staff of the libraries and archives who have provided access to historical materials and assistance with images: Bishopsgate Institute (special thanks to Stefan Dickers); British Library Newspaper Archive, Hull History Centre; Labour History Archive at the People's History Museum; LSE Reading Room; Marx Memorial Library; Modern Records Centre, Warwick University; Southwark Local History Library; Tower Hamlets Local History Library; TUC Library Collections; Wandsworth Heritage Service; Women's Library at LSE; and the Working Class Movement Library. Thanks to City Lit students who road-tested several walks and gave invaluable feedback. Special thanks to Chris Browne at Pluto Press for mapping the walks so imaginatively and helping with photos, and to musician, activist and fellow West Ham fan, Billy Bragg, for his foreword. Finally I would like to thank Julia Bard for expert editorial advice and personal encouragement and support.

FOREWORD

Half way up Whitehall, there's a massive equestrian statue in the middle of the road. A rotund figure sits astride his horse, nose in air, wearing a cocked hat, a field marshal's uniform and sporting huge mutton-chop sideburns. Inspection of the plinth reveals this to be George, Duke of Cambridge. No, me neither.

He's one of a number of martial figures impeding the traffic down Whitehall, few of whom would be readily recognisable to the British public. Recent years have witnessed a laudable attempt to democratise this space, with statues to those who fought and served in the two world wars, but this is still a thorough-fare peopled with memorials to those who defended the British Empire.

Where are the statues to those who fought and struggled for the rights of the British people? Their memorials are all around us: the universal franchise; the eight-hour day; the NHS. None of these great monuments bears the names of those who battled to win them.

The stories of those men and women have been largely overlooked by imperial history, but the Britain they lived in is still tangible if you have a willing guide. Step forward David Rosenberg, who invites us to follow in the footsteps of the London radicals who shaped our modern society. The stories he reveals will resonate with anyone who keeps abreast of current affairs.

Rosenberg highlights the politics of identity in Fournier Street, where a Huguenot chapel, converted into a Jewish synagogue, is now a mosque. The free speech debates on Clerkenwell Green, with their orators, listeners, disputants and mockers remind one of the daily discourse on Twitter. The fight against those who would blame immigrants for all of society's ills colours many of the pages and, even in the drawing-rooms of Bloomsbury, we find ourselves in the midst of the unending struggle against inequality.

As in our post-industrial times, the closer we look, the more we see that the battle lines, rather than being all about ideological differences, were more often focused on the challenge of holding those in power to account.

David Rosenberg's intervention could not be more timely. As the British state is devolved into its composite nations, the English, deprived of the union jack, will be forced to construct a post-imperial identity. By offering us a guide book to our radical past, Rosenberg reminds us of the strong tradition of dissent that has shaped our history and made us who we are.

Billy Bragg

INTRODUCTION

On 13 May 1833 around 3,000 people gathered for a political rally in London's Coldbath Fields – an open space lying in the shadow of London's largest prison, the Middlesex House of Correction. That prison occupied the plot of land between Farringdon Road and Gray's Inn Road where Mount Pleasant Postal Sorting Office stood throughout the twentieth century. Until 1850 this prison housed men, women and children – some as young as six years old – usually serving short-term sentences. Its capacity rose from 600 in 1825 to 1,150 by 1832. Its inmates were typically described through their economic roles, 'beggars, tramps, thieves and debtors', though this prison occasionally held political radicals too. In 1820 it had temporarily housed the 'Cato Street conspirators' who had been accused of plotting to murder the Prime Minister and his entire Cabinet. Five of the conspirators were later hanged and beheaded at Newgate prison.

After 1850 the Middlesex House of Correction housed only male offenders over the age of 17. It became notorious for its widespread use of solitary confinement, its adoption of the 'silent system' which forbade conversation between prisoners, its use of leg-irons restricting prisoners' movements, its paltry bread and water diets, and its rigorous application of 'hard labour'. Some of these tasks were unproductive, making them especially humiliating for the prisoners. The poets Coleridge and Southey coined a verse:[1]

---

1 'The Devil's Thoughts', 1835 version published in Walter Thornbury, *Old and New London*, Vol. 2, 1878.

As he went through Cold-Bath Fields, he saw
a solitary cell;
And the Devil was pleased, for it gave him a hint
for improving his prisons in hell.

Barely a stone's throw away, stood another prison, Clerkenwell Bridewell House of Detention. Less than a mile further east was Whitecross Street debtor's prison.

Harsh and demeaning as the treatment was in these institutions – and Coldbath Fields certainly evoked the most fear – the rally in May 1833 was not about the treatment of prisoners or even about prisons at all. It was protesting about more mundane matters: rising prices, low pay and increasing unemployment, all compounded by the complete lack of political representation for the people suffering economic hardship. The much vaunted 'Great' Reform Act of 1832, passed by a Whig government, had got rid of some of the rotten boroughs, such as Amersham, represented by two MPs from one large-landowning family – the Drakes – on a tiny electorate from the 1600s. It created new constituencies in the larger cities that had grown up in the Industrial Revolution but the electorate was still tiny. Around one in six adult males now had the vote, all of them men of property. Birmingham, Leeds and Manchester gained their first MPs, but, in general, the newly emerging urban centres were still poorly represented.

The organisation that mobilised London's discontented people at that moment was the grandly named National Union of the Working Classes (NUWC). Its constitution proclaimed three key principles:

- to secure for every workingman the full value of his labour;
- to protect workingmen against the tyranny of masters and manufacturers;
- to bring about parliamentary reform (including suffrage for all adult males).

The government was in no mood to tolerate openly rebellious behaviour from the 'lower orders'. The Home Secretary, Lord Melbourne, declared the gathering at Coldbath Fields illegal. The NUWC, convinced that its protest was justified, went ahead with the rally anyway. However, their numbers were soon more than matched by those of the police, who kettled the demonstrators. When the protesters were completely penned in, the police attacked them in order to break up the rally.

It was just four years since Sir Robert Peel's Act of Parliament had established the Metropolitan Police. The novice force had hardly any experience of handling demonstrations, though they would soon get more practice than they might have wished for. On that day the demonstrators fought back and three policemen were stabbed. Sergeant Brooks and PC Redwood later recovered from their knife wounds. PC Robert Culley stumbled into a nearby inn, announced that he wasn't feeling well, then collapsed and died.

An inquest was held with a jury comprising 17 men, most of them bakers from the nearby Gray's Inn district. The coroner set out the case and sent the jury to deliberate. He directed them to record a verdict of 'wilful murder'. They discussed the evidence for 30 minutes, then announced that they had a verdict on which 16 of the 17 jurors were agreed. PC Culley's death, they declared, was not wilful murder but a case of 'justifiable homicide'. Describing the police behaviour as 'ferocious, brutal and unprovoked', their foreman reported: 'We are firmly of the opinion that if they [the police] had acted with moderation the deceased would not have been stabbed.'

The coroner might have seen this verdict as perverse but it was popular among ordinary people. So popular that cheering crowds carried the jurors through the local streets that night in a torch-lit procession. Their rebellious stand, defending the right to protest, won support beyond the working poor. Moneyed supporters laid on special treats for the jurors: a boat trip along the Thames to Twickenham and a free theatre visit to see 'A Rowland for Oliver'. Each juror also received a medallion inscribed 'in honour of the men who nobly withstood the dictation of a coroner ...'

This single incident reveals so much about London in the early 1830s. Economic divisions were widely acknowledged, though use of the term 'working classes' – plural – indicated that there was still a long way to travel before those exploited in different sectors would perceive their more profound commonality. Oppositional forces, though, had begun to use the tools of mobilisation and protest – leaflets, placards and posters – and could mobilise beyond an immediate locality. Public protest was on the agenda and activists acquainted themselves with suitable outdoor venues. They were not cowed by the threats of politicians, backed by an emergent police force ready to use violent means to quell protest, and courts freely dishing out severe sentences.

Over the next hundred years London was a great centre of agitation and protest. Assorted groups organised and campaigned for political and economic goals and fought for rights they believed they were absolutely entitled to claim. Certain locations became especially associated with great protest rallies and platforms for free speech by political agitators: Trafalgar Square, Hyde Park (Speakers' Corner), and Parliament Square in central London; Kennington Common and Southwark Park in south London;[2] and Clerkenwell Green and Victoria Park, north of the river heading east. As more and more areas gave birth to their own significant individuals and campaigning organisations, these groups established local pitches from which to share their concerns and demands with their public. Politics moved from the austere, forbidding surroundings of the House of Commons in Westminster, to street corners, squares and public spaces.

This book tells stories of how defiant grassroots Londoners responded to their circumstances from the beginning of the 1830s until the end of the 1930s. It takes the reader into the heart of several localities where campaigning groups were born and developed; where they declared their agendas, captured the imagination of their wider public, mobilised for actions, took on powerful forces, suffered great setbacks but also won important victories.

The book explores these people's lives to find out what motivated and inspired them to act. It illuminates the methods they adopted and, with the aid of specially commissioned maps and suggested routes for each chapter, invites you to walk in their footsteps. The skyline of our city is rapidly changing. The traces of a rebellious history are being literally erased before our eyes. This book attempts to resist that process. It cannot put back the bricks and mortar of the buildings where momentous decisions

---

2 In 1854 the government enclosed Kennington Common, converted it into a park and banned political meetings.

were made or powerful words spoken but it can help to preserve our collective memory of these struggles for better lives for people in the capital.

Londoners today are not short of issues to protest about. And as we continue to march through the streets of our capital city, holding placards and banners, singing, blowing whistles, chanting slogans and voicing our demands, we are walking on well-trodden ground. But we are also elevated, as we stand on the shoulders of those rebels who came before us, who refused to accept the status quo, and who set out on the paths of protest.

This book honours and celebrates these rebels who dreamt of a better life and aims to ensure that their ideals continue to live in the hearts and minds of those who campaign for justice and equality in our metropolis today.

1

REBELLIOUS CITY

London from the 1830s to the 1930s

[A]gainst those who laud the present state of society, with its unjustly rich and its unjustly poor, with its palaces and its slums, its millionaires and its paupers, be it ours to proclaim that there is a higher ideal in life than that of being first in the race for wealth ... Be it ours to declare that health, comfort, leisure, culture, plenty for every individual are far more desirable than the breathless struggle for existence, furious trampling down of the weak by the strong, huge fortunes accumulated out of the toil of others, to be handed down to those who had done nothing to earn them.

Annie Besant, *Our Corner*

The writer and activist Annie Besant wrote these extraordinary lines in the mid-1880s, when she was living in the comfort of London's West End but becoming increasingly immersed, albeit transiently, in the struggles for better lives led by impoverished Eastenders. She depicts a city mired in conflict between the powerful and the marginalised, the exploiters and the exploited, and the brazen sense of entitlement by those who were ravaging the lives of an underclass. Her description reads just as hauntingly

7

today as the struggles for a more equal city that marked the decades after the Second World War have given rise to a widening gap between London's rich and poor. The wealthy classes are rampantly recolonising significant pockets of inner London, expanding the number of gated communities, installing exclusive boutiques, gyms, restaurants and luxury outlets, while pushing longstanding residents towards the city limits, where new pound shops open weekly.

But Besant was writing, speaking and acting in the middle of a remarkable era of campaigning and protest, in which significant numbers of London's citizens of all ages showed that they refused to accept injustice. Five decades earlier, the class-conscious Chartist movement placed the struggle for political rights firmly on the map, unimpressed by a 'Great Reform Act' that failed to live up to its title, offering crumbs to elements of a rising urban bourgeoisie. It adopted its People's Charter at the Crown and Anchor pub on the Strand and launched the first mass struggles for democratic rights in London. Fifty years *after* Besant's blast at inequality, the people of the East End and of Bermondsey built barricades on the streets to thwart the ambitions of Oswald Mosley, a true son of the aristocracy, who had focused his attention especially on the capital city. He had mesmerised segments of all London's classes including significant numbers of workers, and built a para-military movement, spreading hatred and promoting dictatorship.

In the intervening decades Londoners continually gave proof that this is indeed a rebellious city. The fear stalking London's elites in the late 1840s brought troops into the capital to guard strategic buildings, while Queen Victoria was spirited away from potential harm. In the 1860s protesters demanding political reform unceremoniously removed the railings enclosing its most elegant park. The 1880s saw bloody battles for free speech in Trafalgar Square and an explosion of industrial struggles, spontaneously ignited by atrociously paid women workers in London's original and largest manufacturing area – the East End. During the 1900s and 1910s, women's economic struggles in London were temporarily overshadowed by political battles. Rebellious women were imprisoned for smashing windows of shops along London's showpiece thoroughfare of Oxford Street, attacking government property and randomly setting fire to pillar boxes, as they forced politicians to notice and respond to their agenda for change. Even behind bars they found ways to continue to challenge the authorities. In the 1920s, two London prisons – Brixton and Holloway – temporarily hosted elected councillors who refused to accede to demands on them that they considered an injustice and an outrage to the people who democratically elected them.

But rebellion has not always taken such sensational forms. Other dissenters adopted peaceful means to challenge and subvert the orthodoxies of the age, expose hypocrisies and pose questions and demands, using the power of the written word. They published radical newspapers, wrote incendiary pamphlets and generated mass petitions that simultaneously shook the powerful and gave heart and inspiration to those struggling for change.

This book shines a spotlight on a dramatic set of interlocking struggles that took place in London from the early nineteenth century to the eve of the Second World War. Rebellious Londoners spoke several different mother tongues but had a common campaigning language. They learned from each other's struggles and derived strength from each other's efforts and victories. Many participants in these rebellious struggles had their eyes open to the wider world and were convinced internation- alists. Some among them found creative ways to give solidarity to their counterparts in other countries and publicise their causes here, but their efforts were primarily focused on democracy, freedom and equality in the city where they lived and worked.

Who were these Londoners? In 1831 this was a city of 1.7 million people; a century later the population of inner London alone had reached 5 million, with another 3 million in the growing suburbs of outer London. The development of the railways from the 1850s and 1860s displaced several very poor communities, without any compensation, but also enabled a massive expansion of factories and workshops. This drew new communities to the capital and, in turn, provided a basis for large numbers of workers to come together to fight collectively for better pay and conditions within their workplaces. The trade union movement expanded, especially among men in skilled work. An all-London Trades Council was formed in 1860, and towards the end of the nineteenth century local trades councils emerged, enabling workers across industries to support each other's struggles. By the 1890s a 'new unionism' was adding swathes of low-skilled and unskilled workers to a bigger and more combative trade union movement in London.

At the time when Annie Besant was writing, one out of three Londoners had been born outside of the metropolis. Some had travelled to the capital from other towns and villages within Britain; others arrived as international migrants seeking oppor- tunities for economic advancement. In many cases they also sought greater freedom, security and refuge from persecution and oppression. London had long been a city of migrants, but the numbers increased dramatically towards the end of the nineteenth century and in the early part of the twentieth century.

The influx and settlement of these people coincided with an upsurge of rebellious political movements. But this was not just a coincidence. Although new migrants were reluctant to put themselves in a position of confrontation with the authorities here, they were also determined that their children should have freer and more prosperous lives than they had done. They arrived with a finely tuned sense of the necessity to fight for their rights, and with a determination not to let those rights slip away once they had grasped them. Many new Londoners threw themselves into struggles for better lives and played an outstanding role in London's rebellious campaigns. Chapters 2 and 6 feature the contributions of individual migrants of Caribbean and Indian heritage, Chapters 3, 4 and 10, those of migrants from Jewish and Irish heritage.

Grassroots Movements

This book is about grassroots movements for change. To the extent that it celebrates outstanding and iconoclastic individuals, it highlights those who based their hopes for change on a collective movement. Some of these individuals are more well known, such as the docks' strike leader Ben Tillett, suffragette Emmeline Pankhurst, secularist and anti-war campaigner Bertrand Russell, writer and activist, Eleanor Marx and Labour politician George Lansbury, but readers will also meet individuals with whom they may be less familiar, such as the Chartist leader William Cuffay, whose father was born into slavery in the Caribbean (Chapter

2), the sweatshop worker and anarchist campaigner Milly Witkop (Chapter 3), Rosa May Billinghurst, a suffragette who undertook courageous acts of civil disobedience from her wheelchair (Chapter 7), the veteran East End brushmaker Mrs Savoy, who made a powerful impact on the Prime Minister, Herbert Asquith, when they met in June 1914 (Chapter 8) and Charlie Goodman, whose anti-fascist activism took him from the charge room at Leman Street police station on the day of the Battle of Cable Street, over the Pyrenees to Spain where he joined the British Battalion, Fifteenth International Brigade (Chapter 10).

The word 'rebel' derives from the Latin *rebellis*, which signified a fresh declaration of war (*bellum*) after a defeat. Many of the rebels celebrated through this book were true to this spirit. They were resilient people, undaunted by temporary setbacks, who believed they would ultimately triumph. All of them challenged the status quo, some from the most marginalised and embattled starting points, others more comfortably ensconced within the mainstream, but their common attributes were their fervent refusal to let injustices go unchallenged, their belief that change was possible, and their determination to see their battles through to a conclusion.

In keeping with its 'history from below' approach, this book particularly celebrates those movements that have been less conspicuous in mainstream narratives. Much has been written about the Chartist movement, but less about its predecessors such as the National Union of the Working Classes, whose ideas and activities are outlined in the Introduction and Chapter 2. The Women's Freedom League, whose motto was 'Dare to be Free', fought for the vote but also for equal opportunities, equal rights and equal justice for women. History records them as being less 'militant' than Emmeline Pankhurst's Women's Social and Political Union but, as Chapter 7 argues, they were more politically radical. The Battle of Cable Street in October 1936 was an extraordinary event that dealt a severe blow to Oswald Mosley's fascist movement. But it was one battle in a long war and the complementary actions of the people of Bermondsey who took to the streets and built their own barricades exactly a year after the Cable Street conflagration, are described in Chapter 10.

The book ends on the eve of the Second World War, by which time many of the causes for which rebel Londoners and their counterparts nationwide had mobilised, marched, petitioned, demonstrated and endured imprisonment, had chalked up several significant gains. Fascism had been defeated domestically and within years would be defeated internationally; trade unions were an accepted part of society; the Labour Party was a mass party seeking redistribution of wealth, whose members were drawn largely from the working class; there was free universal education, and higher educational opportunities were about to expand. With very few exceptions, all female and male adults could vote, basic freedoms were guaranteed, and organisations such as the National Council for Civil Liberties (now Liberty) were monitoring and challenging breaches of civil rights. A freely-speaking national press was widely read and, although ownership of newspapers was still largely concentrated in the hands of Conservative political and economic elites, newspapers such as the *Daily Worker*, the *Daily Herald* and the *News Chronicle* flourished and provided accessible and affordable alternatives. The post-war Labour administration brought in further radical reform, reflecting a broad consensus in society, demanding greater fairness, democracy and equality of opportunity.

This war, in which for the second time in three decades, ordinary workers had proportionally made the greatest sacrifice, was a watershed for Britain and especially for its capital city, which suffered so much damage during the Blitz. Thousands of homes were destroyed and communities dislocated. Slum clearance and renovation of the city's infrastructure, which had been taking place all too slowly from the end of the nineteenth century, suddenly presented itself as an urgent necessity. The economic divisions in British society and in its capital city remained conspicuous but the rebels and protesters taking to London's streets in the 1950s, and in the decades immediately beyond could generally undertake their activities from a more comfortable and stable starting point. Protests in London became focused on a more diverse and eclectic, though no less urgent set of issues – for example, the environment, lesbian and gay rights, women's equality, antiracism, disability equality, nuclear disarmament, the Vietnam War, apartheid in South Africa, trade justice – all of which are much more difficult to locate specifically within the London context as opposed to the national or global context.

Areas Covered

Most of the events described in this book took place within inner London boroughs and central London areas. London developed unevenly as a city. The financial centre developed first. Its legal and political institutions developed to the west of the financial area. Industry in London was founded towards the east. The development of the East India and West India docks there brought a host of related industries into existence. Gradually the urbanisation combined with industrial development that occurred in the east was replicated across the capital. But this meant that the demands of rebellious movements for change were first fought out and often took their most dramatic forms in east London, so four of the chapters and the walks that accompany them are in different parts of the East End.

Several areas south of the river underwent a rapid urbanisation and industrialisation later than east London, towards the end of the nineteenth century and the beginning of the twentieth century. The two southern districts that developed particularly strong radical movements, motivated and energised by extraordinary individuals, were Battersea and Bermondsey, and they are the south London areas represented in the walks.

The most central location represented is Westminster. In contrast with the east London and south London districts, this was not at the heart of a local community struggle but rather the focus of a broader movement – the suffragettes – spread over several areas, that concentrated its rallies and public protests on visible centres and symbols of political power, which were plentiful in Westminster.

Although the complete period the book covers ranges from the beginning of the 1830s to the end of the 1930s, most chapters with their corresponding walks relate to narrower slices of time. The Bermondsey chapter, for example, covers the 1890s to the 1930s. The Bloomsbury chapter is the exception to the pattern. This area was a hothouse for the development of radical ideas throughout the period the book covers and that is reflected in a wide-ranging walk. The other important location that the book will lead you through is where our story begins – Clerkenwell.

Using the Book: Text and Maps

The chapters follow a roughly chronological pattern, although several are more thematic. Each chapter conveys accounts of rebellious individuals, movements, incidents and campaigns that occurred principally within that specific locality. The walks stop at key points mentioned in the chapter, and indicate physical remnants that recall this history, but also add other intriguing fragments of historical information. Each chapter, together with its accompanying walk, can be used in a 'stand-alone' manner, although it is worth reading the whole of the relevant chapter first in order to get the most out of the walk. And if you do the walks in the order in which they appear in the book, the way in which different individuals and movements inspired and related to each other will become more apparent.

Old Finsbury Town Hall, Rosebery Avenue

2

TRAILBLAZERS FOR DEMOCRACY
IN CLERKENWELL GREEN

When furious suffragettes aimed their first stones at Downing Street's windows in the summer of 1908, as part of their struggle for the vote, government ministers feigned shock and hurt, and asked naïvely what might have provoked such violent actions. From far away in New Zealand, where women won the vote in 1893, the *Wanganui Chronicle* reminded them of an earlier incident: 'In 1830 the Duke of Wellington declared the House of Commons did not need reform; but when an angry mob smashed his windows and let in a little more light, he saw the matter differently.'[1]

Not differently enough to make real change, though. The following year, Wellington's government fell to the Whigs, who promised a Great Reform Act and won a landslide victory. For the vast majority, long excluded from having any political voice, this election created a rare frisson of excitement. The year 1831 had been unusually wet and thundery, especially August: a sign, perhaps, of imminent political turbulence. But in the early months of 1832, many Londoners were more exercised by the right to live than the right to vote.

---

1   *Wanganui Chronicle*, 3 July 1908.

A few suspected cholera cases in January 1832, the first reported in Limehouse, east London, heralded a major outbreak of the killer disease. It swept across the city's more overcrowded and insanitary areas, where the poorest workers eked out their living. Similar outbreaks in Berlin and Hamburg in 1831 claimed thousands of lives. In Paris cholera killed 9,000 residents in just one month. The government declared that this was 'proof of the judgement of God among us', though the symptoms resembled severe food poisoning. It announced a National Fast Day on 21 March to halt the spread of the disease.

Henry Hetherington's *Poor Man's Guardian* disagreed. Telling the poor to fast was 'superfluous', since they were 'lucky to be able to eat meat once a week let alone be able to forgo it'. This radical penny broadsheet was published at 13 Kingsgate Street, Holborn, in defiance of government-imposed stamp duty.[2] With this paper's support, a newly formed organisation of skilled workers and small shopkeepers from London's poorer communities turned rejection of this government proposal into a physical and political challenge to the authorities.

The National Union of the Working Classes (NUWC) organised on a branch basis with one spokesperson for every 30–40 members. It wanted economic justice and political reform, demanding annual parliaments, full suffrage for adult males, voting by (secret) ballot and, especially, 'no property qualification for members of parliament'. The NUWC argued that 'until intelligent men from the productive and useful classes of society' were allowed to 'represent the interests of the working people, justice in legislation will never be rendered unto them'.

---

2   Stamp duty of four pence imposed on newspapers prevented many poorer people from accessing them.

These were radical not revolutionary demands. However, in a period in which carpenters, shoemakers and tailors were forming unions and organising strikes, Robert Owen's cooperative and communitarian ideas were circulating, and a rising capitalist class was challenging the old landed and financial oligarchy, the ruling elites felt genuinely fearful.[3] They condemned the NUWC as 'destructive revolutionists, pickpockets and incendiaries, meditating an attack on every person of property and the uprooting of law and order.'[4]

The NUWC declared that the cholera outbreak had nothing to do with God, but was caused by 'want, wretchedness and insanitary conditions'. It dubbed the Fast Day a 'Farce Day', and encouraged its supporters to enjoy a 'Feast Day', which, it argued, would benefit the poor far more. It asked its supporters to assemble on the 'Farce Day' at Finsbury Square, on the edge of the City's financial district, 'for the purpose of walking round the Metropolis in procession and enjoying the fresh air'.

Its leaders devised a scenic route through fashionable areas – the City, Fleet Street, the Strand, Piccadilly and Hyde Park – before returning through Oxford Street and Holborn, for the feast in the East End. The organisers wanted to show their disdain for the government's feeble 'explanation' in a militant but disciplined manner. Respecting legal advice, they asked their supporters not to bring banners, flags or anything that might be construed as a weapon. By 12 o'clock on the day of the march, around 40,000 men and women had assembled at Finsbury Square.

---

3   Carpenters and shoemakers in London held strikes in 1825, tailors in 1830.

4   See George Howell's handwritten account, *A History of the Working Men's Association* (1901), held at the Bishopsgate Institute. The NUWC was formed by a group of activists within the British Association for Promoting Cooperative Knowledge.

The newly formed Metropolitan Police placed no such restrictions on its own accoutrements. It had little experience in policing demonstrations but knew how to present a show of force. At Temple, thick ranks of police armed with staves and cutlasses blocked the protesters' path. A cat-and-mouse game followed: marchers turned off route into Chancery Lane, but were blocked again. They headed for Gray's Inn Road. The organisers sent scouts ahead to alert the marchers where police were waiting. A major altercation took place on Tottenham Court Road, near Howland Street, where large numbers of police had hidden themselves in a side alley. A phalanx of police suddenly threw themselves into the march, swinging staves indiscriminately as they tried to split the front ranks from those following. Some protesters threw missiles using whatever materials they could gather. Until then they had been entirely peaceful. The marchers rallied at North Crescent opposite Goodge Street where their leaders, fearing further disorder, advised them to return home and eat.

Three protest leaders – William Lovett and James Watson, both in their early 30s, and William Benbow, in his mid-40s – were arrested in the aftermath and committed for trial at Middlesex Sessions House in Clerkenwell. Prosecutors labelled them 'disaffected and ill-disposed persons', who, 'with force of arms ... made a great riot, tumult and disturbance', causing 'terror and alarm' to the King's subjects for five hours.

Watson had moved to London from Malton, Yorkshire, in the early 1820s, and was a radical publisher based in Finsbury, strongly influenced by Robert Owen's cooperative ideas.[5] He

---

5 Finsbury, formerly a separate borough to the south of Islington, was incorporated into Islington in 1965.

published Tom Paine, and the poets Byron and Shelley. Benbow was apprenticed as a shoemaker in Manchester. He became a non-conformist preacher and joined local radical circles. He had been held on remand in London for eight months during 1817 for political activities, and had no means to return north when he was released without trial. He immersed himself in London's radical publishing milieu, collaborating with the pamphleteer William Cobbett. He was subsequently incarcerated in Coldbath Fields prison, Clerkenwell, for 'seditious libel'.

In the early 1830s, Benbow began expounding his plan for a 'Grand National Holiday', at meetings hosted at the Rotunda, 3 Blackfriars Road, recently acquired by Richard Carlile, a tinsmith and radical publisher.[6] Benbow published his idea as a pamphlet in 1832. The 'holiday' – a one-month general strike – would generate an uprising and force political change. During this 'holiday' period, working-class representatives would draw up a constitution to 'place every human being on the same footing. Equal rights, equal enjoyments, equal toil, equal respect, equal share of production.'

Lovett, who arrived in London from Newlyn, Cornwall, around the same time as Watson, had a gentler introduction to political radicalism, joining a literary association in Soho and political discussion circles at the Mechanics Institute and at various coffee houses. He later opened his own coffee house on Greville Street, Clerkenwell, which had one room full of newspapers and books and the other 'fitted up as a conversation-room ... to separate the talkers from the readers'. In the evenings, the conversation room hosted lectures, debates and classes.

---

6   The Rotunda – a meeting place for radical freethinkers – was a London headquarters for the NUWC.

A society called Social Reformers met there regularly. Lovett actively promoted temperance. He petitioned Parliament in 1829 to open museums and galleries on Sundays as 'want of proper recreation and amusement' was a principal cause 'of drunkenness on that day'. Like Watson, he was strongly influenced by Owen's cooperative philosophy, and joined the British Association for Promoting Cooperative Knowledge.[7]

Watson, Benbow and Lovett represented themselves during their trial eight weeks after the 'riot'. Witnesses testified that the procession was peaceful and orderly. One told the court that he heard police receive an order at Tottenham Court Road: 'Out with your truncheons ... fall on them ... show them no quarter.' The jury acquitted the defendants, to wild cheering both inside and outside the court, scenes that prefigured the response to PC Culley's inquest judgement after the NUWC's 1833 protest on Coldbath Fields, half a mile from the Sessions House.[8]

The Sessions House itself was located on Clerkenwell Green. Devoid of grass for centuries, this space became one of the three most prominent free speech venues in London – the others being Speakers' Corner at Hyde Park, and Trafalgar Square. Gissing captured its atmosphere: '[T]he voices of orators, swarmed with listeners, with disputants, with mockers ... the roar of an enthusiastic total-abstainer blended with the shriek of a Radical politician.'[9]

Branch 1 of the Social Democratic Federation (SDF), Britain's

---

7   W. Lovett, *Life and Struggles of William Lovett in His Pursuit of Bread, Knowledge, and Freedom*, New York: A. A. Knopf, 1920.

8   After the trial Lovett accused Benbow of acting provocatively on the 'Fast Day' procession.

9   G. Gissing, *The Nether World*, London: Smith, Elder & Co, 1889, chapter 21.

first socialist party, was formed in Clerkenwell.[10] The party's leader, a wealthy Cambridge-educated businessman called Henry Mayers Hyndman, who read Marx then saw the world anew, claimed that he first divested himself of inherited class prejudices when he 'addressed a gathering ... of rather debauched looking persons round the old pump at Clerkenwell Green'.

Clerkenwell Green gained a reputation as the 'home of community, commonality and solidarity' among reformers and rebels seeking change, and 'the headquarters of republicanism, revolution and ultra non-conformity' among those defending the status quo. The pardoned Tolpuddle Martyrs, exiled to Australia in 1834,[11] were welcomed back at a rally in Clerkenwell Green. The Green was a venue for rallies and an assembly point for marches of the Chartist movement, established that same decade.

Clerkenwell, an area of 'grovelling starving poverty', which boasted the highest murder rate in early Victorian London, became a pivotal locale for those challenging the authorities, fighting for democracy and championing the rights of London's emerging working classes, especially during the 1830s and 40s. Thomas Beames, a preacher at St James's Church, Westminster, who published a powerful work on London's 'rookeries' in 1850, condemned the slums of St Giles and Seven Dials, and Old Pye Street for their 'squalid misery', 'extreme poverty' and 'abject distress', but ranked Clerkenwell's 'plague spots' second only to St Giles.[12] In Clerkenwell, wrote Beames, 'a most unsavoury black stream of some width, the open sewer of Field Ditch ... [runs]

---

10 Launched in 1881 as the Democratic Federation, its most active branches were in Clerkenwell, Battersea and east London.

11 See p. 114

12 Rookeries were densely populated areas of overcrowded, unhygienic, poorly ventilated, low quality housing.

impetuously between the walls of the houses'. By 'houses' he meant ramshackle buildings populated by 'trampers', 'beggars', 'persons of uncertain occupation', and 'the worst thieves and lowest prostitutes of London'.[13]

Beames's stark observations echoed those published earlier in the *Illustrated London News*. In Clerkenwell's lanes and alleys, wrote its reporter, 'broods the darkness of utter ignorance' where 'the lowest debauch, the coarsest enjoyment ... the most unrestrained vice, roar and riot'. He lent further colour to his descriptions through a set of unflattering ethnic stereotypes:

> Jew receivers, with sharp leering eyes and tangled beards, lurk at corners ... The burglar has his 'crib' in Clerkenwell – the pickpocket has his mart – the half-starved Italian minstrel herds there, crammed with his fellows into foul night cellars – the ragged Irish hodman vegetates in the filth of his 3-pair back. It is the locality of dirt, ignorance and vice.[14]

The short-lived NUWC, and its successor, the London Working Men's Association (LWMA), which drew up the iconic six-point People's Charter in 1837 (drafted principally by William Lovett), did not organise among Clerkenwell's most desperate poor. They built instead among more stable artisans and skilled workers who had formed unions and shown a willingness to challenge their employers through industrial action. Builders, shoemakers and tailors all took industrial action during 1834,

---

13 T. Beames, *The Rookeries of London*, London: Thomas Bosworth, 1850.

14 *Illustrated London News*, 22 May 1849, cited in K Sugden (ed.), *Criminal Islington*, London: Islington Archaeology and History Society, 1989.

and the LWMA, which held organising meetings at 14 Tavistock Street, near Covent Garden, set up sub-committees to investigate the conditions among trades such as weavers, shoemakers, tailors and printers, to arm themselves with propaganda to campaign for better workplace conditions.[15] But those who suffered abject poverty formed the backdrop for political crusades over economic inequalities, which agitators wove together with campaigns to address the democratic deficit. The LWMA's first 'prospectus' stated that:

> No reflecting ... mind can witness the scenes of misery ... can read of the thousand wretched forms under which the demon of poverty tortures the millions, and at the same time reflect on the ample means wasted on folly and lavished on idleness ... without resolving to enquire into the causes of the evils, and to devise ... some means of ... alleviating them.[16]

The LWMA connected industrial disputes with efforts to stimulate education, political discussion and agitation among working-class communities. Its unashamedly vanguardist approach attempted to unify an 'intelligent and influential portion of the working class', to challenge 'cruel laws that prevent circulation of thought'. This required a 'cheap and honest press' which would 'collect statistics about wages ... [and] promote education for the rising generation'. It demanded that 'all public buildings,

---

15 Stonemasons struck in 1841 and 1842. Their strike started among workers rebuilding the Houses of Parliament after extensive fire damage and spread to those working in Trafalgar Square, erecting Nelson's Column.

16 See George Howell's handwritten account, *A History of the Working Men's Association* (1901), held at the Bishopsgate Institute.

museums, galleries of arts ought to be always open to the whole people free of charge'.

The People's Charter, adopted by 'Chartists' at the Crown and Anchor pub on the Strand, defiantly challenged political norms that entrenched power among a narrow elite. It restated four points already drawn up by the NUWC, and added 'equal constituencies' (number of electors), and 'payment of Members of Parliament', which would make it feasible for an elected worker to keep his family afloat. The response from the government and the more conservative newspapers veered from defensive to paranoid, yet the only point still not conceded today is the impractical demand for 'annual parliaments', intended to give electorates the power to dismiss MPs within a relatively short time if they were not performing. A minority of Chartists argued for three-yearly elections.

The government could not acquiesce to the Chartists' demands without risking some shift in the balance of power, but its paranoia about these demands reflected fear of 'the mob' engaging in civil disobedience. The LWMA had stated publicly that, 'those who are excluded from this share of political power are not justly included within the operation of the laws'.

After its London launch, Chartism spread its wings and flew north, gathering strength especially in the northern industrial centres of Lancashire and Yorkshire and in the Midlands, where it focused on economic issues alongside democratic political demands. Although the Charter itself, with millions of signatures, would be taken to Parliament in London, in huge processions in 1839, 1842 and 1848, most Chartists were recruited outside the capital. Feargus O'Connor published Chartism's most popular newspaper, the *Northern Star*, from Leeds, though it relocated to London in November 1844. In London, many Chartists were skilled craftsmen, often self-employed, and Chartism initially had some middle-class participation, but it became a predominantly working-class movement in the capital.

The historian David Goodway identified 1841–2 as the Chartist movement's high point in London, with around 8,000 membership cards being issued there, compared with combined recruitment figures of 7,900 for three other significant Chartist areas, Leicester, Manchester and Sheffield, over the same period.[17] Within London, Chartists were most active in Finsbury/Clerkenwell, east London, the City and St Pancras, north of the Thames, and in Bermondsey, Camberwell and Walworth to the south.

Outside London, there were strong connections between Methodism and Chartism, but London's Chartists tended to be non-religious or actively anti-Christian, seeing the Church as defending the status quo. Ideological influences on London Chartists were more likely to be anti-authoritarians like William Cobbett, and freethinkers such as Thomas Paine, whose birthday was celebrated with annual suppers.

Although Chartists broadly agreed on goals, there were deep divisions over strategy. 'Moral Force' Chartists were committed to peaceful persuasion and education through propaganda, but 'Physical Force' Chartists believed that economic and political elites would not relinquish power and privilege unless compelled to do so by people exerting their own collective power. In Newport, Wales, an armed uprising by Chartists was defeated in 1839.

Lovett, the Charter's principal author, Watson, a co-defendant

---

17 Leicester 3,100; Manchester 2,800; and Sheffield 2,000.

in the 1832 'Farce Day' protest, and Hetherington, founder of the *Poor Man's Guardian*, were all moral force Chartists. So was John Cleave, another radical printer and publisher. He opened a print shop in Snow Hill near Clerkenwell, then moved to Shoe Lane, later opening a bookshop and a coffee house. Cleave urged Chartists to take a stand in favour of women's suffrage too and, in 1840, published a pamphlet called *Rights of Women*, which argued that:

> If a woman is qualified to be a queen over a great nation [she] ought not to be excluded from her share in the executive and legislative power of the country ... If [a woman] be subject to pains and penalties [for] infringement of any laws ... she ought to have a voice in making the laws she is bound to obey ... women contribute to the wealth and resources of the kingdom. Debased is the man who would say women have no right to interfere in politics ... they have as much right as a man.

Women struggled to have influence within the Chartist movement, but its City of London branch had prominent speakers mocked by the press as 'she-Chartists'. Susannah Inge and Mary Ann Walker toured Britain with Chartist leaders, and wrote for the *Northern Star*. Inge dealt confidently with internal critics of women taking on political roles. At a public meeting in 1842, when a male Chartist said women were not physically intended by nature to take part in politics, she replied that it took little physical force to vote! She also discussed why women should be motivated to join the Chartist rebellion: 'Do not ... leave such things for your husbands, fathers and brothers. You have ... a deeper interest than you are aware of. If the country is misgoverned, and bad laws instituted, and good laws perverted, it is on you those laws fall heaviest.'[18]

Another London 'she-Chartist', Emma Matilda Miles, was described by the *Sunday Observer*, when she spoke at a meeting at the National Charter Association hall at 55 Old Bailey, as a 'pretty looking young creature'. She argued the physical force case, saying that Chartist demands would not be granted by justice, but must be 'extorted from the fears of their oppressors'.

Most Chartist orators were men, but women in London played important roles, holding collections for Chartist prisoners, making banners, organising meetings and tea parties, and developing a consumer boycott of shops that did not support the Chartists. The East London Female Patriotic Association, whose object was 'to assist our brethren in obtaining universal suffrage', shared a venue with the East London Democratic Association (ELDA), a stronghold of physical force Chartism that had support particularly among Spitalfield silkweavers.

ELDA, founded by George Julian Harney, later broadened its geographical scope and shortened its name to London Democratic Association. Within London Chartism it challenged the more moderate LWMA. Harney was assisted by James Bronterre O'Brien, who had edited the *Poor Man's Guardian* for Hetherington, a moral force Chartist, and later another newspaper – *The Power of the Pence*, 'intended for those who know the look of a penny better than a pound'. O'Brien was an advocate of class struggle, arguing that disenfranchised workers without property produced all of society's wealth, but it was stolen from them by

18 'Address to the Women of England', *Northern Star*, 2 July 1842, cited by Richard Brown's Looking at History blog 28 November 2007.

government and church, unproductive middlemen and aristo-
crats. After spending 18 months in prison in 1840–41, convicted
for 'seditious libel', O'Brien shifted from his 'physical force'
perspective, and placed more emphasis on Chartists' educational
role than on militancy in his latter years.

Other leading Chartists around the country faced more severe
sentences – they were exiled to penal colonies in Australia. The
revival of London Chartism in 1841 began in January with a large
demonstration in support of three Chartist leaders who had been
deported to Australia. As several leading Chartists in London
were gaoled for their writing and speeches, new leaders came
forward. One was William Cuffay, a tailor less than five feet tall,
born in Chatham in 1788, who rose to the interim presidency of
the Chartists in London during their most active phase.

Cuffay's African grandfather was sold into slavery in St Kitts,
and his father had been born a slave there. Cuffay's father came
to Britain after he was freed and married an English woman from
Kent. William Cuffay's first struggle was with his disabilities – he
had a deformed spine and shinbones – but he became a tailor in his
late teens and worked in tailoring throughout his life. He moved
to London in 1819 and found work mostly in Soho. In 1834 he
participated in a failed tailors' strike for shorter hours and better
pay. He was victimised for his role in the strike, and struggled to
find regular employment afterwards. These difficulties, though,
drew him into political activity, and he joined the Westminster
Chartists. Linking the threads of his political and trade union
work, he helped form the Metropolitan Tailors Charter Association. He spoke powerfully at a crowded meeting at the Owenite
Social Institution in John Street near Tottenham Court Road in
March 1842, urging tailors to support the Chartist petition, which

would soon be submitted. The first Chartist petition had nearly 1.3 million signatories; the one in May 1842 more than 3.2 million.

With Cuffay playing a leading role, *The Times* referred disparagingly to London's Chartists as 'the black man and his party'. Cuffay, though, was not the sole victim of this paper's racism. In due course *The Times* would describe the Chartists as 'tools in the hands of a gang of desperadoes ... a ramification for the Irish conspiracy', claiming that 'The Repealers wish to make as great a hell of this island as they have made of their own.'

Several national and local Chartist leaders were Irish. In London there were radical Irish nationalist societies, whose members included active Chartists. Posters mobilising for the Kennington Common Demonstration on 10 April 1848, when the third national petition would be delivered to Parliament, advertised meeting points for 'the Chartists, the Trades, and the Irish Confederate and Repeal Bodies'. Their interests converged. A large Irish contingent carried a banner of green silk with an orange fringe, a golden Irish harp and the words 'Let every man have his own country.'

Clerkenwell Green was the rallying point that day for marchers of the Chartists' City and Eastern Divisions. Other divisions gathered at Stepney Green, Russell Square and Peckham Fields. Mobilising posters attacked the press for vilifying the Chartists instead of acknowledging their just demands: 'We and our families are pining in misery, want and starvation! We demand a fair day's wages for a fair day's work! We are the slaves of capital – we demand protection to our labour. We are political serfs – we demand to be free.'

Revolutions had erupted in several European cities, and Britain's ruling classes were increasingly jittery about London.

In the early 1820s, the French ambassador Chateaubriand had praised British institutions' stability to Lord Liverpool; Liverpool replied: 'One insurrection in London and all is lost.' A week before the April 1848 demonstration, London's Commissioner of Police declared the planned protest illegal, but the government knew that the organisers would not comply. During that week a volunteer Special Constabulary, drawn principally from shopkeepers, lawyers and government clerks, was formed to bolster the police presence.[19] Armed police were placed outside the Foreign Office the night before, and armed protection organised for prisons, the General Post Office and the British Museum. The Queen was evacuated to the Isle of Wight, and her valuables, royal carriages and horses were removed. Three thousand troops were moved into the capital, expanding the central garrison to more than 7,000 soldiers. On the morning another 450 infantry and 37 marines were mobilised. Meanwhile, 4,000 police were positioned at the bridges, in Kennington, where the demonstration rally would gather, and in Westminster, where the petition would be brought.

With the bridges sealed and such a threatening armed presence in place, Chartist leader Feargus O'Connor met Police Commissioners and magistrates and agreed to abandon plans to march as a body on Parliament from Kennington. He would ask the crowd to disperse after the rally and the petition would be delivered by a delegation in a hansom cab. Many Chartists felt that by crossing the bridges they had been led into a trap. They were willing to test whether the authorities would dare to prevent them marching back. Cuffay condemned O'Connor's 'cowardly' acquiescence.

The press derided the protest as a 'fiasco'. The Prime Minister,

19   The origin of London Metropolitan Police's 'Specials'.

Viscount Palmerston, was more circumspect: 'The snake is scotched and not killed and we must continue on our guard.' His fears were well-founded. Throughout May and June there were fiery Chartist mass meetings, angry marches and mini-riots across the country. These included a running battle on the rooftops of Clerkenwell Green, a militant joint march with the Irish Democratic Federation from Finsbury Square to the West End on 31 May, and a pitched battle between Chartists and police in Bethnal Green in June. Many Chartist speakers were arrested and imprisoned for sedition. The fatal blow against London's Chartists was dealt in August, when police raids on secret Chartist meetings in pubs in Soho, Holborn and Southwark yielded loaded pistols, pikes, daggers, spearheads and swords. In St James churchyard on Clerkenwell Close, 400 hidden ball cartridges were unearthed. Five prominent Chartists were sentenced to transportation, including Cuffay, and 15 others received sentences ranging from 18 months to two years. Most pleaded their innocence, and much of the evidence came from two police spies, Powell and Davis, who had infiltrated secret committees. The defendants claimed that Powell was 'constantly suggesting to his colleagues projects of conflagration and slaughter'. Cuffay protested that his trial was unfair. He wasn't asking for pity or mercy but to be tried by his peers and without an atmosphere of press assassination: 'Everything has been done to raise a prejudice against me, and the press ... have done all in their power to smother me with ridicule.'

He was transported to Tasmania, but pardoned three years later. However, he chose to stay in Tasmania, where his wife had joined him. He worked as a tailor and campaigned for workers' rights and democracy there until his death in Hobart in 1870.

The revolutionary upheavals on the Continent brought several exiled revolutionaries to London as political refugees in the 1850s. Most settled in Soho, and some formed communist clubs and other radical associations here. One Continental revolutionary who preceded them, collaborated with Chartists and operated within Clerkenwell, was Giuseppe Mazzini, founder of the Young Italy movement, which was struggling for a united democratic Italian republic. Arriving in 1837, he was perplexed by London's fog: 'We have had night at mid-day three or four times since our arrival ... during which all the lamps are lit. Imagine an immense cotton cap falling suddenly over the eyes of the town ... passers-by resemble spectres, and one feels himself to be somewhat spectral.'[20]

Mazzini wanted to educate Italian migrant workers about Young Italy and recruit them; instead he helped them improve their practical situation in London. In November 1840 he founded *Unione degli Operai Italiani*, a workers' club and friendly society at 5 Hatton Garden, and introduced the members to ideas of 'association' – unionising.[21] He started an Italian newspaper, *Apostolato Popolare*, modelled on the Chartist press, with assistance from the Chartist printer, John Cleave.

In 1841, he established a Free Italian School at Hatton Garden, backed by Liberal benefactors, which later found bigger premises nearby at 5 Greville Street. The school sought to expand the cultural and educational horizons of adult migrant workers, but it soon had an additional function, as Mazzini responded to the plight of Italian children working as street musicians. Poverty-stricken parents were coerced to sell children to *padroni* – labour

---

20 Massimo Vangelista, http://byronico.com/2013/10/01/giuseppe-mazzinis-houses-in-london.

21 It moved later to 101 Farringdon Road, then 10 Laystall Street.

trafficking gangs – who subsequently enslaved them. Several hundred Italian children gained a basic education at the school's evening classes. This opened opportunities for them once they escaped the *padroni*'s clutches.

The democratic ideals that Mazzini and the Chartists shared were slow to come to fruition. Nearly two decades after London's Chartist movement had been smashed, new generations of reformers and rebels pressed for democratic change. The Chartist movement had organised marches, rallies, petitions, economic boycotts and strikes, and even attempted armed uprisings. It failed to win its goals in its time, but set an agenda for radical change.

When Chartism was launched, around 15 per cent of men had the vote. The Reform Acts of 1867 and 1884 widened the franchise to roughly 60 per cent. In the agitation for changes a militant Reform League demonstration destroyed railings at Hyde Park in 1866. 'The beautiful flower beds with which the road is lined from Marble Arch to Hyde Park Corner were strewn with broken railings and masonry ... having been trampled under the rough feet of a careless multitude.'[22] When the suffragette movement filled Hyde Park in their struggles for democracy in 1908 and 1910, speakers paid homage to those who had fought for democracy on the same turf decades before.

Back in Clerkenwell Green, where Chartists had protested and fought with the police, the London Patriotic Club, founded by the radical liberal, John Stuart Mill, began to meet at number 37a, once a school serving London's Welsh community. The Club spread propaganda supporting republicanism, trade unions, extending

---

22 *Manchester Guardian*, 26 July 1866.

the vote, and equal rights for women. Unusually among London's radical 'workingmen's' clubs, it was open to women. Speakers included the Russian anarchist, Peter Kropotkin, and socialists such as Eleanor Marx and William Morris. By the 1890s many radical liberals redefined themselves as socialists, and Morris – artist, designer, poet, writer and activist, and a wealthy socialist – established a radical publishing house there, the Twentieth Century Press. Much of the Marxist literature circulating in 1890s Britain emanated from this building in Clerkenwell Green.

Today it houses the Marx Memorial Library, acquired in 1933 by a committee seeking a fitting memorial for Karl Marx, 50 years after his death in the city where he had lived for more than three decades. In May that year, after Hitler's Nazi party took power in the land of Marx's birth, the Nazis publicly burnt Jewish and communist literature in Berlin's Bebelplatz. The committee had already planned to create a library of progressive literature, and felt more determined to do so following the Nazis' actions. The building's façade displayed 'Marx House Library and Workers' School' in huge lettering, embodying Clerkwenwell Green's vibrant, rebellious history. In 1967 the words disappeared. An external facelift restored its genteel Georgian appearance – the price of avoiding demolition as several buildings on the Green were being redeveloped. But the echoes of generations of rebels who gathered there and fought for change continue to be heard every spring, when trade unionists, socialists, communists, and young twenty-first-century radicals assemble on the cobbles in front of Marx Memorial Library for the annual May Day march to Trafalgar Square.

JOSEPH
GRIMALDI
1778-1837
Clown
lived here
1818-1828

GARNAULT
PLACE

FINSBURY
TOWN HALL

ROSEBERY AVENUE

EXMOUTH MARKET

SPAFIELD
STREET

NORTHAMPTON ROAD

FARRINGDON ROAD

CORPORATION
ROW

CLERKENWELL CLOSE

COLDBATH
SQUARE

BAKER'S ROW

ST JAMES
CHURCHYARD

AYLESBURY STREET

JERUSALEM
PASSAGE

WARNER STREET

FARRINGDON ROAD

CLERKENWELL GREEN

BACK HILL

CLERKENWELL ROAD

DAILY WORKER

WOOLLEN WORKERS TAKE THE FIELD
MASS STRIKES AGAINST
WAGE REDUCTIONS

HATTON GARDEN

SAFFRON HILL

FARRINGDON ROAD

N

100M

GREVILLE STREET

40

WALK

Start at Old Finsbury Town Hall, Rosebery Avenue, EC1R 4RP

1. *Rosebery Avenue*
The Old Town Hall building was opened by Lord Rosebery in 1895 as the local vestry hall. It became the Town Hall when the Metropolitan Borough of Finsbury was created in 1900. In 1965 Finsbury was incorporated into Islington. In the 1830s the total population of Islington and Finsbury was 137,000, with 100,000 of them in Finsbury. Its largest nineteenth-century industries were brewing, printing and clock- and watch-manufacturing. Turn right into Garnault Place and cross Rosoman Street into Exmouth Market.

2. *Exmouth Market*
The food market established here in the 1890s declined by the 1970s but has benefited from regeneration since the 1990s. Many international foods are sold there today. Halfway along this paved street a plaque commemorates Joseph Grimaldi, the son of Italian immigrants and the original 'Joey the Clown', who lived here. Grimaldi performed as a dancer at Sadler's Wells at three years of age. Italian migrants first settled in this area in the late eighteenth century. The nearby church was built in Italian-renaissance style in the 1880s. Turn into Spafield Street.

3. Spafield Street

To the south and east of this street were fields known as Spa Fields. In November and December 1816, disciples of Thomas Spence, a shoemaker and radical teacher from Newcastle who came to London in the 1790s and died in 1814, organised a series of meetings here attracting thousands of people. The authorities blamed Spenceans for bread riots that broke out in London in 1800–1. Police violently dispersed the meeting on 2 December 1816, arresting several leaders. They were charged with high treason, though the case eventually collapsed. Spence promoted egalitarianism, and supported land nationalisation and universal suffrage. He published a radical paper called *Pig's Meat*. Return to Exmouth Market. Cross over Farringdon Road.

4. Rosebery Avenue (west)

The Post Office's Mount Pleasant Sorting Office, opposite, was opened in 1889 on the site of the Middlesex House of Correction, also known as Coldbath Fields prison. This, in turn, was built on the site of a former prison burnt down in the Gordon Riots of the 1780s. The National Union of the Working Classes demonstration, at which PC Culley was stabbed, took place on the fields behind the prison. Turn left into Coldbath Square.

5. Coldbath Square

The street name recalls the prison, as do the bars voluntarily placed on the windows of this more recent gated development. Continue along the paved pathway and turn right into Baker's Row. Several street names locally refer to bakers. The jury investigating PC Culley's death was comprised mainly of bakers from the nearby Gray's Inn area. Turn left into Warner Street then right into Back Hill. This street was at the heart of the immigrant colony in Clerkenwell known as Little Italy. Italian immigrants in this district worked mainly as knife grinders, lacemakers, street musicians, street food sellers and mosaic and terrazzo craft workers. Turn left into Clerkenwell Road

6. Clerkenwell Road

St Peter's Italian Church was built in 1863. It became a major focus for London's Italian community, functioning also as a labour exchange after Sunday mass. An annual Italian parade (the first one in the 1880s), assembles near the church and along Back Hill. Cross Clerkenwell Road into Hatton Garden.

7. Hatton Garden

Hatton Garden has been the centre of London's jewellery trade for hundreds of years, and in the twentieth century was particularly associated with immigrant Hasidic Jews from central and eastern Europe. At number 5, a stone plaque commemorates the Italian revolutionary nationalist, Giuseppe Mazzini, who established his Free Italian School here. It moved later to Greville Street, opposite where Chartist William Lovett had his coffee house. Turn left into Greville Street. Stop on the corner of Saffron Hill.

8. Saffron Hill

'Near to the spot on which Snow Hill and Holborn Hill meet, there opens, a narrow and dismal alley leading to Saffron Hill', wrote Dickens in Oliver Twist. ' ... [A] commercial colony of itself: the emporium of petty larceny.' Dickens located Fagin's den in that alley – Field Lane (now the southern section of Saffron Hill). Field Lane and Saffron Hill formed a significant part of the Clerkenwell rookery. Turn left into Farringdon Road

9. Farringdon Road

Number 75, William Rust House, a former brushmakers' warehouse, is named after the first editor of the *Daily Worker*, the Communist Party paper launched in 1930. It was printed in this building for several decades from 1948. Rust took a post in Moscow in 1932 and was later the paper's correspondent in Spain during the Civil War, before returning to the editorship. He was in post until his death in 1949 at the age of 45. When the first edition was printed in Farringdon Road, 20,000 supporters blocked the traffic and held a torchlit procession, carrying William Rust to Clerkenwell Green where he auctioned two copies of the first edition for £45 each (the equivalent of more than £1,000 today). Turn right into Clerkenwell Road then left into the Green.

10. Clerkenwell Green

The Sessions House, built in 1779, where leaders of the National Union of the Working Classes were put on trial in 1832, is still standing. Marx Memorial Library is at number 37a. The red flag was hoisted for the first time in London at a rally here in 1871 in solidarity with the Paris Communards, who seized control of their city for a brief two-month period. Eleanor Marx, active in the Socialist League, addressed a large rally of unemployed workers on Clerkenwell Green in October 1887, a few weeks before marching from here to Trafalgar Square on the fateful 'Bloody Sunday' demonstration (see Chapter 3). Walk to Jerusalem Passage on the southeast side of the Green.

11. Jerusalem Passage

This leads towards the Priory of St John of Jerusalem – hence the name. For hundreds of years it was the headquarters of the crusading Knights Hospitaliers. The priory was burned down during the Peasants Revolt in 1381. Its prior, Robert Hales, executed during the revolt, had been appointed Treasurer to Richard II and brought in the hated Poll Tax. A plaque on the corner with the Green celebrates the coal merchant Thomas Britton, a collector of rare books and music, who had a strong interest in chemistry and the occult. He held musical soirées above his shop here, attended by performers and composers including Handel. In the 1830s and 40s, Chartists often met at coffee houses in Jerusalem Passage. Walk across the Green to the corner of Clerkenwell Close

12. Clerkenwell Close

Lenin frequented the Crown Tavern on the corner of Clerkenwell Close. The original tavern incorporated the Red Star Coffee House, established in the 1870s, which served as the strike headquarters for local printing unions in the 1880s.

13. St James Churchyard

In this churchyard, 400 ball carriages were found, leading to the conviction of several Chartist leaders in the summer of 1848. Continue along Clerkenwell Close to the corner of Corporation Row.

14. Corporation Row

The former premises of Hugh Myddelton School, now converted into housing, was the site of Clerkenwell House of Detention.

In November 1867 it held two radical Irish nationalists: Richard O'Sullivan Burke and Joseph Casey. That month saw large demonstrations on Clerkenwell Green in support of Irish prisoners held in London and Manchester. Burke and Casey's associates in London's radical Irish circles plotted to free them by bombing the prison wall. The explosions literally backfired, destroying adjacent housing. Twelve people were killed and 40 wounded. In a letter to Engels, Marx described the event as 'a colossal stupidity ... the London masses who have shown great sympathy towards Ireland will ... be driven into the arms of a reactionary government. One cannot expect the London proletariat will let itself be blown into the air for the honour of Fenian emissaries.' Continue on to Rosoman Street. Turn right to the Old Town Hall.

15. Rosebery Avenue

Next to the entrance, a green plaque celebrates Dadabhai Naoroji, a mathematician, philosopher and one of the founders of the Indian National Congress, who influenced Mahatma Gandhi, and was Britain's first non-white MP. In 1892 he was elected as Liberal MP for Finsbury Central, which he won by three votes.

St James Churchyard, Clerkenwell Close, where weaponry was unearthed in 1848.

Confrontation at 'Bloody Sunday' demonstration in Trafalgar Square.

3

THE SPARK OF REBELLION
IN BOW

*A small deformed boy noticed by no one standing before him
... the face of an old man on the thin body of a child ... a
cold shudder ran through Auban. It was the beginning of the
horror that had always turned him to ice when he returned
from the home of 'the disinherited,' the silent desolation of
the East End.*

J. H. Mackay, *The Anarchists*, 1891

It took the Liverpool-born son of a wealthy ship-owner and corn merchant to uncover the depth of poverty in late nineteenth-century London. Charles Booth had added glove manufacturing and a leather and skins company to his inherited business empire before he researched the victims of London's 'Victorian prosperity'. Initially, Booth set out to refute the claims of another wealthy businessman's son – Henry Hyndman, founder of the Social Democratic Federation – who stated in the *Pall Mall Gazette* that 25 per cent of Londoners lived in 'abject poverty'.

Slums were starting to be cleared. 'Philanthropic' housing developments were expanding. Booth told Hyndman that he 'had greatly overstated the case'. But his own investigation of the East End shook him: 35 per cent of east Londoners lived on or below the 'poverty line' and a third of these were 'chronically distressed'.[1] Several thousand east Londoners slept rough or scrambled for places in shelters and lodging houses, mainly established by religious charities.

Many other Eastenders only kept a roof over their head by entering the workhouse. In 1892 several socialists stood for election to their local Board of Guardians to make these forbidding places more humane while simultaneously organising to abolish them. The elected guardian, George Lansbury, author of a pamphlet, *Smash up the Workhouse!*, described his first encounter with Poplar Workhouse:

> ... [K]eys dangling at the waist of those who spoke to you ... stripped and bathed in a communal tub, and the final indignity of being dressed in clothes which had been worn by lots of other people ... ill fitting and coarse ... floors were polished, but of goodwill and kindliness, there was none.[2]

Workhouses, night shelters, living rough were the lot of the poorest Eastenders. Crowded sweatshops, dingy workshops, factories paying starvation wages, and the daily scramble for a few hours casual work on the docks were grim realities for those one rung higher. Hard-earned pennies disappeared in rent for cramped, dilapidated lodgings. 'The East End', wrote J.H. Mackay 'is labour and poverty, chained together by the curse of our time – servitude.'[3]

---

1   Booth defined the poverty line as the level of income for a family of four or five to subsist on: 18 shillings to 21 shillings a week.

2   G. Lansbury, *My Life*, London: Constable & Co, 1928.

3   J.H. Mackay, *The Anarchists*, Boston: Benj R. Tucker, 1891, p.12.

It seemed inconceivable that such distress could exist indefinitely alongside the stockpiling of vast riches a stone's throw away in the City of London without breeding rebellion. But in April 1888, Friedrich Engels lamented that nowhere were people 'less actively resistant, more passively submitting to their fate ... than in the East End of London.'[4]

Within weeks Engels was proved wrong. A spontaneous two-week strike by 1,400 factory workers ignited a wave of industrial unrest that shook the capital and reverberated nationally. The dispute at Bow's Fairfield Works match factory, owned by the Quakers Bryant and May, spawned a Union of Women Matchmakers and catalysed other dramatic disputes among low-skilled and unskilled, poorly paid workers. By the early 1890s workers were embracing a 'new unionism', and the East End was the cradle of this exciting development.

The striking matchworkers in summer 1888 were female, working class and many were of Irish heritage, but Louise Raw identifies these three 'disadvantages' as positive drivers of change.[5] During the nineteenth century, 100,000 Irish emigrants, mainly from rural southern and western counties, settled near the Thames, in Southwark and London's East End, where work was plentiful though poorly paid and often casualised.

The streets leading towards Bow from Mile End have Welsh rather than Irish names such as Aberavon Road, Rhondda Grove and Morgan Street. Sir Charles Morgan combined his Tredegar-based iron industry with east London's shipbuilding industry and

---

4   Letter to Margaret Harkness who published searing accounts of urban deprivation in London under the male pseudonym, John Law. https://www.marxists.org/archive/marx/works/1888/letters/88_04_15.htm

5   L. Raw, *Striking a Light: The Bryant and May Matchwomen and their Place in History*, London: Continuum, 2009.

developed the land around Tredegar Square from the profits. Many enterprises close to the docks were connected with shipbuilding: rope-makers, candle-makers, sail-makers, and timber yards. Other East End districts had their own distinct industries. Bethnal Green and Shoreditch had a large furniture trade; Stepney and Poplar had many bootmakers and shoemakers. But the East End's most enduring industry was clothing. Flemish weavers settled locally in the fourteenth century. French Huguenot refugees, specialising in silk-weaving, were conspicuous in seventeenth- and eighteenth-century Spitalfields and Bethnal Green. The clothing industry expanded greatly in Whitechapel among Irish and East European Jewish immigrants.

Booth's cousin, Beatrice Potter, was fascinated and repelled by immigrant Jews' sweatshops – a 'new province of production, inhabited by a peculiar people', where minutely subdivided tasks were performed by unskilled, often unregulated workers. Their system, she claimed, super-exploited Jewish and non-Jewish women performing low-status tasks, and harmed indigenous English tailors who followed 'one man, one garment' methods, with regulated pay and hours. Potter noted that even when women performed the same tasks as men they were paid less money. Her sharp economic analysis was blunted by anti-Jewish prejudice: 'love of profit', she wrote, is 'the impelling motive of the Jewish race.'[6]

Labour within east London's industries was sharply divided by gender. Men carried out hard, physical work especially on the docks and in furniture workshops. But wherever workers could assemble products through repetitive, unskilled tasks, performed

---

6   Article on the Jewish community, in Charles Booth (ed.), *Life and Labour of the People in London*, London: Williams and Norgate, 1889.

over exhaustingly long hours, East End employers preferred to hire women, knowing they could pay them less than men.

In Lancashire, many women joined trade unions, especially textile workers, but, until the late 1880s, London's trade unionists were mainly men – builders, carpenters, printers, shoemakers, stonemasons and tailors. The East End's female workers had no vehicle through which to challenge their conditions and most male workers, fearing their wages would be lowered if women infiltrated their industries, offered little solidarity.

During the 1880s a sustained economic depression brought high unemployment. Rumblings of discontent turned into rebellion. The Salvation Army founder, William Booth, claimed that many east Londoners fared worse than a cab-horse, which usually had 'shelter for the night, food for its stomach, work allotted to it by which it can eat its corn'. Regular employment, however poorly paid, had kept families afloat. As unemployment pulled this fraying rug from under their feet, a new wave of political radicals encouraged struggling workers to fight back collectively.

Before 1880, London's political radicals campaigned mainly to expand democracy and challenge the Church's authority. But the 1880s produced new organisations, spreading Marx's idea that the working class was the motor of social change. The Stratford Dialectical and Radical Club emerged from the local Secular Society. It held meetings on Mile End Waste – a space previously dominated by street preachers – and transformed itself into the Labour Emancipation League (LEL). The LEL formed branches in Stratford, Canning Town, Bethnal Green and Hackney, calling for 'political equality with equal social rights for all'. Hyndman's SDF created east London outposts including one on Burdett Road, Mile End. When William Morris's Socialist League split off, it established premises nearby on Bridge Street. But increasingly, new organisations, spreading rebellious ideas in working-class areas focused on outdoor spaces.

East London's liveliest pitches were at Dod Street, Limehouse, Victoria Park in Bethnal Green and Mile End Waste. In Dod Street, to the government's alarm, thousands of workers gathered to hear speakers call for revolutionary change. In 1885, police arrested several socialist activists there, while leaving religious speakers undisturbed. One activist, Annie Besant, formed an organisation to give legal assistance to arrested socialists, and saved SDF member and Jewish tailors' union leader, Lewis Lyons, from a custodial sentence.

Radicals encouraged workers to challenge economic injustice and also targeted Britain's coercive policies in Ireland. The Metropolitan Radical Federation, the Irish National League, the SDF and Socialist League, called a major protest in November 1887 in Trafalgar Square against attacks on Irish civil rights campaigners and the imprisonment of Irish MP William O'Brien. Meanwhile, Sir Charles Warren, an ex-military man appointed to head the Metropolitan Police in 1886, asked the Home Secretary to ban meetings by unemployed workers camping out in Trafalgar Square, London's principal free speech venue, nominally owned by the Crown. Three separate issues – Ireland, unemployment and free speech – each felt strongly in east London, led 30,000 protesters to converge on Trafalgar Square. They endured savage beatings from police and troops in what became known as 'Bloody Sunday'. Hundreds of demonstrators were arrested, including several socialist speakers.

Annie Besant was aggrieved because she *wasn't* arrested. Born Annie Wood in London in 1847, she came to socialism via radical secularism, and felt the Irish issue keenly. 'Three quarters of my blood and all my heart are Irish', she wrote.[7] Educated by an evangelical Christian, Annie married Reverend Frank Besant at 20 and had two children, Digby and Mabel. Reverend Besant's abusive treatment of Annie prompted her to question her faith.[8] After they separated, Annie met secularists and political radicals through South Place Ethical Society,[9] and was strongly influenced by the 'poor-man's lawyer', William Prowting Roberts, a former Chartist who said the poor were 'the working bees, the wealth producers with a right to self-rule [and] justice not to charity'. She began writing for Charles Bradlaugh's secularist *National Reformer*, and told Christians: 'I don't deny God, but deny your [interventionist] God who is an impossibility.' Her pet hate, though, was Christian charity, which gave

... a hundredweight of coal and five pounds of beef once a year to a family who could earn a hundred such doles if Christian justice allowed him a fair wage for the work he performs. It plunders the workers of the wealth they make, and then flings back at them a thousandth part of their own product as charity. It builds hospitals for the poor whom it has poisoned in filthy courts and alleys.[10]

---

7   A. Besant, *Annie Besant: An Autobiography*, London: Theosophical Society, 1893.

8   Besant also attributed her early doubts about Christianity to a 'merciful God' allowing her daughter Mabel to suffer a life-threatening illness in her early years.

9   See Chapter 5.

10 Besant, *Autobiography*, p.182.

In her first major speaking engagement, [11] a lecture in August 1874 on women's political status, Besant said she longed for the day, when women and men would be '[c]o-workers in every labour, co-partners in every righteous project, co-soldiers in every just cause'. They could bring different and complementary talents: 'The man ... his greater strength and more sustained determination, the woman her quicker judgement and purer heart, till man shall grow tenderer and woman stronger, man more pure, and woman more brave and free ... free to grow, to strengthen and to rise.'

A week after the first Bloody Sunday demonstration, at which male police and soldiers hid their tender side, protesters returned to the Square. Again the authorities responded fiercely. A young clerk, Alfred Linnell, was trampled to death under a police horse. Annie Besant organised a mass funeral parade from Central London to Tower Hamlets Cemetery (known locally as Bow Cemetery). The Socialist League's *Commonweal* reported:

> An open hearse with four horses was used; on top ... a shield painted black with large white letters 'Killed in Trafalgar Square' ... behind ... three flags, green, yellow, and red, for the Irish, radicals and socialists ... the train stretched in an unbroken length for nearly a mile, with a large number of banners, mostly red, and several bands playing slow marches. ... Bow cemetery was reached at half past four, when it was already dark.[12]

At the graveside William Morris said that Linnell's 'hard life

---

11 At the Cooperative Hall in Castle Street, W1.

12 *Commonweal*, 24 December 1887.

and hard death' illustrated the need to transform society. Morris sensed that change was in the air. In January 1888, he wrote:

> If rebellion is ... our future, then we must look back at the past year with hope ... no one who witnessed the sympathetic demeanour of the huge crowds that accompanied ... Linnell's funeral procession could ... deny that the masses of London are on our side. Democratic ideas tending towards socialism have been evolved from the Irish struggle and men's minds have been familiarised thereby with resistance to authority; the precariousness of livelihood under the capitalist has been brought home ... the class war is becoming obvious to all.[13]

In June 1888, at a Fabian Society lecture, Besant heard Clementina Black discussing 'Female Labour in London'. From the floor, a former artillery officer called Henry Hyde Champion lit his pipe theatrically, then described conditions at Bryant & May's match factory in Bow, where women worked long hours for paltry wages.[14] Their health was undermined by having to eat at their workstations where they used dangerous materials.[15] The following evening, Besant and three colleagues from her left-wing paper, the *Link*, waited by the factory gates to interview women coming off their shift.

Bryant and May had acquired this former candle, crinoline and

---

13 *Commonweal*, 7 January 1888.

14 Born in Poona India, Champion often wore an eye glass, a dress suit and silk hat. He resigned his army post while on leave, in protest at Britain's Egyptian campaign with which he profoundly disagreed; 'the next night', he said 'I was preaching socialism in Clerkenwell Green'.

15 Charles Dickens wrote an article in 1852 on health hazards in matchmaking. See Raw, *Striking a Light*, p.93.

rope factory in 1861. As Quakers and Liberals, they considered themselves enlightened employers.[16] But the workers corroborated Champion's charges and Besant published a strident exposé in the *Link*. Describing a 16-year-old earning just four shillings a week, Besant said this sum was subject to deductions

> ... if the feet are dirty, or the ground under the bench is left untidy, a fine of 3d... for putting 'burnts' – matches that have caught fire during the work – on the bench 1s ... and one unhappy girl was once fined 2s/6d for some unknown crime. If a girl leaves four or five matches on her bench when she goes for a fresh 'frame' she is fined 3d ... some departments a fine of 3d. is inflicted for talking ... One girl was fined 1s. for letting the web twist round a machine ... to save her fingers from being cut, and was sharply told to take care of the machine, 'never mind your fingers'. Another, who ... lost a finger thereby, was left unsupported while she was helpless.[17]

Besant sent a copy to the company directors. Bryant replied by telegram: 'Nothing but a tissue of lies. Will receive legal attention.' Factory foremen tried to bully the workforce into signing a statement confirming that conditions were satisfactory. When the women refused, the management summarily sacked several 'ringleaders'. In response, the women spontaneously walked out. The next day, a male activist urged picketing matchworkers to stay strong and form a union. The police arrested him for obstruction,

---

16 Quakers had established some early industries of the East End and established some hospitals and schools.

17 'Slavery in London', the *Link*, 23 June 1888.

but were followed to the station by pickets who demonstrated until he was released. He was Lewis Lyons, the Jewish tailors' leader Annie Besant had bailed out in 1885.

During the dispute, she and SDF member Herbert Burrows helped the women form a Union of Women Matchmakers. The women were determined to stay out until the company reinstated those sacked; ended the system of fines; and agreed to create a separate area where they could eat during their twelve-hour shifts without contaminating their food.

The strikers sought community support. On 8 July they held a rally at Mile End Waste featuring Clementina Black, Cunningham Grahame MP, and radical preacher Stewart Headlam. They marched through the City into the West End returning with donations, and stopping for tea and solidarity at a Workers' Club in Berner Street established by Jewish anarchists. Matchwomen took a petition to Parliament with thousands of signatures, and gained sympathetic press coverage. On 13 July Bryant & May declared that nothing would make them concede. They threatened to recruit new workers from Glasgow and talked of relocating to Scandinavia. It was bluster. Within two weeks, they acquiesced to the strikers' demands. The matchwomen's victory provided a template for action by other low paid, low skilled workers.

The factory closed in 1979 but its redbrick buildings remain. Today, Fairfield Works is the gentrified gated Bow Quarter. Its blocks called Arlington, Lexington and Manhattan, mask continuing hardship in the East End with a veneer of New York sophistication. Its on-site leisure centre boasts a pool, sauna, dance studio and gym. Under the Arlington Arch, inside the gate, a large display tells the factory's history, including the strike, but the public are excluded.

Its outer wall has a plaque commemorating the strike, 'led here by Annie Besant'. Bryant & May always claimed that contented workers were radicalised by outside agitators. Counter-narratives also portray the women as passive and docile, needing leadership by educated socialists. The names of those who actually led the strike – Alice France, Kate Slater, Mary Driscoll, Jane Wakeling and Eliza Martin – struggle for wider recognition.

Louise Raw has convincingly shown that Besant was a *supporter*, rather than leader of the matchwomen's cause, who favoured a boycott over industrial action. Raw discovered that the women, largely from close-knit, politically aware Irish communities, had initiated earlier (unsuccessful) strikes and some of them knew Besant from pro-Irish political platforms. She quotes Booth's survey material describing the women as 'a terrible rough lot' displaying insolent confidence rather than docility. '[D]ecent people scarcely dared to go down the street when they were coming out of work.'[18] Excitable behaviour, though, was not new to Fairfield Road: a plaque on the former Poplar Town Hall reveals that the Whitsun Fair, which gave the street its name, was closed in 1823 because of 'rowdyism and vice'.

Annie Besant contributed to east London's progressive campaigns from 1885–90, after which her increasing interest in theosophy diverted her. The strike, though, gave heart to local unskilled workers and had more enduring consequences. London's industrial expansion was powered by gasworkers, including thousands of Eastenders working twelve-hour shifts as at Beckton, near West Ham. An unusual leader emerged among them. Neither Will Thorne nor his wife could sign their names on the register at their marriage because they were illiterate

---

18 Raw, *Striking a Light*, p.151.

Bryant & May match factory, 1890s.

and made a 'mark' instead. At six years old, instead of going to school, he worked twelve hours a day, five-and-a-half days a week turning a wheel at Rob's Rope Walk in his native Birmingham and worked in his uncle's barber shop for much of the remainder of the weekend.

Despite his illiteracy he was a powerful orator and excellent organiser. He was 24 when he first arrived in London in 1881, having lost his job as a gas stoker in Saltley after a failed strike. Leaving his pregnant wife and child behind, he set off for the capital on foot, promising to send for them when he found regular work. He worked at Old Kent Gas Works in south London, but was a victim of the 'last in – first out' rule when the company reduced its workforce the following summer. Returning home, Thorne temporarily found work again at Saltley Gas Works before he came back to the Big Smoke for good, settling in Lawrence Street, Canning Town after being taken on at Beckton Gas Works.

Thorne joined Hyndman's SDF in 1884. His local branch had 14 members and met in a member's house in Lansdowne Road. He added another affiliation in 1885 – the Temperance Union – good for his health and his pocket. Through the SDF he mixed with socialist thinkers and activists such as Eleanor Marx, George Bernard Shaw, John Burns and Tom Mann. He assisted the Federation's struggles to establish outdoor pitches to spread their ideas, especially in east London, and gained experience in addressing mass audiences.

Acutely aware of east London's growing unemployment, he participated in the 'Bloody Sunday' demonstrations, experienced a ferocious police charge and saw colleagues arrested. He returned home injured and more determined to transform the lives of fellow workers and those starving through lack of work. He knew these struggles required patience but, eager to make an immediate difference, he helped to establish a soup kitchen in a temperance bar at 144 Barking Road, East Ham, a venue soon to play a bigger role in Thorne's union struggles. On Saturday nights Thorne and colleagues visited food shops seeking contributions of bread and ingredients for soup. Zibach, who helped run the Temperance Bar, allowed them to use kitchen equipment.

Thorne discussed socialist and trade union ideas at work 'in the lobby, in the mess room, wherever the opportunity permitted'.

Meanwhile, management introduced new technology, called 'the Iron Man', that increased productivity but made the work harder, and compelled randomly selected workers to work 18-hour shifts on a Sunday, instead of twelve. Anger and frustration were growing. Thorne called a meeting in Canning Town for 31 March 1889 with a platform of rousing speakers. Thorne himself led a contingent from Barking, 'with a band I paid for out of my own pocket. We had an old van for a platform ... the atmosphere was electric when I mounted the platform.'

Acknowledging the workers' inhuman treatment by their employers, he greeted the crowd as 'fellow wage slaves'. They responded with a great cheer. He told them:

> ... we have protested, but ... we have been sneered at, ignored and have secured no redress ... you will never get any alteration in ... your conditions or wages unless you join together and form a strong trade union ... it is easy to break one stick, but when fifty sticks are together in one bundle it is a much more difficult job.[19]

He promised the workers that if they organised as a union, 'within six months we will claim and win the eight-hour day, a six-day week and the abolition of the present slave-driving methods in vogue not only at the Beckton Gas Works, but all over the country'.

'Will you do this?' He asked his rapt audience. 'There was one loud roar of "We will!"', he recorded. Thorne described this moment as 'the last birth pain of the union'.[20]

---

19 W. Thorne, *My Life's Battles*, London: G. Newnes, 1925, p.68.
20 *Ibid.*, pp.68–9

Some 800 members enrolled at that meeting. They gathered at 144 Barking Road on Sundays and sent out groups of workers on a 'crusade' to win union members at other gas works and local factories. Within weeks they had 3,000 members and a provisional committee. Union dues were kept at two pence a week, and membership was spread across a range of jobs. Members received a union card with the motto: 'love, unity, fidelity'.

Some workers favoured campaigning for a pay increase of one shilling per day, but most backed Thorne's strategy, to fight for the eight-hour day, 'Shorten the hours and prolong your lives', he said. He recruited able co-workers, including Eleanor Marx – a multi-talented organiser, translator and writer, who drew up the union rules and helped in administration.

When Thorne judged that they had sufficient muscle to challenge their employers, he petitioned the company directors and informed them that thousands of union members were willing to strike, but preferred to negotiate. The petition landed on their desks just as the employers' fear of competition from electric lighting was intensifying. After several weeks Thorne received word that the directors had conceded the eight-hour day. There were still issues to resolve but negotiations concluded with a spectacular victory for the union. Two twelve-hour shifts were replaced by three eight-hour shifts. More workers were taken on, and existing workers whose hours were reduced suffered no loss of pay.

Will Thorne's Gas Workers and General Labourers Union later became the General Municipal and Boiler-Makers Union (GMB). He was proud that this union was 'one of the very few in which men and women are on equal terms', stating 'We want unions of *workers* not of workingmen and workingwomen.' As an Executive Committee member, Eleanor Marx took special responsibility for two all-women branches.

Ben Tillett, another rising figure in east London's labour movement, also began working young. At seven years old he worked long days at Roach's brickyard in Bristol, though he was probably relieved to get away from home, where his alcoholic father and a succession of stepmothers mistreated or neglected him. After two failed attempts to run away, he escaped with a circus troupe, who taught him acrobatics. He took a stray dog with him. The circus troupe gave him a Shetland pony to look after. At night he slept next to the pony and the dog kept rats away. One of Tillett's five sisters tracked him down and took him to relatives in Staffordshire, where he had two years of schooling before being apprenticed to a shoemaker. At 13 he joined the Royal Navy, visiting various European ports, Philadelphia and the Caribbean, and learned to read and write with the help of a Scottish friend. Fittingly, in terms of his future activism, he sailed on one ship called *Resistance*. Between voyages he stayed with his sister's mother-in-law in Bethnal Green, east London. He finally settled there at 16 years old, working at Markie's boot factory, and joined the Union of Boot and Shoe Operatives.

Tillett married Jane Tompkins and they shared her mother's flat in Hunslett Street. Determined to expand his intellectual horizons he became the librarian at his local church, taught himself basic Latin and Greek, and attended lectures at Bow and Bromley Adult Education Institute. He struggled to overcome a stammer by reading Dickens to Jane in the evenings.

He began working on the docks, describing the humiliating 'call-on' system in a powerful speech at Whitechapel in 1887, later published as *A Dock Labourer's Bitter Cry*.

'We are driven into a shed, iron-barred from end to end, outside of which a foreman or contractor walks up and down with the air of a dealer in a cattle market ... choosing from a crowd of men, who, in their eagerness to obtain employment trample each other under foot, and where like beasts they fight for the chances of a day's work.'

A 'day's work' was usually less. Dockworkers often walked great distances to a job, unloaded cargo non-stop for two hours, and were then told to go home. Tillett himself recalled a 40-mile round trip on foot. Beatrice Potter noted the 'hidden irony in the dockers' fate', touching all things but enjoying none as ' ... the luxuries of our elaborate civilisation pass familiarly through the dock labourer's hands'.

The supply of dock labour constantly outstripped demand, driving wages down. One contemporary account describes how dockers 'faint from over-exhaustion and want of food ... are ruptured, their spines injured, their bones broken, and their skulls fractured ... to get ships loaded and unloaded a little quicker and a little cheaper'. This was not a socialist propaganda leaflet but the prestigious medical journal, *The Lancet*.

Tillett was working as a tea cooper at Monument Tea Warehouse in spring 1887 when a dispute broke out among counterparts at Cutler Street Warehouse. They sought Tillett's advice and he helped them to form the Tea Operatives and General Labourers' Association (TOGLA) – a union that would help to challenge the main companies exploiting the dockers.

Tillett was elected as TOGLA's Union Secretary and spent most Sundays speaking and recruiting at the dock gates. His personal diary from 1888 recorded disappointments and successes: frustratingly small meetings in March, when snow still covered the ground after a harsh winter; optimism in April when he met the well-organised stevedores and sold copies of *Bitter Cry*. In June he noted large meetings at the dock gates, while 'enthusiastic crowds' attended indoor evening meetings. When industrial disputes broke out among some dockworkers in October and November, he invited Annie Besant and Herbert Burrows to talk to them about the matchworkers' successful struggle. These dock disputes ultimately failed, but Tillett glimpsed the prospect of wider action. His final diary entry for 1888 recorded, 'Cold worse than ever. Went to chapel. Old year out. Like to live next year a more useful life than last.'[21] He would. By early 1889 momentum was building. Hundreds of TOGLA members paid regular union dues and thousands of dockers expressed growing enthusiasm in meetings around the docks. TOGLA established branches in Tilbury, Poplar and Canning Town.

Participants and historians dispute when the Great Dock Strike began. Will Thorne described a meeting at South Dock gates on Monday 12 August 1889 when he and a stevedore, Tom McCarthy, addressed a large, disgruntled crowd before the eight o'clock call-on. McCarthy listed their grievances and Thorne urged them to form a union and refuse to work. The workers unanimously supported a strike. Simultaneously, dockers unloading the *Lady Armstrong* in the South Dock basin of West India Docks were withholding their labour because a promised bonus had not been paid. Their leader wrote to the dock authorities on Tuesday 13 August with demands that included a minimum four-hour call-on (instead of the usual two or three); wages to be sixpence

---

21   The Modern Records Centre at Warwick University holds Tillett's 1888 diary.

Striking dockworkers, 1889.

an hour (eight pence for overtime), and an end to piecework. Ben Tillett had sent similar demands the previous week, but the dock authorities had not responded. On Wednesday 14 August, Tillett met the *Lady Armstrong* workers. On Friday that week the Amalgamated Stevedores Union announced that dock labourers were on strike, and appealed to 'engineers, fitters, boiler-makers, ships' carpenters, coal heavers, ballast men and lightermen', for solidarity action, and for help from the community.

A collective leadership emerged. Ben Tillett, Tom Mann, John Burns and Tom McCarthy mobilised support. Eleanor Marx took on key administrative tasks and Henry Hyde Champion, whose comments in June 1888 prompted Annie Besant's explosive articles about Bryant & May, acted as press officer. Will Thorne said Tom Mann was 'like a streak of human quicksilver, here, there and everywhere, commanding, pleading, cajoling, enthusing', while Tillett possessed 'a spark of genius' and 'planned a picket system for the whole 50 miles of London's docks'.[22] As well as demands over hours and pay, the strike committee crucially demanded union recognition throughout the port. Without it, companies could break agreements without being held to account.

In the last week of August many East End industries were idle. That week the female workforces of Frost's Ropemakers in Commerical Road and Peak Frean's biscuits in Bermondsey walked out. Women also collected donations and organised rent strikes. In Hungerford Street, near Watney Market, a banner defiantly declared: 'As we are on strike landlords need not call.'

Neither TOGLA nor the Amalgamated Stevedores Union had substantial strike funds, so the committee focused on sustaining the strikers' families through meal tickets redeemable at certain shops. The Salvation Army's hall on Whitechapel Road supplied thousands of loaves of bread each day to strikers' families, and local churches opened soup kitchens. Following the matchwomen's example, striking dockers marched through the area and beyond, holding meetings on open spaces.

On 25 August 1889 a spectacular parade, 50,000 strong, headed for the City. Brass bands, banners proclaiming 'Unity and Victory' and horse-drawn boats carrying strikers in fancy dress, lent it a carnival-like appearance. Street theatre players contrasted dockers' and employers' lives: plates with a director's

---

22 Speakers' Corner orator Bonar Thompson said that Mann's oratory combined 'Fire, vehemence, passion, humour, drama and crashing excitement'.

dinner piled high next to a docker's crust of bread and a tiny herring; puppets represented a docker's scrawny child in rags and a well-fed, well-dressed director's child, and their cats – one thin, the other the director's 'Fat Cat'.[23] They returned with donations of hundreds of pounds. Weekend marches ended in huge rallies, some at Tower Hill, others in Hyde Park, where at the end of August, 100,000 people gathered around 20 speakers' platforms.

On 27 August the *Evening News* estimated that 130,000 workers were on strike, and it was spreading: ' ... [E]ven factory girls are coming out. If it goes on a few days longer, all London will be on holiday ... the proverbial small spark has kindled a great fire which threatens to envelope the whole metropolis.'

That spark had been lit by the 1,400 women who walked out at Bryant & May's Fairfield Works the previous year and became role-models for their brothers, husbands and uncles, many of them dockworkers.

As August drew to a close, the strike entered its most critical period. The extraordinary effort and sacrifice by workers, with solid community backing, had not persuaded the dock employers. Daily collections could not feed all the strikers' families. Hunger was sapping morale. The strike committee considered calling on workers across the capital to come out indefinitely in solidarity. A general London strike might pressurise the employers to settle, but risk losing a significant section of public and press support and be very problematic to sustain. On 29 August the committee took that risk and issued the 'No Work' manifesto, which appealed to 'workers in London of all grades and every calling' to stay at home from Monday, ' ... unless the directors have before

---

23 The expression 'fat cat' may be based on this. Others claim it was first used by political commentators in 1920s America.

noon on Saturday ... officially informed the committee that the moderate demands of the dock labourers have been fully and finally conceded'.[24]

Key members of the strike committee expressed misgivings. Within 24 hours the manifesto was withdrawn but with a face-saving appeal to London's workers to contribute generously towards the strike fund. There were also stresses on the other side; frustrated ship-owners pressured the dock companies to compromise, but the dock employers scented victory, believing time favoured them.

Suddenly a game-changing donation of £1,500 arrived – from the Brisbane Wharf Labourers' Union of Australia – with a message that much more would follow. Over a relatively short period, thousands of pounds were telegraphed to the dock strike committee from their antipodean counterparts, collected though unions and amateur football clubs. The prospect of the docks remaining idle for several more weeks forced the companies to negotiate. A respected local priest, Cardinal Manning, mediated and the strike was settled by mid-September, with the dockers winning their 'tanner' – sixpence per hour (and eight pence for overtime), and a minimum four-hour call-on in most cases.

Within a short time Tillett's pioneering efforts at dockside unionisation had helped to create a Dock, Wharf, Riverside and General Labourers Union with 18,000 members. By 1890, in the light of the matchworkers', gasworkers' and dockers'successes, commentators acclaimed a 'new unionism' born of rebellion, not only against their employers but also against earlier trade unions as small, inward-looking bodies representing what Engels termed

---

24 T. McCarthy, *The Great Dock Strike*, 1889, London: Weidenfeld and Nicholson, 1988, p.125.

'the aristocracy of labour'. East London was the cradle of these struggles.

A more traditional trade unionist, George Shipton considered 'new unionism' too militant. His critical article in *Murray's Magazine* in June 1890, however, gave Tom Mann and Ben Tillett – respectively President and Secretary of the post-strike dockers' union – the opportunity to explain the difference between old unionism and new unionism to its readers. Tillett and Mann said the old unionists '... do not recognise, as we do, that it is the work of the trade unions to stamp out poverty from the land ... We are prepared to work unceasingly for the emancipation of the workers. Our ideal is the Cooperative Commonwealth.'[25]

Although Mann and Tillett cherished the new means of struggle, that transcended the narrow confines of individual workplaces, they valued and honoured 'old union' activists, whose day was passing, as fighters who showed enormous courage, 'when to be a unionist was to be a social martyr ... with the hue and cry against them of police and Parliament'.

By 1892, Engels had cheered up. He described the new unionists as 'rough, neglected' toilers, 'looked down upon by the working class aristocracy', but with an immense advantage, as their minds 'were virgin soil, entirely free from the inherited "respectable" bourgeois prejudices which hampered the brains of the better situated old unionists'.[26]

The rebels who triumphed over powerful economic forces and revolutionised struggles for workers' rights, created new possibilities for those following their footsteps into the twentieth century.

---

25 Their reply was later produced as a pamphlet, *The New Trades Unionism*, London: Green & McAllan, 1890.

26 Kenneth Lapides (ed.), *Marx and Engels on the Trade Unions*, New York: Praeger, 1987, p.163.

The first significant branches of the suffragette movement in London grew in the east, where female matchworkers had fought for their workplace rights. Close to Beckton Gas Works, West Ham returned a pioneering socialist MP in 1892, James Keir Hardie. Tom Mann's grassroots organising in workplace struggles prepared him for a pivotal role in the growth of the syndicalist movement that believed true political advances would come only through economic struggles.

Ben Tillett developed his self-confidence and showed courage in the face of powerful enemies. He urged the next generation of activists to be brave and radical, telling students at Ruskin (trade union) College in 1913: 'I don't want you to be statesmen, don't for God's sake be politicians: they have always been evils. I want you to be idealists.' Unfortunately he didn't follow his own advice, becoming an MP in 1917 in Salford, Manchester, and moving to the right politically, but others continued the grass-roots rebellion.

The Match Girls Strike of 1888
was led here by
ANNIE BESANT
Journalist and Lecturer
1847 - 1933

FAIRFIELD ROAD

WREXHAM ROAD

JEBB STREET

GROVE HALL PARK

BROMLEY HIGH STREET

⑧

⑨

⑪

⑫

⑩

BOW ROAD

BOW CHURCH

TREDEGAR ROAD

MOSTYN GROVE

MALMESBURY ROAD

⑦

GEORGE LANSBURY

BOW ROAD

⑥

HARLEY GROVE

⑤

BOW ROAD

COBORN ROAD

MORGAN ARMS
1892.

③

④

②

TREDEGAR SQUARE

RHONDDA GROVE

① MILE END

WHITE CHAPEL

200M

74

WALK

Start at Mile End Station, E3 4DH.

1. *Mile End station*
The original designation of Mile End was a stone, one mile east of the White Chapel that stood in St Mary's Garden (now Altab Ali Park). Cross the road and turn right to Tredegar Square, passing Rhondda Grove on the way.

2. *Tredegar Square*
Walk through the gardens in Tredegar Square, one of several Welsh names marking the land developed by the iron magnate Charles Morgan. He lived within the block of grand white houses on Morgan Street. The pub on the corner with Coborn Road bears his name. Turn right into Coborn Road.

3. *Coborn Road*
A carved wall stone marks the parish boundary of Mile End Old Town. Earlier it delineated two large estates: Morgan's and Coborn's. It later signified the Metropolitan Borough boundary between Stepney to the west and Poplar to the east. Before 1800, Coborn Road was known as Cut Throat Lane. Stop on the corner of Coborn Road and Bow Road.

4. *Coborn Road/Bow Road*

The building opposite, which started to be converted into housing in 2011, was originally constructed as the City of London Union (Bow) Workhouse in1849, becoming an infirmary in 1874, before being renamed St Clements Hospital in the 1930s. Turn left into Bow Road.

5. *Bow Road/Harley Grove*

A plaque embedded in stone stands in front of the estate that replaced the house of *Daily Herald* editor and rebel Labour MP George Lansbury, who lived here with his wife Bessie. He began his political career as a Liberal but his experiences supporting the dock strike in 1889 helped turn him towards socialism. Continue up Harley Grove.

6. *Harley Grove*

On the right is the side entrance to Phoenix School, built on the former site of Bow Open Air School, which had been constructed out of wood, and designed for children with respiratory problems. The building was destroyed in the Second World War. The Sikh temple at the end of Harley Grove replaced a synagogue that opened in 1927, which, in turn, replaced a Methodist chapel from the 1850s. As Jews settled in east London in the late nineteenth century, the Conservative MP for Bow, Captain John Colomb, said: 'I object to England with its overcrowded population, being made a human ashpit for the refuse population of the world.' Cut diagonally through the estate to the right on to Malmesbury Road and turn right.

7. Malmesbury Road

In the distance you will see the red chimney of the former Bryant & May match factory. Go left under Tom Thumb's archway, along Mostyn Grove, turn right into Tredegar Road, which once housed the Tredegar Silk Mill, then turn right into Fairfield Road.

8. Fairfield Road

Halfway down the road is the gated Bow Quarter estate, converted from the original Bryant & May match factory where the 1888 strike took place. The factory closed in 1979. A plaque celebrates Annie Besant's role in this dispute. Continue along Fairfield Road. Turn left into Wrexham Road, then right into Jebb Street, left into Grove Hall Park then turn right and exit Grove Hall Park through an alleyway alongside the Nunnery Gallery on to Bow Road.

9. Bow Road (island in the middle)

Cross to the road island which incorporates Bow Church. The statue of William Gladstone was donated by Theodore Bryant, a director of the match factory. The factory workers were given half a day off for the unveiling. Annie Besant claimed that matchwomen cut themselves and daubed blood over the plinth when they understood that a shilling had been deducted from their wages to pay for it, although this may be confused with an incident at a fountain donated by Bryant & May further west on Bow Road. In honour of the original story, activists periodically daub red paint on Gladstone's hand. Cross to the south side of Bow Road and turn right.

10. Bow Road/Bromley High Street

At 198 Bow Road (now a block of flats), the East London Federation of Suffragettes had their first shop/office on the site of a disused bakery, and set up a regular street-meeting platform round the corner on Bromley High Street. Continue along Bow Road to the junction with Fairfield Road.

11. Fairfield Road

On the side of the former Poplar Town Hall is a small plaque that recalls the closing down of the Whitsun Fair (also known as the Green Goose Fair) in 1823, as a result of raucous behaviour. Turn back towards Bow Road then turn right.

12. Bow Road/Fairfield Road

The old Poplar Town Hall (now offices), built in the late 1930s, replaced Bromley Vestry Hall. Look up at the mosaic on the canopy entrance of dockers unloading a variety of goods, reflect on Beatrice Potter's observation that 'the luxuries of our elaborate civilisation pass familiarly through the dock labourer's hands', and remember the strikers of 1888 and 1889 who created the 'new unionism'.

East End tailoring sweatshop, early 1900s.

4

COMING IN FROM THE COLD

Immigrant Agitators and Radicals in Spitalfields

In September 1889, as the docks lay idle, the local newspapers claimed that the whole East End was 'infected with Strike Fever': '... [C]oal men; match girls; parcels postmen; car men ... employees in jam, biscuit, rope, iron, screw, clothing and railway works have found some grievance, real and imaginary, and have [come] out on strike.'[1]

There was nothing 'imaginary' about the clothing workers' grievances. They were among London's most exploited workers, slaving 14 to 18 hours per day, six days a week, in 'unhealthy and dirty dens', many on piece rates rather than regular wages. Forming effective unions in this industry was extremely difficult, and owed much to Lewis Lyons' pioneering efforts. Born in 1862 to German-Jewish immigrants, Lyons worked as a tailor from the age of eleven.

As the docks dispute intensified, a strike committee led by Lyons called clothing workers out against the 'unbearable' hardships 'inflicted ... by the Sweater'. Five months earlier, gasworkers at Beckton, led by Will Thorne, opted to fight for shorter hours rather than higher pay, and won the eight-hour day. The clothing workers followed suit. They downed presses,

1 *East London News*, 7 September 1889.

scissors and needles, and left sewing machines idle, until their employers agreed that their 'hours be reduced to 12', including 'one hour for dinner and half-hour for tea', consumed off-site. They further demanded that no work should be sent home to complete 'after working hours'.

Lyons' Strike Committee met at the White Hart public house on Greenfield Street (renamed Greenfield Road), Whitechapel. The pub stood within a triangle bordered by Whitechapel Road, Commercial Road and Jubilee Street that housed an immigrant ghetto of Jews who had fled Tsarist Russia. Many of the 7–8,000 *shnayders*[2] who walked out were first-time strikers. A trickle of Yiddish-speaking Russian and Polish Jews came to London in the 1860s and 1870s, but cataclysmic events in the Russian Empire in 1881 turned a trickle into a flood.

A revolutionary group, *Narodnaya Volya*,[3] threatened to assassinate Tsar Alexander II, who ruled over an authoritarian state. The revolutionaries believed that their action would usher in a period of chaos in which new forms of popular power might emerge. A bomb exploded and the Tsar was dead. But a new Tsar, Alexander III, quickly restored order from chaos and strengthened repression.

One member of the assassination squad was Jewish. Hesya Helfman had found refuge among revolutionaries after escaping a threatened arranged marriage. The new Tsar blamed the chaos following his predecessor's demise on the Jews. Mobs launched pogroms on the Jews in their towns and villages, looting and burning shops and homes, wounding and killing people while

---

2   *Shnayders* – the Yiddish term for 'cutters', used generically to describe tailors and makers of clothing.

3   The People's Liberty emerged from *Zemlya Volya* (Land and Liberty) among peasants, students and workers, especially in the Ukrainian and Volga regions.

the authorities looked on. Fear gripped Jewish communities as the new Tsar's 'temporary measures', intensified the restrictions already undermining Jews' lives. Facing random attacks, bound by discriminatory laws, and struggling economically, many Jews began to migrate towards their 'promised land' – America. Britain was a halfway house, but many stayed. Others paid unscrupulous travel agents in Hamburg for tickets to New York, which were actually marked 'London'. Most Jewish immigrants to Britain gravitated to London's East End, finding work as *shnayders* (tailors), *shusters* (boot and shoemakers) and *stolyers* (cabinet-makers) for employers who spoke their Yiddish mother-tongue.

City and West End firms dominated London's clothing industry. They profited handsomely by subcontracting work to East End sweatshops, where a continuous flow of 'greeners' (new immigrants) enabled employers to depress wages. Middlemen also directed government contracts for army uniforms to East End workshops, which typically employed 10–25 workers, numbers small enough to avoid inspection under the 1867 Factory Act.

The thousands who walked out in 1889, closing hundreds of workshops, struck against co-religionists, including *landslayt* – family members and neighbours from their old towns. Some tailors struggled with this; others had already lost their innocence in Russia's new factories. Jews who had imbibed trade union ideas in Russia assisted Lewis Lyons in forming unions.

Four weeks into the tailors' strike, employers were refusing to compromise and strike funds were almost exhausted. Stitchers, cutters and pressers faced the grim prospect of returning to work having won nothing. But, emboldened by the 'Strike Fever', a tailors' delegation headed for the Wade's Arms, in Jeremiah Street, Poplar, to lobby the Docks Strike Committee.

Many dockers were also immigrants or sons of immigrants – Catholics from the Emerald Isle. As Jews swarmed into Whitechapel, the Irish community shuffled closer to the docks. Stepney became a patchwork of mainly Jewish and Irish enclaves plus seafarers from India, China and Somalia; Italians and Greeks selling food provisions; and German bakers and sugar refiners. But this was no melting pot. Communities kept to familiar streets. Physical confrontations, like today's postcode wars, were commonplace among young Jews and Catholics

Late in life the former dockers' leader Ben Tillett told Jewish trade unionists that he became an agitator in Riga, in 1877, where he disembarked with other sailors. At the market square, local police grinned while young wealthy Russians intimidated Jewish stallholders. Tillett saw an old Jew thrown to the ground. 'As the young Russian lifted his foot to kick [him] I lifted it higher and got him down,' he recounted. The British sailors cleared the police from the square, too.

Tillett saw how Jews suffered under Tsarism. Yet, in the late 1880s, he described Jewish immigrants as the 'dregs and scum of the continent' who 'make more foetid, putrid and congested, our already overcrowded slums'. He told one gathering of Jewish workers: 'You are our brothers and we will do our duty by you, but we wish you had not come.' However, after the tailors' delegation outlined their case, the Dock Strike committee promised £100 – the largest donation the tailors received throughout their dispute.[4] With their strike fund refreshed, they now had the upper hand. Their employers could not afford to suspend production much longer and caved in by the beginning of October. Despite

---

4   Other non-Jewish unions such as the London Society of Compositors contributed funds.

Tillett's antipathy towards immigrants, Irish Catholic dockers' solidarity ensured victory for immigrant Jewish workers.

Cross-community solidarity was further cemented two months later, when a Federation of East London Labour Unions was launched at Mile End's Great Assembly Hall. The *Eastern Post* reported: '2,800 were present ... and speeches were made in different languages and translated.' Non-Jewish union leaders, such as Ben Tillett and Tom Mann, spoke alongside Jewish militants representing tailors, cap-makers, stick-makers, furriers and carpenters. Charles Adams, tasked by the Alliance Cabinet Makers' Association with organising Jewish immigrant carpenters, chaired. He said ' ... if ever labour is to rise successfully ... it must rise as a whole ... This new organisation must be composed of people of all creeds and of all nations', and never let employers 'exploit one against the other'.[5]

A Jewish militant, William (Woolf) Wess, drove this initiative. A shoemaker at twelve, he worked as a machinist in Dvinsk before arriving in London, aged 20, in 1881. Wess lived on Clark Street, near London Hospital, before moving to Cressy House, Stepney Green.[6] He came to London with radical ideas, which developed through involvement in the Socialist League and the 'anarchist-socialist' journal, *Freedom*.[7]

Several years before the tailors' strike, Wess and his comrades laid foundations for activism among immigrant workers by forming unions and establishing an International Workers'

---

5   *Eastern Post*, 4 January 1890.

6   Several immigrant Jewish anarchists lived in Cressy House and its neighbour, Dunstan House.

7   With some breaks, *Freedom* was printed from October 1886 until April 2014, before going online. Freedom Bookshop is in Angel Alley, E1 (stop number 2 on the walk).

Education Club in Berner Street,[8] committed to the 'social and political enlightenment of its members'. It provided a venue for *shnayders*, *shusters* and *stolyers* to eat, drink, play chess or read newspapers after work.

One newspaper they read avidly was *Arbeter Fraynd* (Workers' Friend), a radical Yiddish weekly, later printed on the premises. During major industrial disputes it became a daily strike bulletin. The *Arbeter Fraynd* held a mirror to immigrant workers, reflecting their harsh daily experiences but offering a glimpse, too, of future liberty. It reassured them that workers elsewhere also suffered relentless exploitation but they could challenge their circumstances and change the world, if they acted collectively. This newspaper inspired and motivated immigrant rebels of this period.

One energetic German political exile, born in 1873 and raised in a Catholic orphanage, immersed himself in Jewish immigrants' struggles and amplified these messages. As a teen, Rudolf Rocker was apprenticed as a bookbinder, and joined *Die Jungen* – the German Social Democrats' youth section. *Die Jungen* proved too radical for the parent party. When Rudolf and his friends were expelled, it propelled them towards anarchism. After several of his comrades were arrested, he went into voluntary exile and resurfaced in Paris, where he first encountered Yiddish-speaking revolutionaries. Rocker shared an apartment and working materials with a radical Russian Jewish bookbinder, Shloyme Rappaport.[9]

---

8   Renamed Henriques Street honouring the Sephardi Jew Basil Henriques, who established the Oxford & St George's (boys) Youth Club in Berner Street. His fiancée Rose Loewe later opened a parallel girls' club.

9   Rappaport became a renowned Yiddish playwright after he returned to Russia. Under the pseudonym An-sky, he wrote *The Dybbuk* in 1914, later adapted for film.

In 1895 Rocker moved to London, arriving on a foggy morning into 'a world of ghosts ... people flitted through the murk like shadows. There was a thick clammy yellow mist over everything.'[10] He settled in cosmopolitan Soho, among exiles from the 1848 upheavals. One acquaintance, Otto Schreiber, took Rocker to the city's poorest districts, introducing him to the East End, Deptford and Rotherhithe. Rocker saw

> ... an abyss of human suffering ... squalid courts and alleyways, with dreary tumbledown hovels ... And in these cesspools of poverty, children were born ...
> nowhere was the contrast so vast between assertive wealth and indescribable poverty as in the great cities of Britain. Riches and poverty lived almost on top of each other.[11]

He rented a room in Shoreditch from an immigrant Jewish activist and met campaigners who won reduced sweatshop hours in 1889, but still suffered poor conditions and low pay. He knew these conditions even more intimately after he began dating Milly Witkop, the eldest of four sisters born to orthodox Jews in Zlatopol, Ukraine. Milly came to London unaccompanied, aged 17. Her London experiences challenged her religious beliefs. She witnessed 'pious' Jews operating as heartless slum landlords, or forcing employees to labour on the Sabbath to complete urgent work. Hebrew prophets were trumped by secular profits. Religious observance in London felt devoid of the spirituality she knew in Zlatopol. At an enthusiastic meeting for striking bakers

---

10 R. Rocker, *The London Years*, Five Leaves/AK Press, p.14.

11 *Ibid.*, pp. 24–5.

in September 1894, she encountered the *Arbeter Fraynd*-ers, joined their clan, and rejected God.

The bakers frequently worked shifts longer than 16 hours in poorly ventilated basements. East European immigrants established around 60 Jewish bakeries in the East End, typically employing a few workers based around a family. This made union organisation extremely difficult but workers *did* organise, uniting where possible with Catholic and Lutheran German bakers working nearer the Thames.

When negotiations failed in the 1894 dispute, their fledgling union rented part of 52 Brushfield Street (alongside Spitalfields Market) as a workers' cooperative bakery. The night before the opening, immigrant cap-makers, cabinet-makers, tailors, and shoemakers convened a rally at Christchurch Hall, Hanbury Street urging workers' families to support the co-op.[12] The *Westminster Gazette* reported the opening day:

> ... [O]fficials and organisers among the Hebrew workers ... were seen wheeling about barrows of 'union bread', each loaf properly labelled and supplied to the grocers, restaurant keepers and others who had pledged themselves to patronise 'union bread' ... By 10.30 the crowd surrounding the premises numbered some thousands ... the band struck up the Marseillaise while the doors of the shop opened amid vociferous cheers ... the bakers came out dressed in white hats, shirts and aprons, carrying a large cake on a pole and headed by banners for the various trade unions ... the crowd formed a procession in the

---

12 Christchurch Hall was used for trade union and political rallies. Annie Besant and Eleanor Marx spoke there in support of matchworkers and gasworkers respectively.

midst of which was a cartload of new bread ... meeting everywhere with much sympathy.[13]

Bad debts defeated the cooperative, but consumers' commitment to 'union bread' took hold, workers fleetingly experienced control over hours and pay, and they glimpsed a different world. Wherever workers negotiated acceptable work conditions and the right to organise, master bakers could use the union label. The Bakers Union asked the Chef Rabbi to give this label his *hekhsher* (religious endorsement). He claimed it was beyond his remit and reinforced Milly Witkop's cynicism about religious leaders.

Relations between immigrant radicals and religious leaders were often antagonistic. Rabbis berated strikers in Sabbath sermons and supported the employers whose donations helped maintain the synagogues. In February 1889 a committee representing unemployed Jewish workers asked Chief Rabbi Adler to deliver a Sabbath sermon on sweating, unemployment and demands for an eight-hour day. He eventually refused. However, the *Arbeter Fraynd* had already announced that Rabbi Adler would preach this sermon on 16 March. Nearly 3,000 marchers left Berner Street for his synagogue at Duke Street, Aldgate. Adler was absent. City police prevented the marchers from rallying nearby. They returned to Whitechapel, rallied on Mile End Waste and had further confrontations with the police.

Sabbaths were holy, but *Yom Kippur*[14] holier still. Even many secular Jews fasted and spent the day in synagogue, entreating

---

13 *Westminster Gazette*, 18 September 1894 (see Larry Wayne's *Union Bread*, published jointly by the Jewish Socialists' Group and Socialist History Society, 2009).

14 The Day of Atonement, during which observant Jews fast from sunset to sunset.

God to extend their lives. In London and New York though, Jewish anarchists organised Yom Kippur dances. In 1889, an *Arbeter Fraynd* activist, Benjamin Feigenbaum, held a Yom Kippur meeting in Christchurch Hall, entitled 'Is there a God?' He gave God two minutes to 'kill me on the spot, so that he may prove his existence'. When the time elapsed, Feigenbaum exclaimed, 'There is no God!' and a band struck up the Marseillaise.[15]

Rudolf Rocker first met Milly Witkop when he was living in the West End. She had gone there to sell anarchist papers. He recalled 'a slim young girl ... with thick black hair and deep large eyes ... eager and zealous for our cause'.[16] Their love blossomed in uncertain economic times. They nearly emigrated on to America before settling in Liverpool, where Rocker worked on *Dos Fraye Vort* (the Free Word), a Yiddish anarchist newspaper. He began to master this language with its Germanic-sounding words but mystifying Hebrew script.

Rocker and Witkop returned to the East End when he was invited to edit *Arbeter Fraynd* in 1898. Witkop found sweatshop work but also contributed to the newspaper. *Arbeter Fraynd* activists and supporters inspired and led the struggles locally for democracy and freedom within the immigrant community, rights and dignity in the workplace, and for better lives. They organised Friday night lectures and debates in the back room of the Sugar Loaf public house at 187 Hanbury Street. Rocker marvelled at the commitment shown by 'badly paid and half-starved' workers to these events: 'crowded together on hard benches ... they followed the speaker with rapt attention, and as the discussion afterwards showed, with understanding.'[17]

---

15 See W.J. Fishman's *East End Jewish Radicals*, pp.157–8.

16 See Rocker, *The London Years*, p.39.

17 *Ibid.*, pp.26–7.

These gatherings attracted women as well as men. Rose Robins's parents forbade her from going to the Sugar Loaf where 'free love' was among topics discussed. 'Red Rose' defied them but one night when she returned from the Sugar Loaf, her parents had locked her out and she spent the night on the streets.

A larger venue was needed when the international anarchist celebrity Emma Goldman visited England at the end of 1899. She addressed three packed meetings at Christchurch Hall, offering political analysis and inspiration while raising funds for *Arbeter Fraynd*. Her trip started inauspiciously on an anti-(Boer) war platform at the West End's Athenaeum Hall. 'I had caught a severe cold ... my speaking was painful not only to myself but to the audience.' It was a 'dismal failure'. Hanbury Street, though, was very different: 'I was among my people. I knew their lives, hard and barren everywhere but more so in London. I was able to find the right words to reach them. I was my own self in their midst.'[18]

The *Arbeter Fraynd* struggled financially and there were publication gaps, but from 1903 until 1914, it appeared every week. Rocker was philosophical about the paper's economic circumstances.

> I had been promised £1 a week for my work ... The promise was rarely kept ... amounts owing to me were entered into a book. When the total ... got too large they put a pen through it and the debt was wiped out ... it was a splendid way of keeping the books but it didn't do me any good ... it was only by Milly working and by my odd jobs of bookbinding that we kept going.

18   E. Goldman, *Living My Life*, Vol. 1, London: Pluto Press, 1988 (1931), p.254.

The paper was read not only in London, but also in New York and Tsarist Russia. Across vast distances radical Yiddish newspapers enabled Jewish workers to share and support each other's struggles.[19] Dovid Edelstadt emigrated as a teenager from Russia to New York and worked in sweatshops making buttonholes. He died from tuberculosis aged just 26, but his legacy of labour poems crossed continents through Yiddish newspapers. His poem, *In Kamf* (In struggle) became an anthem sung on May Day marches. 'We are shot and hanged, robbed of our lives and rights, for we demand freedom for downtrodden slaves ... you can kill our bodies but you will never destroy our spirit ... new fighters will come ... we will fight on until the whole world is free.'

Some 25,000 immigrant Jews marched from the East End to a protest rally in Hyde Park after a pogrom in Kishinev in 1903 left 49 Jews dead, approximately 500 wounded and 2,000 homeless.[20] Rocker remembers London's streets lined with people who 'gazed in mute surprise upon the strange procession ... [when] Edelstadt's *In Kamf* was heard the onlookers became very solemn and took off their hats to the marchers'.[21]

The main threat Jews faced in Russia was physical attacks by *pogromchiks*,[22] ignored or even encouraged by the authorities. In America and Canada, Jewish immigrants struggled with overcrowding, exploitation, poverty and hunger, as they did in London. But in the East End an additional threat emerged, which intensified in 1901 with the creation of a grassroots anti-immigrant

---

19 For example, Mr Trushkowsky of 113 Brick Lane was treasurer of a committee formed by several local immigrant unions which sent money to striking workers in Bialystok in 1898.

20 Kishinev is in present day Moldova. In 1903 half of its 125,000 people were Jews.

21 Workmen's Circle, *Mir Trogn a Gezang*, New York, 1977, p.80.

22 Instigators of mob attacks on communities.

movement – the British Brothers League (BBL). These 'brothers' claimed that 'their' territory was being encroached upon and transformed. The BBL's footsoldiers were factory workers, some from Irish immigrant families. Its 'higher-class' leaders included the Tory MPs for Stepney and Bethnal Green South West respectively – Major William Evans Gordon and Samuel Forde Ridley, plus retired army captain William Stanley Shaw. '[T]he other day an Oxford graduate joined us, we have enrolled several city merchants, a bank manager is on our central committee', boasted Shaw. '[M]edical men, clergymen, authors and journalists have written expressing sympathy.'[23] Supportive authors included Marie Corelli, author of the bestseller *A Romance of Two Worlds*, and Arthur Conan Doyle, who donated ten shillings and sixpence to the League.

The BBL held its first public meeting, at Stepney Meeting House, Oxford Street (now Stepney Way), on a Thursday evening in May 1901. The *East London Observer* reported: 'The weather was bad but there was a crowded working class attendance' who were 'enthusiastic and unanimous'. Further meetings in August, October and November were equally packed. Four thousand marchers converged from Hackney, Bethnal Green, Shoreditch and Stepney for the BBL's largest rally at the People's Palace, on Mile End Road, in January 1902. The Hackney contingent's banner proclaimed, 'Britain for the British'. Inside the hall an organ played 'Rule Britannia!' and 'No Place Like Home'. The meeting was protected by '260 stewards ... dock labourers, chemical workers from Bromley and operatives from Shoreditch, Bow, Poplar, Stepney, Bethnal Green and Mile End', who 'unceremoniously ejected ... "foreigners"'.

---

23 *Jewish Chronicle*, 31 October 1902.

The League convinced many local workers that the influx of migrants willing to work long hours for low pay undermined their struggle for better conditions. Instead of unionising migrants, the BBL called for restriction. They denied that their movement was 'aimed at any religious sect or of a racial character'; they were protesting against 'the dumping ... of foreign paupers on these shores'. However, the presence of MPs representing distant unaffected constituencies (such as Orkney and Shetlands) suggests the BBL tapped a deeper, racialised hostility to Jews. Wolverhampton MP, Henry Norman, was applauded when he advised other nations to 'disinfect their own sewage', adding that Englishmen 'would not have this country made the dumping ground of the scum of Europe'. When local agitator Arnold White stated that aliens were not persecuted refugees but came 'because they wanted our money', there were calls from the floor to 'wipe them out'. That year the League presented a petition to Parliament with 45,000 signatures, mostly collected in east London, calling for immigration control.

Individuals struggled to oppose this anti-immigrant rhetoric at such rallies, but immigrant Jewish trade unionists, with support from non-Jewish activists, formed an Aliens Defence League with temporary offices at 38 Brick Lane, and organised public meetings countering the BBL's agenda.

Major Evans-Gordon was invited to head a Royal Commission on Immigration, gathering evidence on allegations that BBL agitators had themselves disseminated: that immigrants arrived impoverished, destitute and dirty; practised insanitary habits; spread infectious diseases; were a burden on the rates; dispossessed native dwellers; caused native tradesmen to suffer a loss of trade; worked for rates below the 'native workman';

included criminals, prostitutes and anarchists; formed a compact non-assimilating community that didn't intermarry; and interfered with the observance of Christian Sunday.

The Commission's report resulted in Britain's first modern immigration law, the 1905 Aliens Act, which permitted government inspectors to exclude paupers unless they could prove that they were entering solely to avoid persecution. The Liberals had opposed this Tory Act, but enforced it when they governed from 1906. Between 1906 and 1910, approximately 2,000 immigrants were refused entry, and more than 1,000 were deported for 'wandering the streets without visible means of support'. The Tories lost many London seats in 1906, but Evans-Gordon held his, using the slogan, 'England for the English. Major Gordon for Stepney'.

Rudolf Rocker and the anarchists campaigned vigorously to defend immigrants and counter anti-Semitic arguments, but simultaneously focused on constructive initiatives. Anarchists opened a social and educational centre for workers – the Jubilee Street Club and Workers Institute – near Stepney Green in February 1906, in a former Salvation Army depot. It held meetings and debates during the week, concerts and dramas at weekends, and offered classes using Francisco Ferrer's progressive pedagogy.[24] Like the previous tenants, Rocker and associates promised salvation, but through workers' own enlightenment, empowerment and self-belief rather than through praying to a deity.

The East End's best known adult education providers at this time were the severe-looking Christian social reformers, Canon

24 Ferrer pioneered the non-competitive, non-punitive 'Escuela Moderna' education philosophy in some schools in Spain.

Samuel Barnett and Henrietta Barnett, who, in 1884, established a university settlement named Toynbee Hall between Commercial Street and Gunthorpe Street. Built in a medieval manorial style, it initially housed 15 Oxbridge graduates, who worked in the City but lived in the settlement, ate and prayed together, and devoted their leisure time to 'provide education and a means of recreation and enjoyment for people of poorer districts', and 'to inquire into the condition of the poor, and advance plans to promote their welfare'.

The Barnetts already worked locally, at St Jude's Church. During the 1870s, Balliol College student Arnold Toynbee was among several Oxford undergraduates assisting them during vacations. He maintained this link as an academic. Determined to see slum conditions at first hand, he frequented dingy, disease-ridden buildings, but contracted tuberculosis and died aged 32. The Barnetts kept his name alive through Toynbee Hall.

The settlement was located close to the poorest people. Canon Barnett instructed the graduates to 'learn as much as to teach', to 'feel out rather than find out what are his neighbours' thoughts' until they themselves become 'the mouthpiece for East London indignation'. Fine aims but coated with paternalism, which groomed residents to act on behalf of poor people rather than encouraging them to liberate themselves. The Barnetts made enlightened statements about changing social conditions, but tasked graduates 'possessing habits and customs of culture' with 'improving the working class'.

George Lansbury admired Canon Barnett's zeal for social reform but noted that Toynbee Hall workers mixed with the poor only within Toynbee Hall's 'fine parlours'. He wondered whether the whole project might prove more a stepping stone for the residents than the recipients. They went to east London full of enthusiasm for the masses' welfare but soon discovered that the interests of the poor

> ... were best served by leaving East London to stew in its own juice, while they became members of Parliament, cabinet ministers, civil servants [who] discovered that the problems of life and poverty were too complex to solve ... that the rich were as necessary as the poor, that nothing must ever be done to hurt the good-hearted rich who keep such places as Toynbee Hall going out of their ill-gotten gains.[25]

One of Emma Goldman's Christchurch Hall lectures deconstructed *tsedoke* (charity). The Yiddish flyers advertising this meeting asked: 'What is charity? Who gives charity and why?' Goldman saw charities as a necessary function of capitalism – an economic system that 'robs man of his birth right, stunts his growth, poisons his body, keeps him in ignorance, in poverty, and dependence, and then institutes charities that thrive on the last vestige of man's self-respect'.

Despite this justified cynicism, many Eastenders *did* benefit from Toynbee Hall's adult education classes, especially literacy classes for immigrants, and advice and support on housing issues through a team of 'poor-man's lawyers'.[26] In 1888, during the matchworkers' strike, four independent researchers from Toynbee Hall examined Bryant & May's books and confirmed

---

25 G. Lansbury, *My Life*, London: Constable & Co., 1928.

26 Forerunners of the National Association of Citizens' Advice Bureaux.

Annie Besant's claims about the system of fines that the strikers described, but the directors denied.

A more radical grassroots initiative to provide adult education, strengthen cultural life, provide practical support, and build collective strength amongst Yiddish-speaking immigrants for their political battles, arose from weekly meetings held in Morris Mindel's tenement flat at 184 Rothschild Buildings – a stone's throw from Toynbee Hall. Mindel was a *Bundist* (Jewish revolutionary)[27] political exile from Lithuania and, like Rocker, a bookbinder. *Bundists*, anarchists and socialists formed a secular friendly society called the *Arbeter Ring* (Workers' Circle). It eventually expanded to 19 divisions (branches), mostly in London – the four biggest in east London. Division 1's committee met at Mindel's flat. In 1912 the organisation rented two rooms at 136 Brick Lane as its activities expanded.[28]

Friendly or mutual aid societies proliferated in working-class communities, providing a non-judgemental mechanism through which individuals could give and receive support. Most Jewish friendly societies were organised through synagogues among *landslayt*. Often, a rich benefactor provided start-up funds. The Workers' Circle developed solely through members' subscriptions, arguing that philanthropic donations would compromise its members' dignity and its beliefs in 'liberty and economic equality'.

Formed by immigrant trade unionists, it met workers'

---

27 The Bund was created by working-class Jewish socialists in Tsarist Russia in 1897. By 1905 it had 40,000 members.

28 The Workers' Circle officially dates its founding to a meeting in 1909 in Sunbury Buildings on the Boundary Estate, Bethnal Green, home of a cabinet maker, Nathan Weiner. A parallel group *Arbeter Ring Farayn* (Workers' Circle Union) hosted weekly literary discussions at Woolf Krasner's home in Umberston Street from 1908. They later merged into the Workers' Circle.

needs beyond the workplace, by establishing a reading room on Whitechapel Road, which later relocated to a large house in Great Alie Street, Whitechapel, with 16 rooms, including two large halls, which the *Arbeter Ring* purchased for £2,000 in 1922 as a workers' social, cultural and educational centre. Every night, circle members sipped lemon tea while playing chess, draughts or dominoes in its teetotal café. On Thursday evenings brothers Alexander and Frank Fine gave free legal advice. On Friday nights, there were political lectures and debates organised by the Circle's 'propaganda committee' featuring Jewish and non-Jewish speakers. On Sunday afternoons, members' children came to a secular Yiddish supplementary school and on Sunday nights there were Yiddish theatre productions, or classical concerts presented by the Circle's own orchestra. On other evenings members attended a range of classes and courses.

A group of Polish Jewish immigrants who arrived in the 1920s commandeered a top floor room and established the Progressive Youth Circle. They invited academics, trade unionists and political activists to lead discussions in Yiddish on topics such as free love, communism, and Zionism, held talks on Yiddish and English writers, and created *Proltet*, an agitprop Yiddish theatre group.

Despite its meagre resources the *Arbeter Ring* provided board and lodging for striking miners in 1914 speaking at London meetings, and donated to the Gresford community in 1934 after a mining disaster. It contributed towards the legal defence of Sholem Schwartzbard, a Jewish anarchist who assassinated the Ukrainian pogrom-leader Petlyura.[29] *Proltet* held benefit

---

29 After Schwartzbard was acquitted he went on tour to thank his supporters. Thousands gathered in the street outside Circle House where a packed dinner was held in his honour.

performances, and Circle members collected clothing, cigarettes and food for the International Brigades fighting in the Spanish Civil War.

Its members – anarchists, communists, Bundists, and left-wing Zionists – held conflicting political views but the Circle's non-sectarian spirit meant it could play a unifying role in London's working-class Jewish life, especially during strikes and in anti-fascist campaigning.[30] Where possible it supplemented strike pay and hosted meetings to mobilise wider support for strikers. The management committees of local workers' cooperatives included Circle members. Rudolf Rocker, who played a key role in the 1912 tailors' strike that struck a powerful blow against the sweated labour system, acknowledged the support given by the fledgling Workers' Circle.

The events of 1912 tested immigrant workers' commit-ment to radical campaigning against exploiters within their own community and the strength of solidarity they could offer beyond that community. In April a strike over pay and conditions broke out among West End tailors, comprised of native English tailors alongside several other nationalities. Their leaders feared that during the strike their work would be subcontracted to East End sweatshops and carried out by poorer tailors desperate to feed their families. Rocker and the anarchists recognised that this could severely damage future relations between the West End and East End tailors, and strengthen chauvinists in the labour movement who labelled immigrant workers as unreliable.

The anarchists seized the moment by building support for the West End strike among East End tailors. Rocker argued that if they struck too, they could help the West End tailors

30 See Chapter 10.

and simultaneously challenge the sweating system which they endured. A mass meeting in Mile End Assembly Hall, attended by 8,000 East End tailors, overwhelmingly supported him. As the strike began to spread, bakers and cigarette workers gave free supplies to workers; Yiddish theatres raised money through benefit performances. Community support enabled the strike committee to provide strike pay and distribute food to their families.

Within three weeks the West End master tailors were forced to agree a settlement, which also included those East End tailors employed in men's tailoring and uniforms. They were guaranteed shorter hours, no piecework, better sanitary conditions and that only union labour would be employed. But the largest group of workers in East End tailoring workshops made women's garments – and these workers continued to strike. Their employers saw the season's trade disappearing. Eventually they offered to meet every demand except one – the right to form a union in every tailoring workshop in the East End. A midnight meeting was held at the Pavilion (Yiddish) Theatre on Whitechapel Road, where the evening's programmed drama had ended. Another was about to unfold. Many tailors remained outside the packed theatre waiting for news. Rocker was not a tailor, but an enormously respected agitator and organiser. He recorded his feelings as he spoke:

> I saw those pale, pinched, hungry faces ... of people who had come together at midnight to decide what to do about the strike for which they had sacrificed so much ... I said that if they held out a few more days ... they would win. If they decided to go back now the Masters would make

them feel they had lost ... You must decide for yourselves. There was an outburst of applause and from all sides came the cry: 'the strike goes on!'[31]

A formal vote to continue striking was unanimous. The next day employers began signing binding agreements so workers would return. For Rocker and the *Arbeter Fraynd*-ers, the strike showed that the most exploited and vulnerable workers could organise themselves to win, give solidarity beyond their own community and locality, and gain esteem among workers who regarded immigrant unions as a weak link.

That commitment to wider solidarity was further demonstrated in the tailors' support for dockers, also striking to improve conditions. In May, tailors and dockers had held joint strike meetings at Tower Hill. As the tailors resumed work, the dockers' families faced starvation. Milly Witkop and other *Arbeter Fraynd* activists formed a committee to place dockers' children in immigrant Jewish workers' homes and give dockers' families fewer mouths to feed. More than 300 dockers' children spent the last weeks of an ultimately unsuccessful dock strike in cramped Jewish ghetto homes. The committee reluctantly refused some offers to take children because the families were already too overcrowded. Many dockers entered Jewish homes for the first time when they visited their children. Jewish workers had remembered the solidarity shown by the dockers in 1889.

The outbreak of war in 1914 curtailed a remarkable period of struggle among a courageous group of immigrant rebels and dreamers. During that war, Rudolf Rocker was interned as an

---

31 Rocker, *The London Years*, p.130.

'enemy alien' and deported. The *Arbeter Fraynd* and Jubilee Street Club were forced to shut down. In 1917, many leading activists of the immigrant Jewish enclave, including half of the Workers' Circle membership, returned to Russia. The land they never truly left behind was in the throes of revolution. Their dreams of liberation for its downtrodden people were only partially fulfilled, their idealism soon betrayed, but few could return to London.

However, in the decades from the 1880s until the First World War, a group of immigrants in a hostile, anti-alien environment, treated with ambivalence by many indigenous workers, oppressed by those who claimed moral authority and held institutional power in their own community, were model rebels. Whatever their internal fears and anxieties as newcomers in a strange society, they gave each other strength by organising collectively, they stood up for their rights in the workplace, formed their own clubs, unions and friendly societies, created their own newspapers to give themselves a voice, broke taboos, challenged employers, rabbis and xenophobes, and built links of solidarity beyond their own community, seeking a better world for all.

WALK

Start at Whitechapel Art Gallery, 77–82 Whitechapel High Street, E1 7QX.

1. Whitechapel High Street

The gallery which opened in March 1901 now incorporates the old Whitechapel Library building which opened in 1892 and became known as the 'People's University of the East End'. The library was relocated near Whitechapel station. More than 200,000 people visited the opening exhibition during its six-week run. Walk a short distance in the City direction and turn right into Angel Alley

2. Angel Alley

Home of Freedom Books which continues the anarchist tradition established by the *Arbeter Fraynd* newspaper (July 1885) and *Freedom* (October 1886). Along the alley wall, an artistic installation celebrates dozens of individuals associated with libertarian or anarchist thought and action internationally. Rudolf Rocker is on the bottom row and Emma Goldman is in the top right hand corner. Go back to Whitechapel High Street and turn right.

3. Gunthorpe Street

Just before turning into Gunthorpe Street look at the sign above Albert's shop, crafted by Arthur Szyk. It marks the former offices of the *Jewish Daily Post* – the first (and short-lived) daily English-language Jewish newspaper in England. On the left, past Canon Barnett School, is the back entrance of Toynbee Hall.

4. Wentworth Street

Turn left into Wentworth Street, cross to the archway inscribed 'Four per cent Industrial Dwellings Company', a remnant of the Rothschild Buildings tenement that stood here until 1973. Workers' Circle founding member, Morris Mindel, lived at Flat 184. Sarah Wesker, who led strikes at trouser factories in east London in the late 1920s and early 1930s, lived at Flat 134.[32] Cross Commercial Street, turn right into Toynbee Street then left into Brune Street.

5. Brune Street

On the right hand side is the remarkable façade of the Soup Kitchen for the Jewish Poor, established by Jewish philanthropists in 1902. It closed in 1992. During the early 1930s depression, it fed more than 4,000 people nightly. Turn right into Tenter Ground, once a field where dyed cloth was dried on frames with hooks called 'tenters' (hence the saying 'on tenterhooks'). Turn left on to Crispin Street.

6. Crispin Street

The sandy-brown building (student accommodation) was a night shelter for homeless women (and later men too) run by the Sisters of Mercy from 1861 until 1988. Looking south to Bell Lane, a sky-blue building towers above the shops and flats – student accommodation for a more elite market. The Jews' Free School

---

32 Sarah Wesker was the women's organiser of the National Clothing Workers Union and was elected to the Communist Party's central committee in 1930. She was the role model for Sarah Kahn in her nephew Arnold's famous play, *Chicken Soup with Barley*.

stood on this site from 1822–1939. Turn right to the junction with Brushfield Street.

7. *Brushfield Street*

The café/restaurant on the corner (number 52) was the site of the cooperative bakery, briefly established in 1894. Turn right, and cross Commercial Street into Fournier Street, named after George Fournier, a philanthropist of Huguenot heritage. Wealthier Huguenot refugee silk-weavers lived and worked in the early eighteenth-century houses in these streets. Turn left into Wilkes Street then right into Princelet Street.

8. *Princelet Street*

Outside number 6, a pavement roundel indicates the East End's first Yiddish theatre. It closed after seven months when a false fire scare led to a stampede to evacuate the building and 17 people were crushed to death. Secular immigrant radicals established a cooperative *folkskikhe* (people's kitchen) in the abandoned building. A delivery of food to the cooperative on the holy day of Yom Kippur in 1904 led to mass street-fighting between religious and secular Jews. Turn back to Wilkes Street, then go right and turn into Hanbury Street.

9. *Hanbury Street*

Christchurch Hall, at number 22, was once a venue for political and trade union rallies. Its upper part has been redeveloped as flats. The anarchist Benjamin Feigenbaum held his lecture 'Is there a God?' here. Eleanor Marx and Annie Besant spoke here in support of gasworkers and matchworkers respectively. Emma Goldman lectured here raising funds for the *Arbeter Fraynd*.

The Kobi Nazrul centre at number 30 is named after a Bengali revolutionary poet imprisoned several times for anti-Empire activities.

10. Junction of Brick Lane/Hanbury Street
To your left, at 136 Brick Lane (Sheba Restaurant), were the Workers' Circle's first meeting rooms. Along Hanbury Street's extension, across the road, a Jewish anarchist, Barnet Ruderman, had a newsagents/bookshop at number 71. He was the first publisher of radical Yiddish books in England. The Sugar Loaf pub, which hosted weekly anarchist meetings in its back room stood at number 187. Turn right along Brick Lane then right again into Fournier Street.

11. Fournier Street
The mosque on the corner was formerly Spitalfields Great Synagogue and originally, in 1743 (look up at the sundial), a Huguenot chapel. In the 1890s, Jewish anarchists taunted religious leaders by eating ham sandwiches opposite this synagogue on Yom Kippur. Rudolf Rocker – a non-Jew – berated fellow Jewish anarchists for this practice. He felt it antagonised ordinary worshippers instead of solely targeting the religious establishment.

Great Strike of London Tailors

A GREAT

DEMONSTRATION

OF

TAILORS

WILL TAKE PLACE IN

HYDE PARK,

On SUNDAY, Sept. 29th, 1889,

Which will be joined by various other Trades and Organisations.

*Among the Speakers the following were invited and are expected
to attend :—*

JAMES MACDONALD,   JOHN TURNER,

WILLIAM MORRIS,   W. M. THOMPSON,

FRANK KITZ,   CHAS. MOWBRAY,   TOCHATTI,

JOHN BURNS,   TOM MANN,

KEILEY,   CLARK,   CONNOR,   and others.

The Procession from the East End will start at 1.30 p.m., from
Buck's Row, and will March by Whitechapel, Commercial Street,
Great Eastern Street, Old Street, Clerkenwell, Theobald's Road,
Bloomsbury, Oxford Street, enter the Park by Marble Arch at 3 p.m.

By Order of the Strike Committee.

"WHITE HART," Greenfield Street, E.

Leaflet published by the Strike Committee of the 1889 tailor's strike.

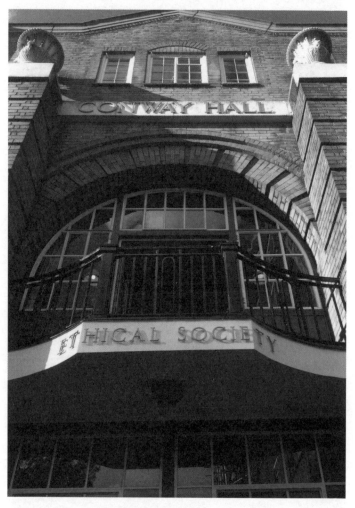

Conway Hall in Red Lion Square, Holborn.

5

NO GODS, NO MASTERS

Radical Bloomsbury

As areas of London are transformed beyond recognition by the scale and pace of rebuilding, Bedford Square, at the heart of Bloomsbury, provides a window on the past. Built between 1775 and 1780, it is London's last surviving fully intact Georgian square. The name 'Bedford' is one of three gracing several streets and squares in this district; the others are Russell and Tavistock. They are one family. William Russell, the 5th Earl of Bedford, became a duke in 1694 and was given the title Marquis of Tavistock. The Bedford Estate is still the largest private landowner in Bloomsbury.

Bloomsbury was kept exclusive partly by property leasing arrangements which listed more than 60 commercial activities forbidden in the squares owned by the Bedford estate. These included: baker, chimney-sweeper, publican, coffin-maker, bone-burner, hatter, plasterer, printer, soap-boiler and tripe-seller. Booth's 1889 map of poverty in London West shows a dark blue block just east of Russell Square, indicating 'Very poor ... chronic want', and similar blocks just south of New Oxford Street. Bloomsbury, in contrast, is a sea of red and pink, indicating 'well-to-do middle classes'. Traditionally, its squares were the homes of judges, retired military men, leading professionals and their families, and others of considerable means, including many owners of slaves in the Caribbean. A database created through a 2013 research project, detailing compensation payments made to owners of slaves when the government abolished slavery in the British Caribbean in 1833, reveals many beneficiaries in this locale.[1] Among them are the Whig politician James Baillie, of 45 Bedford Square, who had owned 801 slaves in British Guyana and 202 in St Lucia; Reverend Thomas Harrison of 6 Bloomsbury Square, who had owned 140 slaves in Anguilla; and Benjamin Greene of 45 Russell Square, who received compensation for the loss of his 224 slaves in St Kitts.

An unlikely location, then, for political rebels. But the Caribbean Trotskyist writer, C.L.R. James – who enjoyed staying in its student and young writers' quarter in 1932, living in Heathcote Street and frequenting Student Movement House, where many African radicals socialised – felt he had fitted into Bloomsbury 'as naturally as a pencil fits into a sharpener'. Its vibrant cultural and intellectual atmosphere enthused him: 'Anyone who lives in this place for any length of time and remains dull need not worry himself. Nothing he will ever do will help him. He was born that way.'[2]

By the 1930s this area was associated, especially, with the well-heeled Bloomsbury Set – intellectuals, writers, artists and philosophers whose flexible living arrangements reflected their radical ideas on aesthetics, feminism, sexuality and pacifism. The satirist Dorothy Parker said the set 'paints in circles, lives

---

1 Legacies of British Slave-ownership, www.ucl.ac.uk/lbs/.

2 C.L.R. James, *Letters from London*, Oxford: Signal Books, 2006.

in squares and loves in triangles'. Several members of this elite network shared a common background – public school followed by Trinity College or King's College, Cambridge. The writer, Ronald Blythe, described them as 'Cambridge in London'.[3]

Acres of literature have been written about the Bloomsbury Set's twentieth-century lives – much of it obsessed with their personal dalliances. Unfortunately, this has obscured the rebellious ideas and activities that flowered in this very comfortable area in earlier decades. Several individuals who were living or working within Bloomsbury, more diverse in their origins than the Bloomsbury Set, challenged the political and economic orthodoxies that dominated Victorian and Edwardian Britain: the power and authority of the Church, and belief in God; nationalism and unquestioning patriotism; education as a privilege, not a right; the use of military intervention to settle international conflicts; differing spheres, rights and duties for men and women; and the assumption that capitalism benefits everyone.

Members of the Bloomsbury Socialist Society, formed in 1888, were key organisers of London's first May Day march in which hundreds of thousands of workers participated. The society usually met in the Communist Club at 49 Tottenham Street, close to Goodge Street. Its 1890 manifesto declared: 'We aim at realising socialism ... a condition of society in which wealth will be enjoyed by those who produce it ... removing all conditions whatever that render it possible for an idle class to exist.'

The Society's members, including Eleanor Marx[4] and Edward Aveling, whose home was directly opposite the British Museum

---

3   Ronald Blythe, in David Daiches (ed.), *The Penguin Companion to Literature*, New York: McGraw-Hill, 1971.

4   The youngest daughter of Jenny von Westphalen and Karl Marx.

on Great Russell Street, lived mainly in Bloomsbury, Soho and Fitzrovia. They devoted themselves to producing political propaganda aimed at educating 'the people' in 'social and political matters'. They wanted to put all 'political power into the hands of the people'; their cause – 'the cause of all those who labour'. The Society's manifesto closed with the call: 'Workers of the World, Unite!'

One early proponent of workers' rights based in Bloomsbury was Devon-born Thomas Wakley, MP for Finsbury from 1835–52. He lived at 35 Bedford Square. Wakley came to London in his late teens to train as a doctor at St Thomas's and established a surgery on Regent Street. He became friendly with the radical pamphleteer, William Cobbett, in 1821, and founded the medical journal *The Lancet* two years later, which he used as a vehicle to challenge the autocratic power of the Royal College of Surgeons' governing council.

Wakley was elected to Parliament as a Radical. He spoke in the House of Commons in support of Chartism, Irish independence and medical reform, but his maiden speech defended the Tolpuddle Martyrs, a group of farm workers in Dorset led by a Methodist lay preacher, George Loveless, who planned collective action to protect their living standards. They were convicted for taking a secret oath – which contravened the 1797 Mutiny Act – to form a Friendly Society of Agricultural Labourers, and were exiled for seven years to a penal colony in New South Wales, Australia. A huge protest movement forced the government to remit their sentences two years after their conviction; Wakley was its leading London spokesperson. When the Tolpuddle Martyrs returned to Britain, Wakley was the keynote speaker at a dinner

Invitation to celebration dinner of Tolpuddle martyrs support campaign.

in their honour at White Conduit Tea-House in Islington.[5]

He was an enthusiastic campaigner against stamp duty imposed on newspapers, which restricted the distribution of radical material. Many activists responded by ignoring the Stamp Act and publishing penny papers until they were forced to stop, often by arrest and imprisonment. Wakley published six issues of an unstamped paper called *A Voice from the Commons* – perhaps the nearest thing to a nineteenth-century blog.

He strongly opposed the 1834 Poor Law, condemned by Chartists for creating the workhouse. Wakley was an outspoken

5   A restaurant occupies the rebuilt tea-house site which has 'White Conduit House' etched across its façade. The nearest turning south of this site was renamed 'Tolpuddle Street' in 1986 to mark the 150th anniversary of the dinner for the martyrs.

proponent of Chartist ideas and actions which sought to defend the poor, raise working-class consciousness and expand the political franchise, but he did not support their demand for annual parliaments. He believed that an election every three years was preferable – but the Chartists nevertheless saw him as a strong ally.

Wakley's Finsbury constituency included the Clerkenwell House of Detention and, when he visited the prison in a medical capacity in 1839, he was shocked at the treatment of remand prisoners who were 'subjected to the lowest possible diet' for the first 14 days of their confinement and in some cases made to do hard labour. He told the House of Commons that he 'could not conceive on what principle it was recommended that a man should be subjected to punishment before he was tried'. Wakley also strongly criticised the use of solitary confinement, which he termed a 'demoniacal system'. His concerns about punishment extended to army discipline too, and he demanded an end to the practice of flogging.

The army, though, had high status in Victorian England, and it was hard for critics to get a hearing. London's pacifist movement, which challenged militarism and army practices and campaigned for peaceful conflict resolution, is often considered a twentieth-century creature that surfaced during the First World War and matured in its aftermath, when War Resisters International (WRI) and the Peace Pledge Union (PPU) came into existence. WRI was formed at a 1921 conference at Bilthoven, Holland, on the initiative of Kees Boeke, a Dutch Quaker peace activist, and moved its international secretariat to London in 1923.[6] The

---

6   Originally called 'Paco' – Esperanto for 'peace'.

prominent Independent Labour Party (ILP) campaigner Fenner Brockway was secretary of WRI from 1926–34, and George Lansbury held the post from 1937–40. The PPU was set up in 1935 by Dick Sheppard, canon of St Paul's Cathedral. In a letter, published in the *Manchester Guardian*, Sheppard invited people to send him a pledge on a postcard, saying: 'I renounce war and pledge never again to support another.' Within weeks, some 30,000 people had signed the pledge, and the PPU held its first mass meeting at the Albert Hall in July that year, attended by more than 7,000 supporters.

John Passmore Edwards, who lived at 51 Bedford Square, was a peace activist during the Second Boer War (also known as the South African War), which began in 1899. A carpenter's son from Redruth in Cornwall, he moved to London, became a journalist and later a successful publisher. He was a supporter of Chartism and committed to improving opportunities for working-class people, using his wealth to fund 24 free libraries and several free hospitals, mainly in London, as well as art galleries and convalescent homes, some of which still bear his name. More locally, within Bloomsbury, he funded the Passmore Edwards Settlement, in Tavistock Place, which opened up educational opportunities for people who had little access to them. It moved there from temporary accommodation in 1897. Young professional men, especially lawyers, lived in the Settlement building and, in return for board and lodging, they taught academic and practical subjects to adults, and organised music, chess and debating societies. They also ran classes and recreation sessions for children from the surrounding area, after school, while their parents were still at work. Modelled on Toynbee Hall in the East End, the Passmore Edwards Settlement operated a busy 'poor man's lawyer' service. The settlement's work was led by a Russell Square resident, Mary Ward, who was committed to increasing educational opportunities for women and girls.

Passmore Edwards' record of peace activism went back several decades before the Boer War. He was part of the London Peace Society in the late 1840s, and published its journal *The Peace Advocate*. He actively pursued his pacifist agenda during the Crimean War, arguing that a war commenced for one purpose 'not infrequently originates or develops other blazing issues, which have to be quenched in blood, if quenched at all'.

In 1855, the Stop the War League (STWL) published Passmore Edwards' lecture, *The War Condemned*. In the STWL, Passmore Edwards collaborated closely with Chartist Bronterre O'Brien, the republican journalist John Hamilton and anti-slavery activist George Thompson.[7]

His opposition to militarism also included internal army discipline. Like Thomas Wakley he spoke out against the use of flogging and he argued against all forms of corporal punishment in prisons and schools.[8] In a period when wars were fought between professional rather than conscript armies, Passmore Edwards identified the effect on 'the common people' who, he said, 'suffer most by wars ... can do most to prevent wars, and would be the greatest gainers if wars were prevented'.

One campaigning trade unionist, who worked in the West End and later became a Liberal MP, expressed similar sentiments. William Randall Cremer was a carpenter and joiner who moved to London in 1852 in his mid-20s. He was a strong campaigner for

---

7   See P. Laity, *The British Peace Movement, 1870–1914*, Oxford: Clarendon Press, 2002, p.18.

8   Passmore Edwards was a member of the Committee for the Abolition of Flogging in the Army and Navy.

the nine-hour day (which cost him his job) and a founder member, alongside Karl Marx, of the International Workingmen's Association, which emerged from a conference of socialists, anarchists and radicals who met in St Martin's Hall in Covent Garden in 1864. He was a close friend of Mazzini and Garibaldi and strong supporter of the radical Italian unification movement. In 1870, Cremer, with support from other working-class activists, formed the Workmen's Peace Association in London, later rebranded as the International Arbitration League (IAL). Like Passmore Edwards, he foresaw that ordinary workers and civilians would suffer most from future wars.

His organisation campaigned for disarmament and for international conflicts to be resolved through arbitration. His decades of work for this cause were recognised at a banquet held in May 1904 at the Holborn Restaurant in Bloomsbury, a popular venue for local radicals and peace activists.[9] The event also celebrated Cremer as the very first winner of the Nobel Peace Prize. He received £8,000 but donated £7,000 of it to the IAL for its campaigning work.

If Cremer was ahead of his time in his concern about civilians during wars, he was behind the times when it came to political equality for women. He was one of the founders of the Anti-Suffrage League in 1906, arguing that women were 'creatures of impulse and emotion and did not decide questions on the ground of reason as men did'. The founding president of the Anti-Suffrage League was Mary Ward, of the Passmore Edwards Settlement, who advocated strongly for women's education but against their political participation.

---

9   Close to Cremer's office in Lincoln's Inn Fields where he lived, with a turn-up bed and a small gas stove, after the death of his second wife.

In the early twentieth century, Bloomsbury's tradition of anti-war activism was upheld by one of the Duke of Bedford's family members – Bertrand Russell. From 1911 to 1916 he lived in Bury Place, close to both Little Russell Street and Great Russell Street. A mathematician and philosopher, his political views veered between liberalism and socialism, but his abiding commitment was pacifism.

Shortly after Britain entered the First World War, he joined a newly established group called the Union of Democratic Control (UDC). This organisation was less sinister than its name suggests: it called for democratic parliamentary control over foreign policy, believing that Britain had been dragged into war by secret treaties with France and Russia. The UDC announced itself to the public through letters to the press in September 1914 and soon won support from well-known political and cultural figures and built a national membership of 10,000 organised in 100 branches.[10] In London, apart from its West Central and Hoxton branches, its support mainly came from the suburbs. It built up a speakers' panel of 45 lecturers undertaking outreach work, and during the first few months of 1915 its London membership soared from around 600 to over 1,500. The 'patriotic' press characterised this Union as pro-German. The *Daily Express* whipped up public hostility, labelling a UDC event in Farringdon in November 1915 as a 'meeting to promote British surrender'. A group of soldiers obtained forged tickets and stormed the platform.

During that month the No-Conscription Fellowship was founded, and Russell shifted his active involvement from the

---

10 There was some cross over with suffragette activists. Muriel Matters and Israel Zangwill were prominent members (see Chapter 7). It agreed a resolution in February 1915 that 'democracy must be based on the equal citizenship of men and women'.

UDC into the Fellowship. Conscription became government policy in January 1916, and came into force in March of that year. As well as campaigning against conscription the Fellowship gave material and legal support to families of conscientious objectors. Russell was fined in June 1916 for publishing a leaflet supporting conscientious objection and exposing the case of Ernest Everett, an objector who had been sentenced to hard labour for two years. Russell was forced to leave his academic post at Trinity College, Cambridge because of his anti-war views, and was eventually himself imprisoned for six months in February 1918 after publicly urging that Britain should take up Germany's offer of peace talks.

Throughout the twentieth century, Tavistock Square Gardens, at Bloomsbury's northern end, accumulated peace memorials in the form of trees, statues, plaques on benches remembering peace activists, and, since 1994, a large stone dedicated to conscientious objectors. Sitting serenely in the middle of the gardens is a statue of Mohandas Karamchand 'Mahatma' Gandhi, pacifist and advocate of non-violent struggle for change.[11]

When Russell was incarcerated during the First World War, a prison warder, fulfilling administrative duties, asked him his religion. He replied 'agnostic', a term the warder didn't recognise. In situations where he could express his ideas more freely, Russell described religion as a harmful phenomenon that impeded knowledge and fostered fear. Religion still commanded great respect in First World War Britain, but Bloomsbury was known for comprising both individuals and institutions that challenged belief in God and the authority assumed by the Church.

The most significant local institution to challenge religious

---

11 'Mahatma' means honourable or venerable.

authority was University College London (UCL). It was founded in 1826 in the face of strong opposition from the Church of England, as a secular alternative to Oxford and Cambridge, which accepted Anglican Christians alone. A battle with the Church raged for ten years before UCL obtained a Royal Charter confirming that it could award degrees. The university was proudly secular and no minister of religion was allowed to sit on its College Council. This earned it the designation, 'that Godless institution in Gower Street' from Thomas Arnold, Head of Rugby School (and grandfather of Mary Ward). Its very existence provoked a formal educational response, and King's College on the Strand was created as a religious rival to UCL.

Jews comprised one of the categories excluded from Oxford and Cambridge universities at this time, but the investors in the UCL site, who included Isaac Goldsmid, a Jew, were adamant that their college was created for students of all faiths and none. The college's enlightened and progressive philosophy sat uneasily, though, with the origins of its investors' wealth. Council members, such as the merchant banker Alexander Baring and the coal industrialist John William Ward (Earl of Dudley), had acquired considerable wealth through slavery in the Caribbean, and Goldsmid accrued much of his wealth through his work for the British East India Company, which made huge profits exploiting workers in India.

Many secular radicals who stayed within the Bloomsbury area, though, had either studied or taught at UCL. Edward Aveling, the son of a non-conformist minister, later became a central figure in the Bloomsbury Socialist Society. He took an unusual academic trajectory, completing his initial studies at UCL and then taking a teaching post at King's College. He ran into conflicts at King's over his increasingly strident atheistic and socialistic views. These came to a head after Aveling became vice-president of the National Secular Society, and published a book on Charles Darwin's religious views, which claimed that Darwin was an atheist. Aveling was encouraged to seek an academic post elsewhere, and became a lecturer in anatomy and biology at the London Hospital.

On Bloomsbury's eastern edge, Richard Congreve, a Leamington-born Comtean philosopher,[12] who worked closely with Edward Beesly, a history professor at UCL, established a 'positivist temple' in 1870. Beesly had chaired the first meeting of the International Workingmen's Association. Their atheistic project ultimately became known as the Church of Humanity and was located, ironically, in Chapel Street.[13] In this 'church', human achievement was honoured in secular ways through rituals that had no reference to a god. Congreve told his congregants, 'We meet as believers in humanity' who used the 'wise utterances of the past' including those developed through religion, 'but we admit of no revelation and no being outside of man.'[14]

In the same year that his positivist temple was founded, the Education Act supported a national primary education system and insisted that this included religious education. Through the Church of Humanity, Congreve established a 'free school' for local children and adults, which included no religious instruction or worship. One of its unanticipated functions was to teach English to children of radical refugees, who had fled from France

12 The French philosopher Auguste Comte was the founder of positivism which rejected religious belief as unscientific and argued for belief only in that which can be proven by science, mathematics and logic.

13 Later renamed Rugby Street.

14 See 'Not the Messiah' by Alain de Botton, *New Statesman*, 19 July 2010.

after the Paris Commune was crushed in 1871. This atheist church suffered a serious schism in 1878; a number of members left, complaining that Congreve's rituals had become too religious in nature, but they eventually reunited and the church continued to function until 1932.

The Bloomsbury building that most clearly symbolises this questioning of religious ideas and authority by local thinkers and writers through the Victorian period and early twentieth century was established in Red Lion Square, near Holborn, in 1929 by the South Place Ethical Society. Conway Hall was named in honour of the nineteenth-century Unitarian-cum-freethinker and American anti-slavery activist, Moncure Daniel Conway. The South Place Ethical Society started life as a dissidentchurch congregation in the 1790s, rebelling against the doctrine of eternal hell. During the nineteenth century it evolved through Unitarianism to secularism and, ultimately, to atheism/humanism. Conway had played a leading role helping to steer it through these transitions from the 1860s to the 1890s. In the foyer of Conway Hall, a board commemorates successive leaders of the Ethical Society. All those who preceded Moncure Conway had the appellation 'Revd'. Conway had 'Dr' instead, as have all those who came after him, symbolising the move away from any religious trappings. Conway Hall, like its predecessor in South Place, has provided a regular meeting place and platform for radicals.

Another Bloomsbury institution constructed in the 1850s within an older establishment, did not deliberately set out to provide a rendezvous for radicals, but fulfilled precisely that role. The British Museum, built in the 1750s, opened an attractive circular reading room in May 1857. This was the brainchild of its principal librarian, Anthony Panizzi, who had arrived in

Britain as a political exile via Switzerland, from Modena, where he had been active in a radical Italian nationalist society.[15] Before it was officially launched, the doors of the Reading Room were opened for the public to view, and had 62,000 visitors in eight days. Its handbook confirmed its democratic access policy: 'The reading room of the British Museum is open to men and women of any country, or shade of political or other opinions.' Users had to apply for a reading card, be at least 21 years old, have a literary purpose – 'study, reference or research' – and needed to supply a reference confirming their 'respectability'.

Karl Marx used the Reading Room for nearly three decades, and wrote the first volume of *Das Kapital* there, which was published in 1867. Many pamphlets, polemics and manifestos of London's burgeoning socialist movement were researched and written in this beautiful space. Annie Besant began to use the Reading Room in 1874. Clementina Black, whose lecture on female labour in London had prompted Besant to investigate and campaign about the matchworkers in Bow, obtained her reading card in 1877, the same year as Eleanor Marx, who lived nearby from 1884 with Edward Aveling. Charlotte Despard, a vegetarian socialist of part Irish background, who was to play a major and dissident role in the early-twentieth-century suffragette movement, began using the library in 1894. During the same decade, a fellow vegetarian socialist of Irish background, George Bernard Shaw, a prolific writer of socialist polemics, penned many lectures and pamphlets in the Museum's Reading Room, mainly for the Fabian Society.

The novelist Edith Nesbit, a founding member of the Fabian society whose work included *The Railway Children*, wrote many

---

15   Panizzi was friendly with Giuseppe Mazzini, when Mazzini was exiled in London.

of her stories in the Museum's Reading Room, and she frequently met there with Annie Besant and Eleanor Marx. Nesbit described George Bernard Shaw as a 'clever writer and speaker' with an 'irresistible' fund of dry Irish humour. She also said he was 'the grossest flatterer I ever met ... horribly untrustworthy ... very plain like a long corpse with dead white face – sandy sleek hair, and a loathsome small straggly beard, and yet is one of the most fascinating men I ever met'.[16]

Untrustworthy or not, George Bernard Shaw's pithy one-liners encapsulated many of the challenges to late Victorian and early Edwardian orthodoxies that emerged from Bloomsbury's radicals. 'I'm an atheist and I thank God for it', he said, adding that 'All great truths begin as blasphemies.' He described patriotism as: 'your conviction that this country is superior to all others because you were born in it.' Shaw advised people not to 'waste your time on Social Questions. What is the matter with the poor is Poverty; what is the matter with the rich is Uselessness.' At the turn of a century in which forces of hate would display an unimaginable barbarism, he wrote about the importance of human empathy and solidarity: 'The worst sin toward our fellow creatures is not to hate them, but to be indifferent to them: that's the essence of inhumanity.'[17]

In 1902, the British Museum's Reading Room was frequently visited by a revolutionary exile in his early thirties, who stayed with his wife, also a revolutionary, close to King's Cross. Mr I. Mitchell, secretary of the General Federation of Trade Unions, provided the necessary reference for one Jacob Richter, who

---

16 Julia Briggs, *A Woman of Passion: The Life of E. Nesbit*, London: Penguin, 1989.

17 *The Devil's Disciple*, 1901.

obtained a reader's card at the Museum in April 1902. Richter was the pseudonym of Vladimir Illich Ulyanov Lenin, who was taking extra precautions to avoid surveillance by the authorities. He continued to use the Reading Room library on intermittent trips to London over the next few years, his last recorded visit being on 11 November 1911.

The presence of so many women among the radicals using the Reading Room was emblematic of the high profile that radical women thinkers and activists had in the area. In Coram Street, south of Tavistock Square, Emily Faithfull opened a women's publishing company called Victoria Press. She had been part of the Langham Place Group, a circle of middle-class female social reformers, struggling, in particular, for more diverse educational and employment opportunities for girls and women. She had herself been trained in the almost exclusively male profession of typesetting, by a secularist publisher called Austin Holyoake.[18]

Faithfull, who lived on Taviton Street, near Gordon Square, cascaded her skills down to 16 other women who worked at the press alongside male printers. Facing down criticisms that 'the female mind is not mechanical', that women would 'sink under this fatigue and labour', and that women engaging in printing would drive down wages in the industry, her press printed the *English Women's Journal*, the *Law Magazine*, the *Journal for Promoting Social Science* and also poetry collections. It was successful enough to move to bigger premises in Farringdon after a few years.

Researching the hazards of the printing industry, Faithfull discovered that the average life expectancy of printers was 48

---

18   His brother was the Chartist and freethinker, George Holyoake.

years, and that they often died from breathing disorders. She made sure that her premises had excellent light and ventilation, and she bought in specially commissioned high-stools so women could sit rather than work on their feet all day. There was a staff kitchen, and the women had regular lunch breaks; there was also a degree of profit-sharing. In 1865 Faithfull launched a penny weekly journal aimed at working-class women called *Work and Women*, and in the early 1870s undertook lecture tours in America on this theme. The 1860s and 1870s saw the beginnings of campaigning in London for women's political rights, and, from the 1880s, one of the earliest prominent campaigners, Millicent Garrett Fawcett, lived in Gower Street, close to Bedford Square.

The radical writer and lecturer Annie Besant, who lived close to Regents Park, often combined a session in the Reading Room with a visit afterwards to 8 Russell Square, where Emmeline and Richard Pankhurst settled in 1886 after moving to London from Manchester. In the 1850s Richard graduated in law from UCL and in 1867 was called to the bar at Lincoln's Inn, just south of Bloomsbury. During their time in Russell Square, Emmeline Pankhurst created the Women's Franchise League, which campaigned for votes for women in local government, a precursor to her later militant activism in the Women's Social and Political Union. Their three young daughters, who all became political activists, grew up knowing Annie Besant, William Morris and the Russian anarchist, Peter Kropotkin, as family friends and frequent visitors.

Many Bloomsbury rebels who developed their ideas for the radical transformation of society, nevertheless continued to live bourgeois lifestyles. In 1883, Thomas Davidson, a Scottish philosopher and educationalist, brought together a set of ethical socialists who attempted to 'live' the politics to which they aspired. They formed the Fellowship of the New Life. Some of its members established a commune at 29 Doughty Street, where they sought to practice 'harmonious living' based on 'unselfish regard for the general good'. Members of the Fellowship included the gay rights campaigner, Edward Carpenter, the feminist activist Edith Lees, her future husband, the sexologist Havelock Ellis, animal rights activist Henry Salt and the novelist Olive Schreiner. The tension between campaigning to change their own lives while also campaigning for change in the wider society eventually led to a schism, and a significant faction broke off in 1884 to form a new group which they called the Fabian Society. George Bernard Shaw joined this new group soon after it was established.

Social justice and women's rights were recurrent combined themes among the agitators, reformers and rebel thinkers of Bloomsbury who were challenging the mainstream orthodoxies of the age. These themes were embodied *par excellence* in Eleanor Marx, thinker and activist, socialist and feminist. She joined the Social Democratic Federation, then the Socialist League, and was a co-founder of the Bloomsbury Socialist Society. As a radical activist who moved in both the rarefied political circles of Bloomsbury and the harsh streets of east London, where she assisted with campaigns led by the poorest and most exploited workers, she was perhaps more acutely aware than many in her immediate environment of the contradictions of class.

In her 1886 pamphlet, *The Woman Question*, co-authored by Edward Aveling, she wrote:

Women are the creatures of an organised tyranny of men, as the workers are the creatures of an organised tyranny of idlers. Both the oppressed classes, women and the immediate producers, must understand that their emancipation will come from themselves. Women will find allies in the better sort of men, as the labourers are finding allies among the philosophers, artists, and poets. But the one has nothing to hope from man as a whole, and the other has nothing to hope from the middle class as a whole.

The personal is political and the political is personal. Sadly for Eleanor, her belief in the man with whom she spent her adult life – who, she thought, shared both her political philosophy and basic values – was betrayed in 1898. After nursing him back to health from a serious illness, she discovered he had cheated on her and had secretly married a young actress called Eva Frye. Eleanor committed suicide on 31 March at just 43 years old. Many of the leading radicals of both the West End and the East End spoke at her funeral, including Will Thorne of the Gasworkers' Union, with whom she had worked so closely in fighting for better lives for East London's workers.

BEDFORD SQUARE

TAVISTOCK SQUARE GARDENS

① ② CORAM STREET

WOBURN PLACE

BEDFORD WAY

⑤ ⑥

GOWER STREET

MONTAGUE PLACE

④ ③ RUSSELL SQUARE

RUSSELL SQUARE

GREAT RUSSELL STREET

MONTAGUE STREET

SOUTHAMPTON ROW

MUSEUM STREET

⑦ ⑦

⑧ QUEEN'S SQUARE

BURY PLACE

BLOOMSBURY WAY

⑬

GREAT ORMOND STREET

LCC

JOHN HOWARD
1726 - 1790
Prison Reformer
Lived Here

⑫

EMILY WILDING
DAVISON
BORN OCT. 11TH 1872
DIED JUNE 8TH 1913.
DEEDS NOT WORDS.

⑩

THEOBALDS ROAD

LAMB'S CONDUIT STREET

RUGBY STREET

⑪

RED LION
SQUARE

100M

WALK

Start at Gandhi's statue, Tavistock Square Gardens, WC1.

1. Tavistock Square Gardens

Mahatma Gandhi's statue is the centrepiece of this garden dedicated to the peace movement. Gandhi began to study law at nearby UCL in 1888. He spent most of the next two decades in South Africa. When he returned on a visit in 1906, he was very impressed by the non-violent direct action tactics of the suffragettes. Opposite the northeast corner of the square is the British Medical Association building, formerly Tavistock House. Charles Dickens lived in its spacious and salubrious accommodation when he wrote *Hard Times*. Exit the square and turn right along Woburn Place, then left into Coram Street.

2. Coram Street

Named after a retired sea captain, Thomas Coram, who set up a foundling hospital in 1739. Emily Faithfull established the Victoria Press with the women typesetters she trained at 9 Coram Street. Return to Woburn Place then turn right. Cross over into Russell Square.

3. Russell Square

The square was developed around 1800. Its houses started with number 1 on the southern corner of the Russell Hotel and went anti-clockwise around the square to number 64. A Christian socialist,

Frederick Denison Maurice, lived at number 5. He founded the Working Men's College in 1854, which offered evening classes in arts, culture and humanities to workers. The Pankhursts lived at number 8 (northern corner of the hotel) from 1886–93. Mary Ward, leader of the Passmore Edwards Settlement, lived at number 61. Cross the square diagonally, then cross the road and turn right then immediately left into Montague Place.

4. Montague Place

This is the back of the British Museum, whose Reading Room, opened in 1857, was a place where Bloomsbury's radicals met, researched and wrote lectures, pamphlets and books. Marx wrote the first volume of *Das Kapital* here, and made notes for the second and third volumes, which were published posthumously by Engels. Continue along Montague Place, turn right into Gower Street.

5. Gower Street

Millicent Garrett Fawcett, a leading figure in the National Union of Women's Suffrage Societies, lived at number 2 from the mid-1880s, after her husband – the blind Liberal MP, Henry Fawcett – had died. Cross over to Bedford Square.

6. Bedford Square

Walk anti-clockwise round the last intact Georgian square in London. Its houses have since been converted internally into offices. The garden in the middle is only accessible to selected key-holders. The Radical MP, Thomas Wakley, lived at number 35.

Elizabeth Jesser Reid, a social reformer and anti-slavery activist, founded a women-only higher education institution at number 46. John Passmore Edwards, peace activist, supporter of the Chartists, publisher and philanthropist, lived at number 51. Return to Gower Street. Turn right, then left into Great Russell Street.

7. *Great Russell Street*

Margaret Harkness, author of six novels exposing working conditions in city slums, lived at number 45; Eleanor Marx and Edward Aveling, stalwarts of the Bloomsbury Socialist Society, lived at number 55. Turn right into Museum Street, then left into Bloomsbury Way.

8. *Bloomsbury Way*

St George's Church hosted the funeral service of the suffragette, Emily Wilding Davison, who was fatally injured by a horse as she made a protest at the Derby races on 14 June 1913. She had lived at 31 Coram Street, northeast of Russell Square. Her coffin was borne on a horse-drawn carriage amidst a march by 6,000 suffragettes. Her body was taken to Morpeth and buried in a family plot. Her gravestone was marked with the suffragette slogan, 'Deeds not Words'. Turn left into Bury Place.

9. *Bury Place*

A plaque marks the house where pacifist activist and humanist philosopher Bertrand Russell lived. Return to Bloomsbury Way. Turn left. Cross into Theobalds Road, then across again to Red Lion Square.

10. Red Lion Square

At the west end of the square, just inside the garden, is a statue of Fenner Brockway, who became a Liberal early in his life but switched to the Independent Labour Party after interviewing James Keir Hardie in 1907. He was an energetic member of the No Conscription Fellowship and War Resisters International and active later in the anti-colonial movement, Liberation. He was also active in the secularist movement. The opposite end of the square has a bust of Bertrand Russell. Exit the gardens along the north side and turn right to the humanist centre, Conway Hall. On the first floor is the Humanist Library. Inside its grand hall above the stage are the words spoken by Polonius in *Hamlet*, reincarnated as a humanist statement: 'To thine own self be true'. Continue along the alleyway, turn left and cross Theobalds Road into Lamb's Conduit Street. Turn right into Rugby Street.

11. Rugby Street

Rugby Street was formerly called Chapel Street, and number 20 was renumbered from 19. The original 19 Chapel Street was the location of Richard Congreve's atheist Church of Humanity. Return to Lamb's Conduit Street; turn right, then left into Great Ormond Street.

12. Great Ormond Street

At number 23 a plaque commemorates John Howard, a Hackney-born social reformer who campaigned to ameliorate conditions in prison. The Howard League for Penal Reform was created in 1866 in his honour. Continue to Queen's Square.

13. Queen's Square

The Passmore Edwards Settlement, now called the Mary Ward Centre, moved here in 1982 from Tavistock Square. The after-school activities that Mary Ward established there in the early 1900s initiated the playcentre movement. Mary Ward herself described the settlement as 'a place for ideals, a place for enthusiasm'.

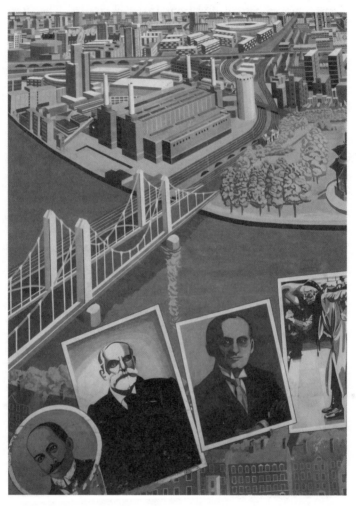

'Battersea in Perspective' mural by Brian Barnes, Dagnall Street.

6

STIRRINGS FROM THE SOUTH

The Battersea Four

In 1863 a railway station opened in south London, and transformed the local area. A joint venture of two railway lines created a new terminus called Clapham Junction, a name that would soon become a byword for a crowded, noisy, chaotic scene. Clapham already had an upmarket resonance for Londoners, but the terminus was actually located in the depressed and impoverished district of Battersea, which at that time had a population of 20,000. By the 1890s a new industrial landscape had appeared, and the local population had grown to more than 160,000, boosted especially by immigrants from Ireland. Battersea's northeastern area, around Nine Elms Lane, became known as the 'Irish Island'.

This rapidly growing workforce was herded into new factories where women made candles, soap, pencils, cigars, hats and caps, army clothing, biscuits, boxes and envelopes, or worked in huge laundries. Men also did factory work but mainly found jobs on the railways and within its allied industries. With a continuously expanding population, employers could keep wages low. Housing development, based on minimal investment, struggled to keep pace with industrial development. The area soon became as notorious as the East End for its overcrowded, insanitary conditions, and shared similar social problems, especially alcoholism, criminality and prostitution, with the latter centred around Clapham Junction.

Battersea was crying out for people with the vision and capability to turn these circumstances on their head. Between the 1880s and the 1930s the area was blessed with four 'tribunes of the people',[1] who attempted in their own ways to do just that. Each of these outstanding figures had the personality and inner strength to make a sustained difference in their own right, and, more importantly, to inspire others with their ideas and optimism that collective effort could bring positive change. One was a powerhouse of energy from a Scottish background; one, an aristocratic widow from Kent with an Irish father; another, a Liverpool-born photographer of Caribbean background and pan-African political leanings; and the last, a quixotic Indian figure from a Zoroastrian background. Each had their own progressive dreams, and believed they could help to turn dreams into reality.

The powerhouse was John Burns, the youngest of 16 children, born to an English mother and a Scottish father in Vauxhall in 1858. After the father deserted the family, they moved to a basement in Battersea. When he was ten, Burns was apprenticed as an engineer and, in his late teens, when he was working at Mowlem's construction and engineering company, a French work colleague introduced him to socialist ideas. That colleague was Victor Delahaye, a political exile who had participated in the 1871 uprising that heralded the short-lived Paris Commune. Burns absorbed these ideas and was soon enthusiastically conveying

---

1   In ancient Rome a 'Tribune of the People' was a champion of the ordinary people's rights elected by them.

them to others at open-air meetings. He was first arrested in 1878 for defying a police prohibition, and speaking on Clapham Common.

Burns founded a vibrant local branch of the Social Democratic Federation (SDF) in 1885. The trade union activist Tom Mann, who lived in Battersea in the mid-1880s and joined that SDF branch, said Burns possessed 'a voice that could fill every part of the largest hall or theatre, and, if the wind were favourable, could reach a 20,000 audience in the parks'. Henry Snell, a fellow SDF member and later a Labour MP, claimed that Burns's power as a street orator 'was probably unequalled in that generation'.

Burns organised unions locally at Vauxhall gasworks and at the Nine Elms goods yard and locomotive works. He was one of the key organisers during the Great Dock Strike in 1889. That same year, the SDF and progressive Liberals established the Battersea Labour League. John Burns's credibility grew not only among workers in Battersea but in London as a whole through his determined campaigning against unemployment. On Sundays he led processions of London's unemployed into fashionable churches, forcing their congregations to take notice. He was arrested at the Bloody Sunday riots of 1887 and spent six weeks in prison.

Burns knew, though, that change would not come solely through protest but by getting hands on the levers of power. Having built a considerable support base among both socialists and liberals, he contested and won two key elections. He was elected on to the newly formed London County Council in 1889, and defeated the Tory candidate to win the parliamentary seat of Battersea and Clapham in 1892 as a socialist, with significant Liberal Party support. The cooperative relationship he forged between local Labourites, Liberals and Radicals through the

Battersea Labour League enabled a broad Progressive Alliance to come into being. Adopting the motto; 'Not for me, not for you, but for us', it took control of the local vestry in 1894 and held power until 1909.[2] By then the partnerships within it were sufficiently strained for the Tories to regain control for three years. But during those initial 15 years, with John Burns as its driving force, the alliance enabled Battersea to become the beacon of municipal socialism in London. Gold-coloured bees, symbolising unity and cooperation, adorned the beautiful mosaic floor of its new Town Hall on Lavender Hill, where progressive polices were proposed and adopted.[3]

The Alliance reduced the working week to 48 hours for all council employees; created London's first municipal health visiting service – paying special attention to maternity and child welfare; established a sterilised milk depot providing free school milk; and built more libraries, swimming baths and a municipal laundry. But its proudest achievement was one that began to challenge Battersea's biggest problem – poor quality and overcrowded housing. In 1902 Battersea Council opened its first municipal housing estate – the Latchmere Estate. Wired for electricity from the council's own generating station, it comprised 173 two-storey dwellings at rents that were affordable for skilled workers. Most properties on the estate had two front doors and housed two families. At the opening ceremony John Burns said: 'The land has communal origin, the streets bear democratic names, the whole plan, history and achievement is redolent of the common victory of the common people.'[4]

---

2   During which Battersea became a Metropolitan Borough (1900).

3   The former town hall building is now the Battersea Arts Centre.

4   S. Creighton, 'Latchmere Estate: Celebrating its 100th Anniversary' (talk given in 2005), www.seancreighton.com/bwhistory.htm; http://hawkley.ctie.org.uk/History/latchmere_estate.htm.

On the estate, Freedom Street runs parallel to Reform Street. One street is named after a Boer general (Joubert), another after William Matthews, a stonemason who chaired Battersea's Stop the War Committee during the Second Boer War. All a far cry from the streets a few hundred yards west, such as Candahar Road, Cabul Road and Khyber Road, which celebrate British military adventures of the late 1870s.

Anti-war activism locally was complemented by republicanism. In honour of Edward VII's coronation in 1902, local authorities were instructed to seal a loyal address and organise public rejoicing. When Battersea's ruling Progressive Alliance voted narrowly to refuse to do so, the Liberal-inclined *Daily Chronicle* described it as: 'Battersea versus the British Empire'. Another Liberal paper, the *Pall Mall Gazette*, lauded Battersea as 'the only borough council which has the courage to flout the King on his coronation'. The Alliance's anti-war stance and proud republicanism had popular support. Councillors adopting these stands continued to be elected, and Burns held the Battersea and Clapham seat in 1900 despite the national Tory surge at the 'Khaki Election'. On Empire Day (24 May), Battersea Council regularly flew its municipal flag rather than the Union flag.

Burns frequently sniped at the style and character of the wealthy classes. He said: 'The better the dress and position, the bigger the snob and the greater the rogue.' He laid great stress on the virtues of the 'common people', declaring, 'I am not ashamed to say I am the son of a washerwoman.' Nevertheless, an aristocratic widow called Charlotte Despard, who lived in Battersea's most deprived area, Nine Elms, observed that, on the day in 1892 when John Burns and

James Keir Hardie entered Parliament as the country's first elected socialists, Keir Hardie wore plain clothes and a cap, whereas Burns wore an exclusive suit paid for by his supporters. While Keir Hardie consolidated the Independent Labour Party during the ensuing years, Burns edged closer to the Liberals.

Despard was neither shocked nor surprised when Burns accepted a post in the Liberal government that won power in 1906, becoming the first working-class Cabinet member. He argued that it provided an opportunity to make practical policies benefitting working-class people and claimed that many trade unionists supported him. Others regarded it a betrayal of his socialist principles. His radicalism began to fade in government, but some old habits die hard. Having been promoted to President of the Board of Trade, he resigned from the government in 1914 when Britain went to war. He stepped down from political life altogether in 1918, devoting himself to cricket and studying London's history.

Charlotte Despard, of half-Irish background, grew up in Ripple, Kent, as Charlotte French, in spacious countryside accommodation – a dramatic contrast with Burns's circumstances. By the age of ten, though, her naval commander father had died and her mother, who suffered mental health problems, was committed to an asylum. Charlotte was packed off to relatives in London and attended by nurses and governesses. As Burns enjoyed upward mobility into the corridors of power, Despard's opposite trajectory found her increasingly immersed in the daily struggles of Battersea's most impoverished residents.

She had married a wealthy businessman, Maximillian Despard, in 1870 and spent many years nursing him. In her spare time she wrote romantic novels. After Maximillian's death in 1890, she threw herself into radical political activity, initially as a campaigner on the Lambeth Board of Guardians, and then on the London School Board. During that decade she joined Hyndman's Marxist SDF and Keir Hardie's ethical socialists of the Independent Labour Party (ILP), campaigned against sweated female labour, and became a Catholic, drawn by spiritual ideas which ultimately led her to Theosophy. Her Catholicism also gave her a strong affinity with the largely Irish population in the congested neighbourhood of Nine Elms – sandwiched between gasometers, a brewery, a coalyard and a railway depot – where she settled.

When Charles Booth interviewed Despard at 2 Currie Street in 1898 for his poverty survey, he found a home converted into a community centre with a club for factory boys, subsidised meals, a dispensary, and a room for mothers' meetings. Booth described her as 'one in 10,000', saying: 'Hardly one I have seen in the whole course of the Inquiry has left so strong an impression ... If I wanted to read a district with sympathy I should be inclined to borrow her eyes, and if to influence it I should be content with her heart.'[5]

Despite the poverty and degradation around her, Despard believed that the twentieth century would see the 'rise of two great movements: Labour and Women'. Teresa Billington-Greig, who came to know her a few years later in the suffragette movement, described Despard as 'a visionary and optimist' of 'untiring energy' whose appeal was 'ethical and emotional'. She was 'a dreamer who gave hope and inspiration and courage to those with whom she worked'.[6]

---

5   C. Booth, *Notebooks*, miscellaneous districts 36/37, Battersea, LSE archive.

6   Teresa Billington-Greig papers, Women's Library archive, LSE.

As well as providing everyday practical help to people struggling with their circumstances, she articulated her radical ideas for
social change at large outdoor gatherings, speaking regularly at
Battersea Park, Wandsworth Common and Clapham Common,
and at indoor campaigning meetings in Battersea Town Hall.
Alongside her local work, she was the leading personality, nationally, in the Women's Freedom League, a suffragette organisation
campaigning not just for the vote but also for equal economic
opportunities for all women and against women's oppression in all spheres.[7] Charlotte Despard was extremely effective
in supporting the political causes of London's Irish minority,
eventually moving to Ireland to campaign there directly.

In 1913, however, newspapers noted Battersea's support for
a different minority. An article in the *Chicago Defender* under
the headline 'England More Civilised Than US' reported that a
London council had elected its first black mayor. But only just.
John Archer, born to a Barbadian father and an Irish mother,
triumphed by 30 votes to 29 over a West End tailor, W. G. Moore.
The Daily Mail announced 'Coloured Mayor – Majority of One
at Battersea – Dramatic Speech'. In his acceptance speech Archer
declared: 'My election tonight marks a new era. You have made
history ... That news will go forth to all the coloured nations
of the world and they will look at Battersea and say, "It is the
greatest thing you have done. You have shown that you have no
racial prejudice, but recognise a man for what you think he has
done."

Thetford in Norfolk elected *Britain's* first black mayor (in
1904), but Archer's appointment to office was novel enough to

---

7   See Chapter 7.

generate considerable press speculation, much of it uncompli-
mentary, about his and his parents' ethnic origins. He clarified
the issue with delicious sarcasm:

> I am a son of a man born in the West Indies. I was born
> in a little obscure village in England, that maybe you have
> never heard of – Liverpool ... My mother was not born in
> Rangoon. She was not Burmese. She belonged to one of
> the grandest races on the face of the earth. My mother was
> an Irishwoman.[8]

He entered local politics as a Liberal, through Battersea
Labour League, and was one of six councillors elected to
Latchmere ward in 1906, where he had also opened a photographic studio. But his political interests were wider. He attended
the Pan-Africanist Conference in London in 1900, organised by a
Trinidadian barrister, Henry Sylvester-Williams, which called on
Britain to give 'the rights of responsible government to the Black
colonies of Africa and the West Indies'.[9] Archer was elected to
the conference's Executive Committee. The conference moved
to different national locations over the years and Archer chaired
it when it reconvened in London in 1921.

Following his mayoral election, Archer received congratula-
tions from across the world, but was shocked at the volume of
hate mail he received. A month after his election he told a meeting
at the Town Hall

---

8   *Daily Mail*, 10 November 1913.

9   Sylvester-Williams was also elected as a Progressive councillor in 1906 in St Marylebone, where Progressives were the minority.

I have had letters since I have been Mayor calling my mother some of the foulest names ... I have been made to feel my position more than any man who has ever occupied this chair ... because I am a man of colour. My dead mother has been called in question because she married a coloured man.[10]

The Progressive Alliance, which resumed control over the borough in 1912, did not last through the First World War. Labour was emerging as a strong independent force, and the Liberals split off. Archer became a key figure in the local Labour Party, respected particularly for his efforts on behalf of the unemployed and ex-servicemen. He argued that a government that spent millions of pounds a day prosecuting a war 'should be able to find sufficient money to keep out of the workhouse the men who helped to win that war'.

Labour's candidate in the parliamentary election in December 1918 was Charlotte Despard, who had taken a strong pacifist stance during the war. Her manifesto put demands of justice and equality for Ireland and India high on the agenda alongside adequate food for children, better education and housing, land nationalisation and a minimum wage. Archer worked hard as Despard's election agent but she couldn't withstand the backlash against pacifists that dominated this election nationally, and lost the seat to Richard Morris, a Coalition Liberal. Archer proved more fortunate with the candidate he promoted at the next election, a man who entered the ranks of political pioneers for his affiliations as much as his ethnic origins.

10 M. Phillips, *Black Europeans: A British Library Online Gallery Feature, John Archer (1863–1932)* www.bl.uk/onlinegallery/features/blackeuro/pdf/archer.pdf

At a session on colonial freedom during the 1921 Pan-Africanist Congress, Archer welcomed a Parsee Indian, Shapurji Saklatvala, to the platform. In the following months, Archer became Saklatvala's principal backer for the Battersea North parliamentary seat, aiding his victory in 1922. Saklatvala narrowly failed to keep the seat in 1923 but, with Archer's help, regained it in 1924, holding it until 1929. Saklatvala fought these elections as a Communist Party (CP) member with Labour support. John Archer, a Labour representative, chaired Saklatvala's final election rally in 1924. When he represented Battersea North, Saklatvala was Britain's third Indian MP and its first Communist MP.[11]

Born in Bombay in 1874, Saklatvala came to Britain in 1905 to recuperate from malaria and work in his maternal uncle's firm, the Tata Corporation, in Derbyshire.[12] In his late 20s, Saklatvala had become politically rebellious and spoke out against the damaging effects of British rule. His family thought he would benefit from a change of scenery! In Derbyshire he married Sally Marsh, a local working-class woman who had left school at 13. She worked as a waitress at the health centre where Saklatvala was recuperating. Through Sally he began to learn the realities of working-class life in a country enriched by its enormous empire, and just how little of that wealth filtered down to the lower classes. He was drawn into left-wing activism after seeing the conditions of ordinary people in Manchester and London.

Saklatvala joined the Social Democratic Federation in 1907 and became a keen follower of Sylvia Pankhurst, whom he first heard speaking at a Votes for Women demonstration in 1908.

---

11 Excluding MPs born in India but of white British ethnicity.

12 The corporation established itself in 1868 working initially in steel, energy and textiles.

The following year he joined the City of London branch of the ILP. He continued to live in two worlds, supremely conscious of immediate issues in his adopted country, but equally aware of the ongoing struggles of Indians under British rule. He tried to connect the two through campaigning work with socialists and trade unionists. He joined the Workers Welfare League for India, set up by two socialists including Arthur Field, a Battersea-based ILP member. The Russian Revolution had an enormous impact on him, and after the British Communist Party was established, he was part of a segment of the ILP that split off and joined the Communists in 1921.

Saklatvala mainly lived north of the Thames but had increasing contact with John Archer and Battersea's strong trade-union movement. He knew both Communist and ILP activists in Battersea, and was invited to speak at a rally for striking Welsh miners in 1921 at the Town Hall. When Saklatvala was nominated by Battersea's Trades Council to fight the parliamentary seat, he was backed by the local Communist Party and Labour Party branches. Joint membership was permitted until the Labour Party and CP became locked in internecine warfare in 1924.

He had strong support from Charlotte Despard, who made a special appeal 'to my fellow Irish countrymen and women in North Battersea' to 'support the Party and support the man, Saklatvala – that will be on your side in the great struggle which is bound to come'.

In his maiden speech to the House of Commons on 23 November 1922, Saklatvala spoke of his constituents who suffered from unemployment. He commented on workers' wages in Bengal too, but his main focus was Ireland, denouncing the Anglo-Irish treaty, which he said was not acceptable to the

Irish people as a whole, adding, 'I put forward not my personal views but the view of 90 per cent of those Irish men who are my electors.'

According to the communist writer J. A. Mahon, Saklatvala's constituents enthusiastically supported his work inside and outside Parliament:

> ... he was known in every [Battersea] working class district as 'Sak'. He placed his legal ability and untiring energy at the disposal of anyone in trouble ... his frequent meetings were crowded with men, women and even children, who absorbed his simple but eloquent explanations.[13]

Saklatvala's speeches in the House were witty, and his behaviour in Parliament occasionally unconventional. He was slapped down for addressing the Speaker as 'Comrade'. In a debate about the Indian Civil Service, he said it was 'not Indian', had 'no reputation for being civil', and it was 'a domination and usurpation'. Barring these 'great defects, they are all right', he said. His style did not endear him to opponents. One Liberal, Leslie Hore-Belisha, who entered the House in 1923, deplored Saklatvala's 'turbulent' and 'loosely phrased' rhetoric, 'spoken in a slightly raucous voice [with] wild gesticulation'.

As the only Indian MP, he endured racist jibes but answered critics with panache. In a 1924 health debate Saklatvala claimed that the Russian revolutionary government cared more about workers' health than did the British government. Austen

---

13 Saklatvala file in the Dictionary of Labour Biography archive, Hull History Centre.

Chamberlain MP began his reply, 'When Mr Saklatvala knows this country more intimately ...'. Saklatvala, who had lived in Britain for nearly 20 years, told the *Sunday Worker* that he had 'too good a knowledge of the British ruling class and their politics ... much more than he considers it good for an Indian to know'.

> Against one Chamberlain I have the voice of 15,000 British workers in Battersea and during my visits to the provinces ... I have reason to know that there are as many thousands elsewhere who know I have a far more intimate ... knowledge of the conditions ... of the workers of Britain than ever Mr Austen Chamberlain will be able to possess.[14]

The wrangles at national level between the Labour Party's rival wings impacted on Battersea's unique situation. Labour's conference in October 1924 forbade party branches from supporting Communist candidates, but Battersea Labour Party rebelled. It voted overwhelmingly to continue supporting Saklatvala. It would not stand a candidate against him, and he retained the seat on a Communist ticket. As a result the local Labour Party was temporarily disaffiliated from the national party.

Battersea and Bermondsey were south London's most militant supporters of the May 1926 General Strike, called by the TUC in support of miners refusing to accept a pay cut and increased hours of work. The miners' slogan was 'not a penny off the pay, not a minute on the day'. Around the country, Councils of

---

14 S. Saklatvala, *The Fifth Commandment*, Manchester: Miranda Press, 1991, pp. 282–3.

Action (COAs) were formed through existing networks of trade unionists. These COAs aimed to maximise local participation in the strike by picketing large workplaces where production was continuing and persuading workers to join the strike; facilitating distribution of food to local strikers and their families; and conveying information about the strike's local and national progress in a situation where national newspapers were temporarily closed down.

The Lower Hall in Battersea's municipal headquarters was given over to a COA formed by 70 local organisations – mainly trade unions – within a day of the strike starting. The local Unemployed Workers' Movement marched through Battersea Square, Battersea Church Road, and along York Road to Nine Elms, stopping to hold meetings outside factories and calling workers to join the strike. Every evening, strike updates were given at the Prince's Head pub on the corner of York Road.

But Battersea North's MP could not be present at these updates. He was in jail. Saklatvala had addressed a mass meeting in Hyde Park at the beginning of the strike. Troops were camped nearby. He called on troops to defend the people and not to follow orders to act against them. He was charged with sedition and imprisoned for two months. A huge crowd attended a rally at Battersea Town Hall on 8 May in support of the strike. The main speaker, a South Wales miner, Noah Ablett, was arrested as he left the meeting for supporting Saklatvala's request to the troops.[15]

In the aftermath of the General Strike, the hostility between the Labour Party and Communist Party was ratcheted up further

---

15 Ablett was bound over for 12 months and ordered to pay £10 10s costs. In 1911, Tom Mann served six months after making a similar call during the transport workers' strike.

and John Archer, ultimately, fell out with Saklatvala, fell back in with Labour, and supported a successful Labour candidate against him in the 1929 election.

Between 1932 and 1943, Battersea's four outstanding activists – each of whom had stamped their personalities on the area over the preceding decades, refused to accept the status quo, inspired hope and supported radical change by courageous personal example – departed this earth. John Archer died first, in 1932, a few weeks shy of his 70th birthday. He was Deputy Leader of the council at the time, representing Nine Elms, where the fight against poverty continued. He was buried in Croydon after a service at Our Lady of Carmel Church, on Battersea Park Road, where mourners said he left a multitude of friends and not a single enemy.

On 20 January 1936, the Bombay-born writer Rudyard Kipling was cremated in a private ceremony at Golders Green in northwest London, his coffin draped in the Union Flag. The few mourners were surprised to find the grounds littered with red flags and insignia, left behind from a cremation earlier that day. Hundreds had come to pay their last respects to another of Bombay's sons, Shapurji Saklatvala, who had died of a heart attack at the age of 61.

Charlotte Despard was buried in Dublin in 1939, having lived to the grand age of 95. In Ireland her political energy was transferred from the Labour Party to Sinn Fein, and, following a trip to Russia in 1930, to the Communist Party. Her religious and spiritual journey took her from Catholicism to Theosophy. On her death, the militantly atheist left-winger Harry Pollitt described her as 'the only real saint I've ever met'.

John Burns, who had retired early from active politics in 1918, outlived them all. He was buried by St Mary's Church, Battersea, in 1943. A local primary school is named after him, as is a street leading into the Latchmere municipal housing estate.

In the decades in which these four individuals were so prominent, Battersea gained a reputation both for radicalism and internationalism. During the period in which they passed away, Battersea's people combined these traditions to great effect, especially in their solidarity with the fledgling Spanish Republic's struggle against fascism.

Within days of the Civil War breaking out, the Communist Party organised a public meeting at the Railwaymen's Unity Hall in Falcon Grove, entitled 'Support Spanish Workers Against Fascism'. Speakers included a local communist, Tom Oldershaw, who was cycling for pleasure in Spain when the Civil War broke out. Alongside him was a fellow party member, poet and painter, Clive Branson. Both later joined a band of 'volunteers for liberty' from Battersea who fought in Spain. Six of them, including Oldershaw, never returned. Branson spoke at the next major campaign meeting at Battersea Town Hall in September, which attracted an audience of more than 400.

An ad hoc Aid for Spain Committee helped overcome the tensions between Labour and the CP that persisted from the 1920s. The CP invited the fiery Labour left-winger, Aneurin Bevan, to speak at a meeting about Spain at Battersea Town Hall. Bevan explained it would be difficult to appear on a CP platform, so the ad hoc committee was formed. More than 1,000 people heard Bevan make a dramatic, prescient speech in which he warned: 'If Madrid fell to fascism, it would be Paris next, and then London.' In December the Trades Council formally established an Aid for Spain Committee that collected food, money and supplies for the Spanish Republic, through an Aid for Spain

Week and house-to-house collections. The week concluded with a public meeting, with more than 20 organisations represented on the platform.

Two venues on Lavender Hill close to the Town Hall became organising and collection centres for the Aid for Spain Committee: the Labour Party headquarters at number 177 and the CP's People's Bookshop at number 115. Inside the People's Bookshop during this period, a group of women knitted garments that were sent as aid to the Republic. The shop's manager, David Guest, a Cambridge mathematics and philosophy graduate – and son of the playwright and suffragette Carmel Goldsmid and a Southwark Labour MP, Leslie Haden Guest – had a more ambitious project. He wanted to raise £750: the amount needed to send an ambulance to Spain. By the end of January 1937, only £100 had been raised. Guest made arrangements with the central London HQ of the Aid for Spain movement, guaranteeing any shortfall himself. Fellow Battersea communists, Percy Cohen and Joe Ilean, drove the fully equipped ambulance to Spain. In April 1938 Guest himself joined up with the 15th Brigade, but was killed by a fascist sniper as the brigade attempted to capture a key hill in the Battle of Ebro three months later. Guest's sister, Angela, also volunteered for Spain doing medical work, without training at that stage. She survived and became a doctor in 1945.[16]

The local anti-fascist campaigns directed towards Spain from July 1936 gave heart and inspiration to the fight against fascism on their own doorsteps. Battersea was one the few areas in London where the British Union of Fascists had established a working-class base before 1934. Hundreds of campaigners attended

---

16 Angela Guest later worked for the World Health Organisation but was killed in a car crash in 1965.

Saturday morning open-air meetings. Their local organiser was J. P. D. Paton, a Covent Garden porter, formerly active in the National Unemployed Workers' Movement. Battersea Borough Council repeatedly refused to allow Mosley's movement the right to meet at Battersea Town Hall.

In April 1938, Mosley himself attempted to hold an open-air rally in the area. Fascist supporters were outnumbered by hundreds of anti-fascists. Instead of speaking from the platform, Mosley had to give his speech from inside a van, through two microphones and six speakers. The rally was abandoned amid a mini-riot by anti-fascists, during which ten of them were arrested. The following month, when the fascists announced a march from Clapham Junction to Clapham Common, fewer than 100 fascists turned up and they were met with huge opposition every step of the route. An area that had provided London with one of its first two socialist MPs in the 1890s, its first black mayor in 1913, its first Communist MP in the 1920s, and had sent at least 17 of its most idealistic younger people to Spain to fight for democracy, was in no mood to give ground to those who would destroy these ideals.

JOHN
RICHARD
ARCHER
1863-1932

ENGLISH HERITAGE

BIRLEY STREET

DAGNALL STREET

CULVERT ROAD

REFORM STREET

FREEDOM STREET

EVERSLEIGH ROAD

HOLDEN STREET

GRAYSHOTT ROAD

SHEEPCOTE LANE

ST JAMES'S GROVE

BATTERSEA PARK ROAD

IVENS ROAD

JOUBERT STREET

MATTHEWS STREET

LATCHMERE ROAD

LAVENDER HILL

LATCHMERE ROAD

FALCON PARK

CABUL ROAD

CANDAHAR ROAD

DOROTHY ROAD

AFGHAN ROAD

FALCON GROVE

ESTE ROAD

LAVENDER HILL

FALCON ROAD

GRANT ROAD   CLAPHAM JUNCTION

100M

WALK

Start at Clapham Junction station, Grant Road exit, SW16 2PE.

1. Grant Road
The creation of Clapham Junction station in 1863 brought considerable economic development to Battersea and a huge influx of workers over the next four decades. Turn left into Falcon Road, then right into Este Road.

2. Este Road
Mary Gray, who lived at number 72, was an active member of the Social Democratic Federation and founder, in Battersea, of London's first Socialist Sunday School. Go back to Falcon Road, then turn right.

3. Falcon Road
Battersea Labour Club, on the right, is not officially connected to the Labour Party but part of the strong local labour movement tradition. Battersea Labour Party was established in 1908, and Battersea was one of the first areas of London to have a local Trades Council. Battersea Labour Party was established by a group of Trades Council activists. Continue along Falcon Road. Turn right into Falcon Grove.

4. Falcon Grove

The building at number 5 with long windows used to be the National Union of Railwaymen's Unity Hall. In addition to union meetings, it was used to promote radical political campaigns. During the Spanish Civil War, the first of a series of meetings to 'Support Spanish Workers Against Fascism' took place here. Return to Falcon Road. Turn right and stop on the corner of Afghan Road.

5. Afghan Road

The Prince's Head public house opposite, took its name from an earlier demolished pub 200 yards further north, which housed nightly meetings in 1926, during the General Strike, updating workers on the strike and mobilising for local support actions. Several streets in the next section of the walk honour British military campaigns between 1878–80. Continue along Afghan Road, turn left into Candahar Road then right into Cabul Road, past Sacred Heart Catholic school. Catholic schools in Battersea reflect the large numbers of Irish heritage children in the area. Pass the former Milton Congregational Hall at 21 Cabul Road, go through Falcon Park, under the railway bridge, left into Latchmere Road then right into Burns Road.

6. Burns Road

This road celebrates John Burns, trade unionist, later Liberal MP for Battersea, and first elected as a socialist in 1892. It leads into the Latchmere Estate – Battersea's first municipal housing project, which opened in 1902. Turn right into Matthews Street, named after the chair of the local Stop the War Committee during the Second Boer War. Mr Goodman, who lived at number 21, was active in Battersea Labour League and helped to develop the Workers' Educational Association. Turn left into Sheepcote Lane.

7. Sheepcote Lane

Sheepcote Lane was a traditional area for Gypsy families, who camped in the neighbourhood for parts of the year. Continue along Sheepcote Lane. Joubert Street to the left was named after a Boer general; Odger Street recalls a Chartist shoemaker and trade unionist, George Odger, Secretary of the London

Battersea Stop the War Committee, formed in 1900.
Photo courtesy of Wandsworth Heritage Service

Trades Council from 1862–72, and one-time president of the International Workingmen's Association (First International). Turn left into Freedom Street. Social Democratic Federation (SDF) activists, Ellen and William Humphreys lived at number 1. Ellen was active in Battersea Women's Socialist Circle and helped organise the Socialist Sunday School. Turn right into Reform Street.

8. Reform Street

The recreation ground facing Reform Street once housed a controversial brown dog statue, unveiled in September 1906. Anti-vivisectionists, with strong local support, commissioned the statue following a campaign about vivisections taking place during medical students' training at University College London. The statue's plaque read, 'Men and Women of England, how long shall these things be?' Speakers at the unveiling included George Bernard Shaw and local socialist and anti-vivisectionist Charlotte Despard. 'Anti-dogger' students frequently vandalised the statue and a 24-hour police guard was instituted in 1907. Battersea's Progressive Alliance council supported the anti-vivisectionists, but the Conservative council, elected in 1909, was unsympathetic and in March 1910 it authorised council workers, accompanied by 120 police officers, to remove the statue at night. There were protests calling for its return. It is believed to have been smashed and melted down. In 1985 a new statue was commissioned by the Anti-Vivisection Society and unveiled in Battersea Park. Walk part-way round the recreation ground and turn right into St James Grove, then right into Battersea Park Road.

9. Battersea Park Road

A plaque above number 214 celebrates John Archer, London's first black mayor, elected in 1913, who had a photographic studio/shop first at number 214, then at number 208. Turn right into Culvert Road then left into Dagnall Street.

10. Dagnall Street

Along the side wall of the first building on the right (formerly the Haberdashers Arms public house) is a remarkable mural called 'Battersea in Perspective', painted by Brian Barnes in 1988. It features nine local heroes. The first four from the left are: black mayor and radical pan-African nationalist John Archer; trade unionist and MP John Burns; Communist MP Shapurji Saklatvala; and wealthy socialist widow, activist and suffragette Charlotte Despard. Turn back then left into Culvert Road. Go through the tunnel over the railway bridge, left into Eversleigh Road, right into Birley Street, then right into Holden Street.

11. Holden Street

John Burns founded the Battersea Branch of the SDF in 1885, at his home at number 8. The houses in these streets are part of the Shaftesbury Park Estate, built as a semi-philanthropic venture by the Artisans, Labourers and General Dwelling Company in the 1870s, which provided affordable rented accommodation for skilled workers. The seventh Earl of Shaftesbury – a social reformer – laid the estate's foundation stone. Burns spread the SDF's message on Clapham Common to the south and gained support from many residents in these streets. Turn left into Grayshott Road, then left into Lavender Hill. Cross the road.

12. Lavender Hill (1)

In the 1930s, the Communist Party's People's Bookshop, was at 115 Lavender Hill, run by Noreen and Clive Branson. Noreen, who sang with the Bach Choir, was Secretary of Battersea Communist Party. Later it was managed by David Guest, who volunteered to fight against fascism in Spain in 1938 and died there. Turn back and walk westwards along Lavender Hill.

13. Lavender Hill (2)

This building, which has housed Battersea Labour Party for many decades, was purchased for the Party by Charlotte Despard. Continue along Lavender Hill and cross to Battersea Arts Centre.

14. Lavender Hill (3)

Battersea Arts Centre occupies the former Battersea Town Hall, built in 1893 to Edward Mountford's design. After Battersea Council was absorbed into Wandsworth in 1965, this building, in which several radical political initiatives were launched, was threatened with conversion into a swimming pool. A vigorous local campaign saved the building. The lobby area floor has a mosaic of bees, representing cooperation and unity. Go through the lobby and up the central stairway. What look like books on a shelf actually form a timeline of Battersea's history including several radical episodes. The books with red covers have been adapted inside to convey that history through laminated photographs and texts. The Communist Party first held its National Congress here in the Grand Hall in 1922. In 1926, the Lower Hall became the headquarters of the Battersea Council of

Action during the General Strike, organising support for strikers and their families. In 1927 Bertrand Russell gave a seminal lecture here entitled, 'Why I am not a Christian', later published as a pamphlet. The Arts Centre sees itself as heir to Battersea's radical traditions.

15. Lavender Hill (4)

At number 263, Oswald Mosley's British Union of Fascists established an Unemployed Workers' Centre. Members of this centre, known as the Battersea Boys, were noted for their contribution to Mosley's stewarding force. His movement established a Fascist Union of British Workers to help it recruit among the working class. Its first branch was in Battersea. Today it is used for healthier purposes as a doctors' surgery.

Arrest of suffragette, central London.

7

SPEAKING TRUTH TO POWER

Suffragettes and Westminster

In 1883, an imposing venue with two large public halls opened on Caxton Street, Westminster, half a mile from Parliament. This redbrick and pink sandstone building, which began life as Westminster City Hall in 1883, was renamed Caxton Hall and became a celebrated concert hall, a registry office for the marriages of Elizabeth Taylor, Orson Welles, Diana Dors, Ringo Starr and others, and a venue for meetings and conferences touching the further reaches of the political spectrum.

Lenin's notes on the three-day conference on 'Nationalities and Subject Races' there in June 1910, describe 'speeches by various people living under foreign rule: Egyptians, Indians, Moroccans, Georgians, negro races of Africa, South American Indians and also European nations such as the Irish and Poles'. Any surviving delegates would have been disheartened by the event there nearly 60 years later, when supporters of three marginal far-right groups – the League of Empire Loyalists, the British National Party and the Racial Preservation Society – came together to form the National Front.[1]

---

1 The NF was founded in February 1967. When it split in the early 1980s one faction revived the name 'British National Party'.

The Ministry of Information hosted its wartime press confer-ences at Caxton Hall, and a plaque celebrates Winston Churchill's presence. On the third anniversary of the outbreak of the war, a Polish Jewish Marxist, Szmul Zygielbojm, stunned a large Labour Party meeting there, when he revealed the Nazis' first use of gas as a weapon of mass murder, against 40,000 Jews incarcerated in Chelmno, Poland.[2]

On 13 March 1940, Caxton Hall had hosted an equally dramatic meeting organised by the East India Association and the Royal Central Asian Society. The platform speakers included 75-year-old Michael O'Dwyer, former Governor of Punjab, who presided over the Amritsar massacre in 1919 when British troops fired on a peaceful protest by Hindus, Sikhs, Muslims and Christians. The British authorities admitted killing 379 protesters; most Indian sources estimate that more than 1,000 died. O'Dwyer described the troops' behaviour as the 'correct action' in the circumstances.

Udham Singh, an Indian revolutionary, had visited Caxton Hall a week earlier. On the night, as the meeting closed, he fired a revolver towards the platform. O'Dwyer was hit twice in the back. One bullet passed through his heart and right lung, another through both kidneys. O'Dwyer was killed instantly. Lord Zetland, Secretary of State for India, and two other speakers were wounded.

On his arrest, Singh reinvented himself as 'Ram Mohammed Singh Azad' – names representing Indian's diverse religions. In his witness statement he said that O'Dwyer 'wanted to crush the spirit of my people, so I have crushed him', adding at his trial, 'I

---

2   In May 1943 Zygielbojm committed suicide at his Paddington flat as a political protest at the allies' passivity at Nazi genocide. A plaque was mounted on Porchester Road, W2, in 1996, near to where he lived.

have seen my people starving in India under the British rule ... I am not sorry for protesting. It was my duty to do so ... I am not afraid to die. I am proud to die'.[3] He was hanged and buried at Pentonville prison. The judge rejected Singh's request to return his remains to India.[4]

Not every meeting at Caxton Hall had such melodrama but assemblies there felt very significant, because the venue was so close to Parliament. It became a favoured venue for, arguably, London's most successful rebel movement, Emmeline Pankhurst's Women's Social and Political Union (WSPU) or 'suffragettes', which first gathered there on 19 February 1906. Hundreds of East End women sang 'The Red Flag' before formal proceedings opened that day.[5] From 1907, the WSPU held 'Women's Parliament' meetings at Caxton Hall which coincided with the male Parliament nearby reopening after recess. As their alternative sessions closed, the chair would encourage participants to march on Parliament.

With the *Daily Mail*'s unwitting help, the WSPU became popularly known as the 'Suffragettes'. *Mail* reporter Charles Hands covered the trial of two members, Christabel Pankhurst (Emmeline's eldest daughter) and Annie Kenney, held after they disrupted a speech by the Liberal minister, Sir Edward Grey. Kenney, who worked in a cotton mill in Saddleworth, Yorkshire from the age of ten, was fearless. The arresting officer claimed they assaulted and spat at him. When Pankhurst and Kenney

---

3 See Florian Stadtler's chapter in R. Ahmed and S. Mukherjee (eds), *South Asian Resistances in Britain*, London: Continuum, 2012, pp. 27–9.

4 In 1975 Singh's exhumed remains were returned at the request of the Punjab authorities. His casket was paraded through Punjab's major urban centres, including Amritsar, to Singh's birthplace, for cremation.

5 See Andrew Rosen, *Rise Up Women!* London: Routledge & Kegan Paul, 1974.

were convicted they refused to pay the fine, and became the first activists for women's votes in Britain to be imprisoned. The news reverberated nationally and Hands, searching for words to match his outrage at their impudence, mocked them as 'suffragettes' attempting to demean them. But the movement embraced the name exuberantly, as a simple means of distinguishing themselves from more longstanding *Suffragist* campaigners committed, on principle, to staying strictly legal.[6]

Two early suffragists, Emily Davies and Elizabeth Garrett Anderson,[7] handed a petition to MPs Henry Fawcett and John Stuart Mill several months before the 1867 Reform Act, which doubled the existing franchise to approximately 30 per cent of adult males. Mill proposed an amendment granting equal numbers of women the vote. It fell by 196 votes to 73. When the male franchise doubled again in 1884, women were still excluded at national level. Within a decade, though, the Women's Franchise League, founded in Russell Square in 1889 by Emmeline Pankhurst, whose family had temporarily moved to London (in 1886), won a limited franchise for women in local government. Pankhurst returned to Manchester, but the ball was rolling.

When Emmeline Pankhurst resettled in London, in 1907, local suffragette branches were springing up across the capital, the largest among women workers in east London. But the movement concentrated its mass outdoor activities in Westminster – in Parliament Square, Trafalgar Square, Whitehall, Downing Street and Hyde Park. It held large indoor meetings at the London

---

6 Suffragist societies in Britain which formed in London and Manchester in the 1860s coalesced into the National Union of Women Suffrage Societies (NUWSS).

7 Stepney-born Anderson became the first female doctor in London. Her sister Millicent married Henry Fawcett in 1867.

Opera House and London Pavilion[8] as well as Caxton Hall, and ostentatious rallies which filled the Albert Hall seven times between 1908 and 1913.

The movement's first major outdoor show of strength was in Hyde Park in June 1908. Seven separate processions bedecked with green, white and purple flags converged on the park. The *Daily News* said that 'suffragettes have cultivated the art of popular magnetism for all it is worth. Those who dominate the movement have a sense of the dramatic'. *The Times*, not normally given to hyperbole, stated that the organisers 'had counted on an attendance of 250,000 ... Probably it was doubled; and it would be difficult to contradict anyone who asserted confidently it was trebled.' Eighty speakers on 20 platforms promoted the suffragette message. The *Daily Mail*, which already had form for demeaning women activists, dug itself even deeper when its Special Correspondent opined:

... men take politics so seriously. Women blend with their determination to get votes a delightful resolve to enjoy themselves as much as possible in the getting of them. The idea that the women who want the suffrage are plain, severe, be-spectacled middle aged frumps, was ... exploded long ago. But ... a great many people ... never realised until yesterday how young and dainty and elegant and charming most leaders of the movement are.[9]

---

8   This theatre, opened in 1885 on the corner of Piccadilly Circus and Coventry Street, was converted to a cinema in the 1930s. It is now part of the Trocadero Centre.

9   *Daily Mail*, 22 June 1908.

Men were present too. The pacifist-socialist Laurence Housman had formed a Men's League for Women's Suffrage together with three radical writers, Israel Zangwill, Henry Nevinson and Henry Brailsford. Zangwill brought his sardonic wit to their campaigning, saying: 'A man likes his wife to be just clever enough to appreciate his cleverness and just stupid enough to admire it.' At the 1910 general election, sympathetic men scrawled 'Votes for Women' over their ballot papers.

Suffragettes wanted to speak truth to power, directly. On 9 March 1906, Annie Kenney led 30 suffragettes to 10 Downing Street intent on meeting the Prime Minister, Henry Campbell-Bannerman: unthinkable today, when electronic gates guarded by armed police bar entrance to the whole street. Activists then could simply approach the door of Number 10, where a policeman greeted them. When Kenney was told that the Prime Minister was unavailable, she clambered on to his parked car, using it as an impromptu platform to address her sisters.

The suffragettes used traditional protest methods – mass rallies, petitions, lobbying, propaganda through leaflets and their own newspapers – but also pioneered new tactics, some to shock, outrage and draw publicity, others provoking the authorities, to force a government response. In 1909, sculptor Marjorie Dunlop slipped unnoticed into St Stephen's Hall in the Houses of Parliament and left a message with an indelible rubber stamp: 'Women's Deputation. June 29. Bill of Rights. It is the right of the subjects to petition the King, and all commitments and prosecutions for such petitionings are illegal.' Charged with wilful damage she was sentenced to one month's imprisonment. The previous year, Dunlop had shared a cell with a child killer, after being convicted for obstruction at a protest. This time, she demanded recognition as a 'political prisoner'. When the authorities refused, she started a hunger strike. The government panicked and released her after 91 hours, not wanting a dead suffragette on their hands. Suffragette leaders hadn't authorised Dunlop's strike, but quickly grasped its potency.

Many courageous suffragettes came forward, knowing they would endure tortuous attempts at force-feeding. In 1913, the government passed the 'Cat and Mouse Act'. [10] This sanctioned the release of prisoners when they were weakened by their hunger strike and their rearrest as their health returned. Several suffragettes continued their own cat and mouse game by adopting disguises after release.

In 1908, London suffragettes began smashing windows, at first targeting government property, then, from November 1911, attacking private property as well – including West End shops, hotels and newspaper offices.[11] This was controversial within the movement. The Women's Freedom League (WFL), led by Battersea socialist Charlotte Despard, which had split from the WSPU in 1907, threw stones at government property alone.

In March 1912, the *Daily Graphic*, founded by the social reformer William Thomas, reported: 'an unexampled outrage [by] militant suffragists ... Bands of women paraded Regent Street, Piccadilly, the Strand, Oxford Street and Bond Street, smashing windows with stones and hammers', adding that 221 women and three men were arrested. The *Graphic*'s reporter seemed particularly affronted that Burberry, Liberty and Marshall & Snelgrove were attacked.

The new tactics increasingly relied on individual acts of

---

10 The Prisoners (Temporary Discharge for Ill Health) Act 1913.

11 Window-smashing incidents occurred before this date but it became official policy that year.

militancy, usually undertaken by middle-class members, substi-
tuting for mass collective action involving large numbers of
working-class women. The earlier mass demonstrations, which
aimed to build and strengthen pro-suffragette public opinion,
ultimately looked to Labour to emerge as a credible force for
change. Christabel Pankhurst introduced direct action tactics
to shift the movement in a more militant direction, defining
'militancy' as a 'great upheaval, a great revolution, a great
blasting away of ugly things'. She rebranded the movement as a
radical middle-class pressure group that Liberals and Tories had
to take notice of in the here and now. Teresa Billington-Greig,
who left the WSPU with Charlotte Despard in 1907 to form the
WFL, criticised random militancy and the class politics behind it.

In 1903, Emmeline Pankhurst had sent Preston-born Teresa
Billington[12] to London with Annie Kenney to expand the fledgling
movement there. Later she sent her to Glasgow to build branches
in Scotland. Apprenticed as a milliner, Billington also attended
night school and became a teacher. She remained conscious,
though, of her roots. The WSPU, she claimed, 'gradually edged
the working-class element out of its ranks', becoming 'socially
exclusive, punctiliously correct, gracefully fashionable'.

Christabel Pankhurst recognised that violent acts of civil
disobedience might divide the public, but, she argued, 'public
opinion' was: 'shamefully tolerant of hideous wrongs and indig-
nities inflicted upon women ... The sufferings of the militant
women they have not felt keenly enough, and the cost of repairing
government windows has fallen on them too lightly. That is why
private property has now been attacked.'

---

12 When she married Glasgow socialist Frederick Greig, their pre-nuptial agreement insisted
    both adopt the name Billington-Greig.

Few suffragettes would have disputed her moral justification: ' ... there are cases where law may be broken to vindicate a higher law and where violence may be done to prevent a greater violence ... suffragist violence is committed ... to put an end to the violence done to sweated women, to white slaves, to outraged children.'

However, her defence of these tactics sanctioned women acting on behalf of others, rather than encouraging all women to liberate themselves: 'No militant could go to prison merely for her own sake ... . It is for the sake of other people more helpless and more unhappy than themselves that the militant women are prepared to pay a heavy price.'[13]

---

13 C. Pankhurst, 'Broken Windows (1912)', in J. Marcus, *Suffrage and the Pankhursts*, London: Routledge & Kegan Paul, 2005, p. 123.

Arson was another dramatic form of militant action that caused establishment panic. Lillian Lenton, a dancer and seasoned window-smasher, began a series of arson attacks in London with her colleague Olive Wharry in early 1913. In a 1960 interview Lenton said:

> Whenever I was out of prison my object was to burn two buildings a week ... to create an absolutely impossible condition of affairs in the country, to prove that it was impossible to govern without the consent of the governed ... no one could ignore arson.[14]

In November 1910, when the Prime Minister, Herbert Asquith, ruled there was no time within the parliamentary session for the Conciliation Bill – which would have enfranchised some women – to reach its conclusion, 300 angry suffragettes marched on Westminster. The clash with the authorities, recorded as 'Black Friday', was marked by police brutality and mass arrests. Israel Zangwill believed that this day altered suffragette psychology, after which they resolved, 'to inconvenience oneself as little and society as seriously as possible'.

That day was etched in the memory of Rosa May Billing-hurst, secretary of the Greenwich suffragettes. Billinghurst was paralysed from the age of five months. Her legs were strapped in irons and she moved around on a manually-propelled invalid tricycle. Her interest in suffragette activism emanated from her work helping to rescue young girls from prostitution. On 'Black Friday', she said, the police

---

14 See Jessie Street's 1960s interviews of Lenton and other former suffragettes in the Women's Library archive at LSE.

... threw me out of the machine on to the ground in a very brutal manner ... when on the machine again they tried to push me along with my arms twisted behind me in a very painful position ... [Then] they took me down a side road and left me in the middle of a hooligan crowd, first taking all the valves out of the wheels and pocketing them so that I could not move the machine.[15]

A hundred years later – almost to the day – students protested on the same Westminster streets about increasing tuition fees. Many were shocked by video footage of Jody McIntyre, pulled roughly from his wheelchair by police. Few would have known of the precedent a century earlier.

Police brutality failed to intimidate Billinghurst. She was arrested just four days after Black Friday, steering her invalid tricycle into a police cordon. In March 1912 she served a one-month prison sentence for participating in a window-smashing spree. While her sisters rampaged with hammers, she kept a supply of stones under the blanket covering her paralysed legs.

She served her final term of imprisonment in January 1913 for setting fire to a pillar box. Facing eight months inside she began a hunger strike. The prison authorities attempted to force-feed her violently, damaging her teeth and leaving a deep gash in her cheek. The Home Secretary ordered Billinghurst's release after ten days. She immediately stepped up her campaigning to stop force-feeding of suffragette prisoners, alongside campaigning for women's votes.

---

15 See Rosa May Billinghurst papers in the Women's Library archive, LSE.

Between 1912–14 the suffragettes escalated their tactic of burning pillar boxes, aiming to disrupt civil life until their demands were addressed. One of the first activists imprisoned for this offence was Emily Wilding Davison, who ultimately gave her life for the movement on Epsom Racecourse in June 1913. On 14 December 1911, she was arrested in Parliament Street. Inspector Powell told the court:

> She was wearing a long coat, which hid her arms ... When she got close to the letter-box ... she appeared to be striking matches ... She was holding a small packet in the left hand, one of the top corners of which was slightly alight. She held it in that position for a minute ... I seized the packet ... and ... extinguished the flame. I took her into custody ... she sat in a room; as I was leaving ... [she] said, 'Do you know I set fire to two in the City this morning, a pillar-box in the middle of Leadenhall Street ... the other was facing the Mansion House'.[16]

She told Inspector Powell that she had also set fire to a post office in Fleet Street on the previous Friday. Before she was sentenced, Davison told the Recorder that she had acted without malice:

> It was a purely political act ... to draw the attention of the public to the iniquitous state of affairs ... Technically ... I must be judged to be guilty, but morally ... you before whom I stand ... are guilty; you, the private citizens of this country and the Government that you choose to

---

16 www.oldbaileyonline.org/browse.jsp?div=t19120109–20.

represent you, who keep women out of their just rights as citizens ... so long as you exclude women from these rights, upon you lies the blame for any act that they may have to commit in order to procure those rights.[17]

Public suffragette activity was heavily focused on the Westminster precinct – marches on Parliament, static protests in Parliament Square, women chaining themselves to railings, delegations lobbying the Prime Minister – so officers from Cannon Row Police station, including those guarding government buildings, had the most frequent contact with the suffragettes.[18] One officer, Harold Brust, recalled a lone suffragette bringing a petition to 10 Downing Street:

She was recognised as a suffragette wanted by the police under the Cat and Mouse Act. She was ... seized by Sergeant Gough ... In a flash the unfortunate sergeant was surrounded by a score of women who sprang into Downing Street from all sorts of odd corners and doorways ... [we] were hopelessly outnumbered, and then the women began to strip the clothes off poor Gough! ... it was an astounding sight to see him, the centre of a plunging, struggling, shrieking mob ... being divested of hat, coat and vest. In shirt sleeves, his face one crimson blush, the sergeant howled protest as they began to unfasten his trouser braces. It was too much.

---

17 *Ibid.*

18 On 17 January 1908, suffragettes Edith New and Olivia Smith chained themselves to railings outside 10 Downing Street. They were charged with disorderly conduct and imprisoned for three weeks.

Gough released his prisoner and disaster was averted by two brace buttons.[19]

The suffragette movement achieved most of its goals by 1918. The new Representation of the People Act abolished most property qualifications for men over 21 and enfranchised women over 30 who met minimal property qualifications or those who were graduates of British universities. This created a national electorate of 21 million potential voters in the December 1918 general election, of whom 8.4 million were women. Given the numbers of men killed during the war, and a clause that voters had to be resident in the UK for the twelve months before the election, women would have constituted the majority of the electorate if the government had granted equal suffrage then. Full voting equality was inevitable, but took another ten years. Millicent Fawcett, veteran of London's 'law abiding' suffragist societies of the late 1860s, lived to see that day. She died in 1929. But Emmeline Pankhurst, who had transformed the movement into one unafraid to step outside the law, that developed new and powerful forms of rebellion, died on 14 June 1928, less than three weeks before the Conservative Government finally passed the Act giving all adult females the vote on the same basis as men.

Victoria Gardens abuts the Houses of Parliament. In the section nearest to Parliament, a 1930 statue, with two blocks added in the 1950s, commemorates Emmeline Pankhurst and the suffragette movement. Even with the later additions it is fascinating for who and what it omits.[20] Eldest daughter Christabel is honoured on

---

19   H. Brust, *I Guarded Kings: Memoirs of a Political Police Officer*, New York: Hillman-Curl, 1936.

20   The statue was made by Arthur George Walker and the base by Herbert Baker.

one side. On the other is an etching of the 'Holloway brooch' – a portcullis-shaped medal, with a chain, overlaid with a triangle of green, white and purple bars, which was presented to suffragettes on release from prison. Emmeline's second daughter, Sylvia, a dedicated suffragette from the WSPU's foundation and a leading figure in its radical east London section designed the medal. But Sylvia is not recognised.

The overwhelmingly working-class East End suffragettes were increasingly at odds with West End suffragettes over principles and tactics. They allied their activity to daily economic struggles for better lives, and sought 'universal suffrage' rather than 'votes on the same basis as men', which West End WSPU leaders were willing to accept, as this would still exclude many working-class voters.[21] In March 1914 Emmeline and Christabel Pankhurst, temporarily staying in Paris to escape police harassment, summoned Sylvia. On the pretext that Sylvia had disobeyed an instruction not to speak at a meeting organised by George Lansbury in support of striking Irish workers during the Dublin lock-out, they expelled her, freeing the east London suffragettes to become an independent movement.[22]

Sylvia's younger sister Adela, imprisoned several times for suffragette activism, is also unacknowledged, although her latter political involvements may have embarrassed a movement advocating equal rights. After Adela fell out with her mother in 1914, Emmeline bought her a one-way ticket to Australia. In Melbourne, she worked closely with the suffragist and feminist Vida Goldstein's anti-war Women's Political Association. Adela

---

21 Before 1918, approximately 60 per cent of men had the vote on a property-related qualification.

22 See Chapter 8, p.206–7

and her husband Tom Walsh were founder members of the Australian Communist Party but she later had a major political *volte face* that drew her to pro-fascist ideologues. She ultimately joined Australia First, which advanced Nazi biological race theories, and was interned during the Second World War for pro-Japan activity.

Emmeline Pankhurst performed a U-turn too. When she began campaigning for women's political rights, she was active in the Independent Labour Party (ILP) and the Fabian Society,[23] and a close associate of Keir Hardie. In 1926 she was adopted as the parliamentary candidate for the East End seat of Whitechapel and St Georges – for the Conservative Party. She died before the election, which Harry Gosling comfortably won for Labour.

The East/West divisions of 1914 exposed the continuing class conflict among London's suffragettes. However, the movement's first major fracture took place in London as early as 1906 and, ironically, given the movement's democratic goals, it concerned lack of democracy inside the movement. Teresa Billington-Greig had drafted a constitution. At the meeting of 350 suffragette delegates where this was to be discussed Emmeline Pankhust 'announced that there was not to be a constitution or any voting membership, but that she ... had assumed dictatorship and would direct-govern ... through her selected colleagues or subordinates'.[24]

Emmeline Pankhurst tore up the draft document, theatrically trampled it underfoot, announcing that 'the WSPU was not a society but a volunteer army enrolled by her and her officers for one purpose only and that no interference from the ranks could be

---

23 Many of the early WSPU leaders and a high proportion of the first suffragettes sent to prison were ILP members.

24 Teresa Billington-Greig papers, Women's Library archive, LSE.

contemplated'. Billington-Grieg describes 'stunned surprise and confusion ... the meeting broke up in disorder'. Delegates asked how they could 'claim the right to vote as citizens of the country and agree to be voteless in the management of our own society'. Seventy committed activists departed, later forming the Women's Freedom League (WFL), which had its own charismatic figure – the vegetarian socialist Charlotte Despard – but elected officers at an annual conference and made binding policy decisions by majority vote. The League could not match the WSPU's scale of operation but was a key player, campaigning alongside the WSPU in major mobilisations while largely working in parallel, with its own approach. The WFL is unacknowledged at the Pankhurst statue.

The novelist and playwright Christabel Marshall[25] described seeing Despard at a suffragette demonstration in Hyde Park:

> The arms were raised, Cassandra like; the whole thin, fragile body seemed to vibrate with a prophecy ... the white hair, the familiar black lace veil ... On the edge of the great mass of listeners ... I could catch no word, but I seemed to know the thoughts as they passed.[26]

Despard was nearing 60 when the WSPU was formed. She had joined Hyndman's SDF and Keir Hardie's ILP, and saw women's struggle for political rights as intimately linked with wider struggles for equality. In a 1910 letter to a friend, Mrs Solomon, she wrote: 'It is my dream, when the first step is won, to make our

---

25 Also known as Christopher Marie St John.

26 Appreciation by Chistopher St John in C. Despard, *Women in the New Era*, London: Suffrage Shop, 1910.

league international – for women's freedom everywhere and the lifting up of the oppressed through her ... our cause is not only votes for women but the binding together of all womankind with human rights.'

The pamphlet she published that year, called *Women in the New Era*, articulated demands beyond the WSPU's single issue campaign, ' ... for equal rights, equal opportunities; equal reward for our work; equal justice'. The WFL supported women's workplace struggles, such as the 1908 strike of London teashop waitresses. When negotiations with their employers broke down irretrievably, Despard helped them start a cooperative café in Leicester Square.

She urged women to become more self-aware and to prepare for wider equality battles:

> We women have been cajoled or forced into a false conception of ourselves. We work first for enlightenment ... using our own capacities, seeing with our own eyes and not with the eyes of men to understand ... what are our duties and our rights.[27]

Tactically the WFL supported civil disobedience such as window-breaking targeted at state institutions, but, it 'gave every form of protest a reasoned ... background', said Teresa Billington-Greig. Its campaigning was 'more marked by sacrifice of self than by aggression against others'. Many members were pacifists regarding international conflicts, and challenged conscription during the First World War, but were combative in the face

---

27   C. Despard, *Women in the New Era*, London: Suffrage Shop, 1910.

of heavy-handed policing.[28] Charlotte Despard's first prison sentence resulted from her leading large numbers of women from a Women's Parliament meeting directly into police lines protecting the House of Commons. The *Daily Mail* said: 'The women fought like tigers and they received and inflicted many bruises.' After Despard's arrest and conviction, she refused to pay the 40 shillings fine, and spent 21 days in Holloway Prison. One of the early WFL branches was formed in the Holloway area and several members visited the district temporarily! Within the WFL's first three years, 300 of its members had experience of prison.

Annie Cobden-Sanderson, a socialist activist in Hammersmith and a prominent WFL member, was arrested at the same protest as Despard and sentenced to two months. She told the court, 'I am a law-breaker because I want to be a law-maker.' Cobden-Sanderson later helped to establish the Tax Resistance League, inspired by her neighbour, Dora Montefiore, an activist in several socialist and suffrage groups and a tenacious campaigner about unemployment, who lived at 34 Upper Mall, by the Thames. She sat on the SDF executive and was a founder of its Women's Socialist Circles.

Montefiore was a tax-rebel before the WSPU and WFL were born. During the Second Boer War of 1899–1902, she refused to pay income tax because it 'went towards financing a war in the making of which I had had no voice'. In 1906, after informing fellow WSPU activists to prepare support, she defied the tax authorities and barred her doors against the bailiff 'who had

---

28 The WSPU suspended most of its campaigning work during the war to display patriotic credentials. The WFL opposed compulsory war service for women as long as they were 'denied their share in the government of the country'.

appeared outside the gate of my house [and] the "siege" of my house began'. Inside were Dora and her housekeeper, who also strongly supported the suffrage campaign. 'The tradespeople of the neighbourhood were absolutely loyal to us besieged women, delivering their milk and bread, etc., over the rather high garden wall ... The weekly wash arrived in the same way and the postman day by day delivered very encouraging batches of correspondence.'[29]

The six-week siege won sympathetic press coverage. There were day and evening meetings. East End suffragettes trekked across town to Hammersmith after work, to show support.

> At the evening demonstrations rows of lamps were hung along the top of the wall and against the house, the members of the W.S.P.U. speaking from the steps of the house, while I spoke from one of the upstairs windows. On the little terrace of the front garden hung during the whole time of the siege a red banner with the letters painted in white: 'Women should vote for the laws they obey and the taxes they pay.'[30]

When the siege ended and bailiffs seized goods sufficient to cover the tax debt, 22 police were sent to protect the auctioneer of the seized goods.

Montefiore attributed the courage and inspiration she needed to take this action to her frequent contact with 'self-sacrificing and self-effacing' Russian political exiles, some of whom had stayed

---

29 D. Montefiore, *From a Victorian to a Modern*, London: Archer, 1927.
30 *Ibid.*

at her house, especially Seraphina, a Russian Jewish woman who had been imprisoned for organising textile workers.

In Russia, the revolutionists sought to overthrow an autocratic monarchy. One suffragist tax-rebel who might have caused consternation among more socialist comrades was Princess Duleep Singh, resident of Hampton Court Palace and a regular speaker at suffragette branches in Kingston and Richmond. She was prosecuted several times and had her diamond ring, pearl necklace and gold bangle impounded.

The WFL popularised campaigns of non-violent defiance – such as refusal to pay taxes, purchase dog licences, or complete census forms – through its own newspaper, *The Vote*, published from its Robert Street offices, near Aldwych. While the WSPU was shifting from mass action in London towards individualised militancy, the WFL continued to develop inclusive campaigns requiring collective action. These included nocturnal activities. During the night of 12–13 October 1908, WFL members plastered proclamations of women's political rights on hundreds of public buildings in London, the provinces and Scotland. London targets included ministers' homes, the House of Commons, Scotland Yard and Holloway Prison, as well as countless pillar boxes.[31]

But the WFL also had members keen to perform individual stunts. Australian journalist and actress, Muriel Matters, had a penchant for aerial activities. She arrived in London in 1905 and became friendly with George Bernard Shaw and the Russian anarchist, Peter Kropotkin. On 28 October 1908, Matters and a WFL colleague, Helen Fox, chained themselves to the grille at the front of the Ladies' Gallery for observing the House of

---

31 The WFL also did daytime visits to ministers' homes, making speeches on their doorsteps until they were removed by police.

Commons, and began to broadcast suffragist ideas to the MPs below. A third activist lowered a WFL proclamation to the parliamentary floor on a string, and a male collaborator in the Strangers' Gallery dropped a flood of handbills. Unable to break the chains, the police removed the whole grille with the women attached. The grille was never replaced. On another occasion Matters flew over London, showering handbills with suffragette messages from a dirigible emblazoned with the slogans 'Votes for Women' and WFL.

During the war, the WSPU suspended its activities, but WFL members and the expelled East London Federation of Suffragettes led campaigns for equal pay, as women filling jobs previously reserved for men were often paid at half or even a third of the wage rate. When the franchise for women rose from zero to 8.4 million overnight in 1918, Emmeline and Christabel Pankhurst believed their work was done. The WSPU dissolved itself but the WFL continued to campaign for full equality and on its wider agenda.

In her most intensive period of activism, Teresa Billington-Greig had argued that:

> The vote cannot secure of itself any single woman's emancipation. It is a tool; and the kind of work that can be done with it depends first upon the nature of the tool, and second, upon the capacity of the person who uses it. Large areas in which emancipation is needed lie entirely outside [its] scope ... a slave woman with a vote will still be essentially a slave.[32]

---

32 Teresa Billington-Greig papers, Women's Library archive, LSE.

When the WFL shut down in autumn 1961, Billington-Greig praised the organisation for insisting that votes for women was 'only the first stage of political emancipation' and 'rejecting dictatorship as a false means to a good end'. She added: 'I feel its death as a tragedy. It was born of the spirit of democracy and rebellion.' In London that included a rebellion within the suffragette movement.

On 28 December 1918, Constance Markiewicz, a Sinn Fein activist married to a radical Polish count, was the first woman elected to Parliament. But she sat in Holloway Prison rather than Westminster that day, locked up for campaigning against the conscription of Irish men into the British army. In any case, Sinn Fein boycotted the British Parliament. A Conservative, Nancy Astor, won a by-election in Plymouth in November 1919 to become Britain's first actual female MP. Dr Ethel Bentham won Islington East for Labour in 1929 to become London's first female MP.[33]

The period from the 1890s until the end of the 1920s, during which the House of Commons was forced to become more democratic and diverse, also saw the first non-white MPs elected – each one of them in London. The Liberal MP for Finsbury Central elected in 1892, Dadabhai Naoroji, and the Communist/Labour MP elected for Battersea North in 1922, Shapurji Saklatvala, were both Indian Parsees and political radicals who supported women's suffrage. A third Parsee, Mancherjee Bhownagree, Conservative MP for Bethnal Green North East in 1895, was, in contrast, pro-establishment and a staunch supporter of the British Empire. Their breakthrough

---

33 Susan Lawrence won East Ham North for Labour in 1923, but at that time it was an Essex rather than London seat.

was short-lived. No other Asians were elected in Britain until Keith Vaz in 1987.

In India, Naoroji had campaigned for girls' education and taught at a girls' school. In 1889, he strongly supported Jane Cobden, one of the first two women elected to the new London County Council. Her official agent was George Lansbury, at that time a Liberal, soon to become a leading east London socialist. Saklatvala's election leaflets were enthusiastically endorsed by women's suffrage campaigner, Charlotte Despard. In summer 1908, he went on his first large demonstration– the suffragette extravaganza in Hyde Park – and was enthralled by Sylvia Pankhurst, who later became a leading figure among east London's suffragettes.

For rebels such as Sylvia Pankhurst and George Lansbury, equality for women was intertwined with the fight for working-class advancement. And east London in the 1910s and 1920s, as the next chapter shows, was the perfect arena for them to play their part in these struggles.

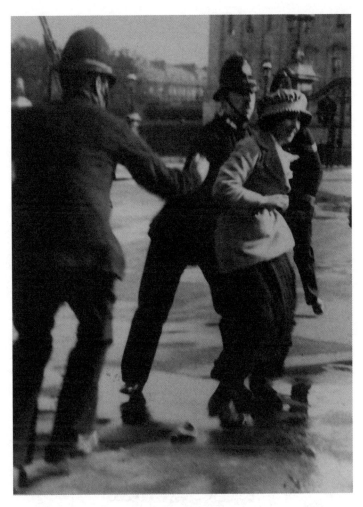

Suffragette being arrested outside Buckingham Palace.

WALK

Start at Caxton Hall, 10 Caxton Street, SW1H 0AQ.

1. Caxton Street

Caxton Hall hosted the Women's Parliament meetings organised by the WSPU. Its Great Hall and York Hall, now demolished, were used for political and cultural events. Its high-society registry office closed in 1979. Cross over into Christchurch Gardens.

2. Christchurch Gardens

Edwin Russell sculpted the 'S'-shaped monument, for the Suffragette Fellowship in 1970. Women's Freedom League member Edith How-Martyn created the Fellowship in 1926 to perpetuate the memory of suffrage campaigns. Former suffragette arsonist Lillian Lenton unveiled the monument. Walk through the gardens, cross Victoria Street into Old Pye Street.

3. Old Pye Street

This area was one of London's worst slums in Victorian times, designated 'the Devil's Acre' by Dickens in *Household Words* and depicted in Gustave Dore's bleak etchings of London's poverty. Slum clearance began in the 1860s and 1870s. Several semi-philanthropic Victorian housing developments remain. Turn right into Perkins Rents.

4. Corner of Perkins Rents and Great Peter Street

The public house, called The Speaker since 1999, was rebuilt in 1794 on the site of an earlier pub – The Castle. The Speaker has three panels on the outside with entertaining facts about parliamentary norms, particularly the role of the Speaker! Turn left into Great Peter Street.

5. Great Peter Street

The plaque for the Gas Light & Coke Company, next to the Seacole Building (one of three buildings comprising the Home Office) marks Britain's first gas works, founded here by a German Freidrich Winzer in 1813. He came in 1799 and changed his name to Winsor. He is also memorialised through Winsor Terrace, which leads to the former site of Beckton gasworks, where Will Thorne organised for the eight-hour day. Turn right into Tufton Street.

6. Tufton Street

A plaque commemorates Eleanor Rathbone MP, both a campaigner for women's suffrage and a beneficiary of the campaign, who lived here. The first woman elected to Liverpool City Council, she later represented one of the former 'Combined Universities' Parliamentary seats. Active within the constitutional National Union of Women's Suffrage Societies, she argued that more militant campaigners 'came within an inch of wrecking the suffrage movement, perhaps for a generation'. In April 1937 she joined a fact-finding delegation to Spain during the Civil War, and co-founded a Dependents' Aid Committee to support the families of International Brigade volunteers. Return to Great

Peter Street, turn right, and cross Millbank / Abingdon Street into Victoria Gardens. Follow the path towards Parliament.

7. *Victoria Gardens*
Near the exit back on to Abingdon Street is a statue of Emmeline Pankhurst sculpted by Arthur George Walker, with two side-blocks added in the 1950s. The ceremony unveiling the original statue, further south in the gardens, in March 1930, included the Metropolitan Police Band performing March of the Women. Continue towards the House of Commons. Cross over to Parliament Square.

8. *Parliament Square:*
This was the site of the 'Black Friday' suffragette demonstration in November 1910. At another demonstration on the Square a year later, 184 protesters were arrested. On 'Census Night' in April 1911 Emily Wilding Davison hid in the cupboard in the Chapel of St Mary Undercroft in the House of Commons, as suffragettes disrupted the census. They said, 'women not considered persons should not be counted as persons'. Hundreds of activists from the WFL and WSPU spent Census Night at Aldwych Ice Rink. Cross to the south side of Parliament Street. Walk towards Whitehall. Turn right into Cannon Row.

9. *Cannon Row*
This police station opened in 1902 (and closed in 1992). Many suffragettes spent the night singing and shouting in the cells here.

Return to Parliament Street. Cross to the north side of Parliament Street and stop outside Downing Street's unwelcoming gates.

10. Downing Street

Suffragette delegations brought petitions directly to the door of Number 10. Barriers were erected at the St James Park end in November 1920. Until 1982 campaigners could walk along Downing Street to hand letters or petitions to the police guarding Number 10. Steel gates were erected in 1989. Walk along Whitehall and turn right into Whitehall Place

11. Whitehall Place

Charlotte Despard's pamphlet *Economic Aspects of Women's Suffrage* originated as a talk given to the National Liberal Club in Whitehall Place in 1908. Women were not admitted as full members of the club until 1976. Cross Northumberland Avenue into Villiers Street.

12. Villiers Street

At 43 Villiers Street, where Rudyard Kipling lived from 1889–91, Ronald Kidd opened a radical bookshop in the 1920s. On 1 November 1932 Kidd observed protesting Hunger Marchers, who were completing a three-week march, being incited into a physical confrontation with police by the use of police provocateurs as they passed Trafalgar Square into Whitehall. He resolved to create a body to monitor and expose such activities, and defend protest rights. He co-founded the National Council for Civil Liberties. Turn back towards Embankment and step down into Watergate Walk. Halfway along, walk up some stairs into Buckingham Street.

13. Buckingham Street

The Women's Freedom League's first premises (from 1907–08) were at 18 Buckingham Street, before they moved to Robert Street. Continue along Buckingham Street and turn left into the Strand.

14. The Strand

The Crown and Anchor public house stood east of here, near where the Strand meets Fleet Street. On 28 February 1837, the six-point People's Charter, drawn up by William Lovett, was adopted there. Turn left to Trafalgar Square.

15. Trafalgar Square:

The first suffragette demonstration held in Trafalgar Square was on 19 May 1906. Charlotte Despard, leader of the Women's Freedom League during the period when women were seeking the vote, spoke many times at Trafalgar Square for women's rights, socialist causes and Home Rule for Ireland. Her last speech in the square was at an anti-fascist rally in the mid-1930s.

Demonstration in support of Poplar Council, 1920s.

8

NOT AFRAID OF THE
PRISON WALLS

Rebel Women and Men of Poplar

'How shall we benefit if instead of electing our master – as we do today – we elect his wife to govern us?' asked Rose Witkop, an immigrant Jew in London's East End, who, like her older sister Milly, joined the anarchist movement. Her barb, aimed at the suffragettes, was fair comment about West End campaigners, dominated by distinctly middle-class activists, who retreated from the slogan of 'Votes for Women' to a less inclusive demand for women's votes 'on the same basis as men'. The 1884 Reform Act increased the franchise but left a property qualification in place that restricted the vote to approximately 60 per cent of adult males. If the government had acceded to the demands of Emmeline Pankhurst's Women's Social and Political Union, it could have equalised the franchise as regards gender, while still leaving 40 per cent of the population living more precarious lives with no political voice.

In Witkop's Whitechapel milieu of sweatshops and small factories, populated by an immigrant underclass, cynicism about political campaigns that gave no voice to the poorest and the most disempowered was understandable. However, it was an unjust slur on working-class women activists a little further east, in Canning

Town and West Ham, who established the first suffragette groups east of Whitechapel and were organising for woman's rights – and every man's too. By 1912, several suffragette groups in eastern districts formed an east London branch of the Women's Social and Political Union (WSPU). They transformed a disused bakery at 198 Bow Road, Poplar, into an organising centre emblazoned with the slogan: 'Votes for Women' in gold letters. They later established a similar centre in Bethnal Green's Roman Road.

As local suffragettes were gaining a higher profile through meetings, processions and protest marches, a controversial decision made in 1912 by a local politician helped thrust debate about women's right to vote into the centre of Poplar's political arena. The parliamentary seat of Bow and Bromley had traditionally swung between the nineteenth-century's powerful political elites – the Tories and the Liberals/Whigs. But in 1910, George Lansbury won this seat for Labour for the first time.

Lansbury was born in Suffolk in 1859. When he was seven, his parents moved to Albert Road, Bethnal Green. Young George loved Victoria Park, a 'mysterious' place for children, where the park-keepers 'wore top hats, frock coats, red waistcoats and carried sticks'. Later, the family moved into a mainly Irish segment of Whitechapel. His political aspirations surfaced early: 'When I was a very small boy I wrote my name in a church prayer book as "George Lansbury MP". I think I even added the name of an East End constituency.'[1] He was at school until 14, with a year's break when he was eleven to work in an office. From 14 he was a factory worker, a manual labourer and a wholesale grocer. In his teens he became involved with community projects

---

1   G. Lansbury, *Looking Backwards and Forwards*, London: Blackie, 1935.

through the Bedford Institute and helped to provide breakfast for 1,000 local homeless people on Sunday mornings.

Married with three children and struggling economically in his mid-20s, he was enticed by adverts encouraging poorer people to seek their fortunes in Australia. His time there was politically formative. 'I knew the bitterness of unemployment, and endured the hardship of being treated just a little worse than a serf.' When he returned, he took a job in his father-in-law's sawmill (which he later inherited), and began attending political meetings. Lansbury became familiar with local anarchists, socialists, radical liberals and freethinkers, and was strongly influenced by Stewart Headlam, Rector of St Matthew's, Bethnal Green, and a pioneer of the Christian socialist movement. Lansbury believed that the Liberals offered the best vehicle for enacting practical change.

He was a successful election agent for Jane Cobden, seeking election to the London County Council's first administration in 1889. That same year, though, he visited Ireland and returned frustrated at the local Liberal parliamentary candidate's dismissive approach to Irish political concerns. When the dock strike broke out, in August 1889, Lansbury campaigned alongside local socialists. Through the local eight-hour day committee he helped to organise London's first May Day march in 1890. In 1892 Lansbury left the Liberals and helped found the Bromley and Bow branch of the Social Democratic Federation (SDF), which he designated 'the cockpit of socialism in East London'.

> Our branch was about 40 strong. We were ... convinced our mission was to revolutionise the world ... Our branch meetings were like revivalist meetings. We opened with a song and closed with one and often read together some

extracts from economic and historical writings ... Every Saturday we ran dances, telling our critics we were going to dance into socialism ... We were firm adherents and supporters of ... equality of the sexes and equal pay for equal work.[2]

In 1903 Lansbury switched to the Independent Labour Party (ILP). He and his wife, Bessie, and several of their children, were already active women's suffrage campaigners by the time the movement hit the headlines in 1905. The suffragettes' story is replete with individuals making personal sacrifices for the movement, and George Lansbury played his part. Having made a priceless breakthrough for Labour by wresting Bow and Bromley from a long succession of Liberals and Tories,[3] he resigned the seat and forced a by-election on women's suffrage. He wanted to confirm that the men who put him in Westminster agreed with votes for women. He had reason to believe they did. In January 1911, he spoke alongside Charlotte Despard at a crowded and very supportive Labour meeting at Bow Baths, advocating votes for all adult women and men.

When he won Bow and Bromley, an enthusiastic voter had written to Lansbury, 'you have earned it and ought to keep it now as long as you like (provided you aren't court martialled or shot as a traitor)'.[4] But contesting an unforced by-election on this issue was risky. Labour's Westminster leaders believed the governing parties were very far from accepting votes for women,

---

2   G. Lansbury, *My Life*, London: Constable & Co., 1928.

3   He won the seat in 1910 by a majority of 683 over a Liberal Unionist candidate who opposed Home Rule for Ireland.

4   From Lansbury correspondence 1910–11, LSE archive.

but could be pressurised into increasing the male franchise. Lansbury took a minority position that the party should only agree to proposals for extending the franchise that enfranchised at least some women.

He contested the by-election without Labour's endorsement. In his last speech before the ballot, Lansbury argued that it was only 'when the women and men are able to stand [together] in the common fight' that they could 'hope to accomplish economic and social emancipation'. His wife Bessie, well-known in the area, appealed to voters through the local press: 'both of us believe that men and women, united as friends and comrades, can and will save this country from the horrors of destitution, prostitution, and misery'. West End suffragettes parachuted in to support him, though some local suffragettes thought his action was premature. Shortly before the by-election, Lansbury's brother James wrote to warn him that the House of Commons 'is no place for a man of conscience'. Lansbury lost by 861 votes to a Tory named Blair.[5] Some months earlier, the *Daily Dispatch* said, 'George Lansbury's defect is that he is impatient to put the world right.'[6]

Despite this setback, he stepped up his campaigning work both for socialism and women's suffrage. Supported by trade unionists including Ben Tillett, he established a left-wing newspaper, the *Daily Herald*, which began life as a strike bulletin for print workers. In 1913 Lansbury was imprisoned for the first time for incitement to civil disobedience after making an Albert Hall speech supporting militant suffragette tactics. Sentenced to six months, he borrowed the suffragette's hunger strike tactic to get

---

5   The Liberals, who opposed suffragette demands, did not stand a candidate.

6   *Daily Dispatch*, 16 June 1912.

released in just a few days: 'I took neither food nor drink,' he recalled. ' ... I refused to change my clothes, would not take a bath, and [refused] to be civil to anyone except to the doctor.'[7]

George and Bessie Lansbury's coupling of women's political emancipation with the struggle against poverty and destitution chimed with the local suffragettes' approach. A far cry from the moneyed 'ladies' who met as the Kensington Society in the 1860s, or those living in London's more fashionable squares in the early 1900s, east London suffragette activists were typically factory workers like Flora Buchan, maids and cleaners like Melvina Walker and Daisy Parsons, laundry workers like Nellie Cressall, barmaids like Charlotte Drake, and housewives, many married to dockers.[8] Local suffragettes built up a strong, mutually supportive relationship with dockworkers.

Working-class suffragettes argued that winning political rights for women would only be worthwhile if they could use these rights to challenge the economic circumstances that blighted the lives of both women and men of their class. As militant campaigners, committed to collective action, they were worthy heirs to the determined women and 'rough set of girls' who rebelled at Bryant & May's match factory in Bow in 1888. George Lansbury described women in Poplar as very politically minded and 'splendid listeners', who 'never fail to argue and heckle anyone who comes to teach them the way they should go. They are ... not at all angelic, and are quite capable of taking care of themselves.'[9]

If the matchwomen benefited from middle-class supporters

---

7   Lansbury, *Looking Backwards and Forwards*.

8   Daisy Parsons was later mayor of West Ham and Nellie Cressall mayor of Poplar.

9   Lansbury, *Looking Backwards and Forwards*.

such as Annie Besant and Henry Hyde Champion, so the east London suffragettes' activism was boosted by the ingenuity of a rebellious middle-class socialist hailing from the Pankhurst family. Estelle Sylvia Pankhurst, who joined the ILP at age 16, had a troubled relationship with her mother and preferred to use her middle name, chosen by her father.

Sylvia was a highly trained artist, who had won a scholarship to study in Manchester, and studied later in Venice then London. As a student she learned important feminist lessons. While male art students were groomed for careers as artists, female art students were guided towards teaching.

She lent her professional talents to her political involvements, decorating halls hosting suffragette events and designing posters and banners; in 1906 she designed a banner for West Ham suffragettes emblazoned with the words 'Courage, Constancy, Success'. When she settled in the East End in 1912, she was already known locally. Sylvia proved less flighty than Annie Besant, whose East End involvements were confined to a few years in the 1880s. In 1912 Sylvia promised: 'I am part of the East End now and if still alive, I shall not leave it.'[10] She left in 1924 but for twelve years was at the heart of every major suffragette and socialist campaign there, demonstrating her commitment and self-sacrifice. She was repeatedly imprisoned during 1913–14, undertaking ten separate hunger and thirst strikes in that period.

Before she settled in east London, Sylvia travelled widely, working as an artist and writer and supporting activism. In 1907 she recorded women workers' conditions in northern England and Scotland through paintings and articles, an experience that

---

10 *TP's Weekly*, 4 July 1914.

strengthened both her socialist and feminist convictions. She spent much of 1911 lecturing in the USA and Scandinavia on the British suffragette movement – but she was in Britain in August when women in jam and biscuit factories in Bermondsey fought for economic justice through spontaneous strikes. She went there to hear first-hand about the conditions they were rebelling against.[11] East London's suffragettes consistently supported women's struggles for equal opportunities and fair pay in the workplace.

Suffragettes east and west showed equal determination in the face of hostility, threats and violence, but differences emerged between them. East London suffragettes, influenced by Sylvia's own attitudes, favoured mass *collective* action by women to emancipate themselves, rather than the individual action on behalf of others favoured by their West End sisters.

East London suffragettes held mass Women's May Day processions that started at East India Dock gates and ended in Victoria Park. These processions displayed the suffragettes' familiar colours – green, white and purple – but many marchers also wore red 'caps of liberty', affirming their political radicalism. Victoria Park's free speech site, which attracted the politically curious and many police too, was the backdrop for an imaginative propaganda stunt by local suffragettes in summer, 1913 – a time of frequent conflict with the police. Dozens of suffragettes carrying folded umbrellas hired boats on the west lake by Crown Gate. Out on the lake and beyond the reach of police, they opened umbrellas overlaid with suffragette slogans in large letters.

The conflicts between East End and West End suffragettes

---

11 See Chapter 9.

came to a head after Sylvia Pankhurst spoke at a public meeting on 1 November 1913, organised by George Lansbury's Daily Herald League, in support of the Dublin workers fighting for trade union rights. Defying her sister Christabel's injunction, Sylvia spoke alongside Sinn Fein supporters and the radical socialist James Connolly, founder of the Irish Citizens' Army.[12] Emmeline and Christabel Pankhurst were simultaneously courting Ulster Unionists, who had promised that an Ulster state would grant votes to women. A few weeks later, Emmeline and Christabel summoned Sylvia to Paris, where they had fled to avoid police harassment. They ordered Sylvia to sever connections between the East London suffragettes and the WSPU.

The expulsion liberated both parties. Mainstream suffragette leaders stopped looking over their shoulders at what working-class sisters were doing in their name, and the east London suffragettes relished the autonomy to campaign without fear of censure from the centre. In March 1914, east London WSPU was transformed into the independent East London Federation of Suffragettes (ELFS), and launched its own newspaper – *Women's Dreadnought*.

'Dreadnought' not only symbolised a powerful battle force, but also signified that women fighting for freedom 'must fear nothing'.[13] A family firm, Arber & Co., based near the suffragettes' Roman Road organising centre, printed the paper.[14] On market days east London suffragettes set up a second-hand goods stall there to raise money for political work and sell the paper. At

---

12 Other prominent socialist suffragettes such as Charlotte Despard and Dora Montefiore also addressed the meeting.

13 Sylvia Pankhurst had proposed *Workers' Mate* as a title but members preferred the *Women's Dreadnought* suggestion made by Mary Paterson, secretary of the Poplar branch.

14 Arber's, established in 1897, finally closed its doors in May 2014.

the stall and through house-to-house sales, they found out about the issues most affecting women's lives locally.

The *Dreadnought* stayed afloat through sales and self-sacrifice. The ELFS organised 'self-denial' weeks, when supporters would go without sugar in tea and butter on bread, would walk to work instead of taking the bus, and stop smoking. They gave the money saved to the paper. Alongside exposés of exploitation in the sweated trades, practical advice on dealing with bailiffs and organising rent strikes, the *Dreadnought* mobilised readers to attend indoor meetings at the Mission Hall in Tredegar Road and Crowder Hall in Bow and outdoor meetings in Victoria Park, Priscilla Road, Morris Road and Chrisp Street. It advertised elocution and speakers' classes to widen the pool of confident public speakers. From May 1914 these classes took place on Monday evenings in the newly acquired Women's Hall at 400 Old Ford Road, adjoining the house of suffragette supporters and shoemakers, Mr and Mrs Payne. Sylvia Pankhurst and fellow activist Norah Smyth shared the Paynes' house. The Women's Hall became an organising and community centre, housing a library, and hosting concerts and strike meetings.

While a choir practised at the Women's Hall on Tuesday evenings, the 'People's Army' trained in self-defence techniques, including ju-jitsu, at Bow Baths. This stewarding organisation, comprised of hundreds of women and men (especially dockers), was set up by the ELFS to prevent police from attacking and closing down suffragette meetings. When police raided an ELFS meeting at Bow Baths in October 1913, two women had arms broken and two were knocked unconscious, including Zelie Emerson, later treated in hospital for a fractured skull. Mounted police, whose horses were stabled behind Bow Road police station, launched a fierce assault two months later on a protest by hundreds of local suffragettes supported by a contingent of gasworkers, outside the Tomlin's Grove home of Conservative Councillor John le Manquais, who campaigned to bar suffragettes from council property.

The east London suffragettes experienced the police as an oppressive force that sought to deny their right to organise, yet on 28 March 1914 the *Dreadnought* published an anonymous 'Policemen's letter' assuring the ELFS that they 'have the sympathy and support of the majority of the intellectual section of the police'.

The 'intellectual section' was clearly elsewhere on 28 May 1914 when the ELFS held their Women's May Day procession from East India Docks to Victoria Park. Sylvia Pankhurst, threatened with re-arrest under the Cat and Mouse Act,[15] marched with 20 bodyguards from the People's Army surrounding her. As they reached Victoria Park, the police tried to arrest Sylvia. Women's hats were torn off, their hair pulled, their faces punched, and arms twisted, but they clung on. The police realised that her bodyguards were all chained together. An inspector demanded the keys but none were given. Police hammered with truncheons until the chains broke. They took Sylvia Pankhurst away and inflicted further blows on her defiant bodyguards. One guard who pulled a policemen to the ground was seized by another who threatened to ' ... break your bloody arm and twist your bleeding neck'. Despite the police actions, the procession entered the park, and speakers from different groups, including the Men's League for Women's Suffrage, the Rebel Social and Political Union, and the Actresses Franchise League, addressed the marchers from nine platforms. [16]

---

15 See Chapter 7.

16 Report in *Women's Dreadnought*, 30 May 1914.

In early June 1914 the ELFS requested a meeting with the Prime Minister, Herbert Asquith, explaining that previous delegations were composed of well-to-do middle- and upper-class women, but the bread-winners, child-bearers and home-makers of East End families wanted to state their views too.

On two previous occasions Asquith had refused to meet the ELFS. This time, Sylvia Pankhurst attempted to force his hand by threatening a hunger strike on the steps of the House of Commons. She said: 'I shall not give way, although it may end in my death.' Asquith finally relented.

Like the Women's Freedom League,[17] the ELFS resented the West End suffragette leaders' autocratic practices, so they democratically elected their delegation at branch meetings. Previous suffragette delegations to Asquith had argued for women's votes on the same (restricted) basis as men; the ELFS delegation, composed of six working-class women, sought votes for all adult women and men. They arrived in two cars accompanied by former MP George Lansbury, and John Scurr of the Dockers' Union, a former SDF member who was president of Poplar Trades Council. Lansbury and Scurr introduced the delegation, which included Scurr's wife, Julia. Asquith received them warmly and spent over an hour with them.

Each delegate revealed poignant details of their everyday lives. Mrs Ford, a widowed mother of two, spoke about her husband, who became an invalid soon after their marriage. She had taken up trouser-making and pressing, but left because of sexual harassment by a foreman. Mrs Scurr said the difficulties facing widows were very common.

---

17 See Chapter 7.

Our husbands die ... at a much earlier age than do the men of other classes. Modern industrialism kills them off ... by accident and overwork... . we know by bitter experience the terrible struggle with absolute want that our widowed sisters have to face from no fault of their own.

Daisy Parsons, a cigarette packer, described her piece-work. Young women, paid two pence a thousand, earned less than a shilling some days. Men were allowed time for lunch, women had to eat surreptitiously in the lavatory. She said that if men had to work under these conditions, 'through their trade union or through the vote they would secure an alteration'.

Mrs Savoy was introduced as 'Mrs Hughes' – her husband didn't want publicity. She handed Asquith a hairbrush valued at ten shillings and sixpence and explained that she received two pence for her share of making that brush. She had done this work for 43 years. 'As I have to work so hard,' she said, 'I feel it is very wrong that I cannot have a voice in the making of the laws.'

Mrs Bird described working in a jam factory from the age of eleven and then in a clothing workshop before becoming a mother of six. Her husband, a transport worker, earned 25 shillings a week. 'I have one of the best men,' she said. 'He is a teetotaller but yet I have a great struggle to bring up a family on the wages he earns.'

Collectively they demonstrated that women could not challenge these appalling circumstances without a political voice. Daisy Parsons also referred to brutal police actions against suffragettes, endorsed by superiors who were 'not fit to help rule the country, while we have no say in the matter'. Mrs Scurr said it was 'gravely unjust' that the government passed legislation affecting women's daily lives 'without consulting the women of this country'.

Asquith conceded that this delegation was more representative than previous ones. He said he understood from their 'moderate and well-reasoned' presentations, that women could not get 'substantial and intelligent reform' either in legislation or administration affecting their economic conditions, unless they 'themselves had a voice in choosing their representatives'.

The meeting had clarified his thoughts about partial changes to the franchise. He said: 'If the change [women's suffrage] has got to come we must face it boldly and make it thoroughly democratic in its basis.'

This crucial breakthrough achieved by a rebellious, marginalised section of the wider suffrage movement was frustratingly put on ice a few weeks later when war broke out in Europe. The war deepened conflict within the suffragette movement and also opened up schisms within east London's labour movement. Just after Austria-Hungary declared war on Serbia, Lansbury's Daily Herald League called a 'united labour and socialist demonstration' in Trafalgar Square for Sunday 2 August stating, 'The war must be stopped'. Lansbury warned the government that the labour movement would 'not allow England to be dragged into this fearful crime', where workers of different nationalities slaughter each other. Speakers' platforms were set up all around the square. At one, dockers' leader Ben Tillett told the crowd, 'We don't want to sing Rule Britannia nor God Save the King ... [but] God Save the People', as they would do 'the fighting and the starving'.

The *Manchester Guardian* reported that, 'the crowd overflowed into Whitehall and some distance up the Strand. It was the largest

Trafalgar Square demonstration for many years'. The *Herald* said a contingent of 5,000 had marched to the Square from the East End 'headed by the striking red banner of the National Transport Workers Federation'.

Two days later, several women's organisations held a massive peace rally in Kingsway Hall, calling on the British government to stay out of the conflict and on Europe's workers not to kill each other. But that week the situation dramatically changed. Germany had declared war on Russia and France, and invaded Belgium. Britain and Serbia declared war on Germany, and Austria-Hungary declared war on Russia. As soon as Britain entered the war, working-class communities were swept up by the wave of patriotic fervour. Several labour and trade union leaders, including Ben Tillett and Will Thorne, now adopted a pro-war position. Mainstream suffragettes ceased campaigning and the government released all suffragette prisoners. The WSPU focused on supporting the war effort and ensuring that women could participate as equals in serving Britain. It later renamed its newspaper *Britannia*.

But rebellious Poplar swam against the tide. Lansbury, the *Daily Herald* and the ILP fought against the war. ELFS leaders instinctively shared these sentiments but stated them less stridently. Many of their supporters' husbands had signed up to fight. They made it clear, however, that they would continue to campaign for equality and women's rights and livelihoods as food prices rocketed, unemployment grew and women were drafted into absent male workers' roles at half or even a third of the normal rate.

On 29 August the *East London Observer* claimed that the best British socialists 'have joined wholeheartedly with the

Government in our hour of trial', except the 'Socialists of Bow and Bromley and Poplar, and the Suffragette garrison at Old-Ford' whom it lumped in with 'social maniacs and desperadoes ... trying to make capital out of the most awful war'.

In early September, an ELFS delegation to the Board of Trade called for government intervention over food prices. However, knowing that government wheels turned slowly (except for the war effort itself), they developed their own initiatives to support and empower struggling local women. On 5 September the *Dreadnought* announced it had opened a 'cost price restaurant' offering two-course meals for two pence, or soup at a penny a pint. Two sisters, Ennis Richmond and Morgan Brown, both health-food enthusiasts, were soon serving 200 dinners a day. At the end of September, another 'tuppenny restaurant' opened in Railway Street, Poplar, serving suet dumplings, gravy and bread. In January a soup centre opened in St Leonard Street, Bromley. The ELFS began to provide work through establishing cooperative factories and workshops, making boots, clothing and children's toys. The most long-standing one – a toy factory – opened on Norman Road.[18] Women were paid five pence an hour, the amount ELFS campaigned for as a minimum wage. Women could work flexi-time and leave their children in a crèche there for three pence a day including meals.

The ELFS transformed a disused pub, the Gunmakers Arms on Old Ford Road, into a crèche and maternity health facility, and renamed it the Mother's Arms. Its principal nurse, Maud Hebbes, later worked at Marie Stopes' pioneering birth control clinic. Women's Freedom League activist Muriel Matters,[19] who

18 Later renamed Norman Grove.
19 See Chapter 7.

was trained by Maria Montessori, set up a small school there.

Meanwhile, the ELFS continued to lobby and protest for equal pay. They lobbied the Board of Trade in April 1915. The following month, ELFS activists also lobbied Home Secretary Reginald McKenna about price controls. As Sylvia Pankhurst was leaving the meeting, McKenna said, 'I must shake hands with you – you are the pluckiest girl I ever knew.' In July, the ELFS organised a large protest march from East India Dock Gates to the House of Commons, demanding equal pay for men and women, that wages should rise with prices, and that women should get the vote.

The ELFS became more openly anti-war, but without diminishing support for East End women affected by the war. After compulsory conscription was introduced, Sylvia Pankhurst was arrested and fined for speaking against the war and the *Dreadnought*'s office was raided several times. In February 1915, Sylvia Pankhurst collaborated with George and Bessie Lansbury to form the League of Rights for Soldiers' and Sailors' Wives and Relatives, which fought for higher allowances and pensions. One ELFS activist who threw herself wholeheartedly into the League's work was Minnie Glassman, who grew up on Chicksand Street, off Brick Lane, one of seven children born to an immigrant Jewish bootmaker, Isaac, and his wife Hannah (Annie). She had joined the ELFS while working as a primary school teacher. Minnie married the Lansburys' son Edgar, a Labour councillor, then left teaching to work full time for the ELFS as assistant secretary to Sylvia Pankhurst. Minnie and Edgar settled in Wellington Road, Bow. Minnie stayed politically close to Sylvia as the *Women's Dreadnought* became the more explicitly socialist *Workers' Dreadnought*.

Much further east, in 1917, revolution gripped Russia. Sylvia Pankhurst's political focus shifted from local to global, and what was once the ELFS morphed into the more revolutionary Workers' Socialist Federation. There was undoubtedly huge support for the Russian Revolution in the East End, not least among the 150,000 Jews who fled here from Tsarist persecution, but east London's workers were more inclined towards radical reform than revolution in their own backyard.

In 1920 Minnie and Edgar Lansbury joined the newly formed Communist Party, but stayed politically grounded in east London, where they contributed to a seismic shift, if not a revolution, that began in 1919. Every adult male still waiting to vote was enfranchised shortly after the war ended, along with 8.4 million women. (Women between the ages of 21–30 remained disenfranchised.) Labour started to gain dramatically from that wider franchise in the 1919 local elections, especially in east London, where the party won impressive majorities for the first time. In Poplar, Labour won 39 of the 42 council seats. As the governing party, they could appoint four aldermen to facilitate the administration. One was Minnie Lansbury; another was John Scurr, who had escorted the ELFS delegation to Asquith.

Janine Booth, author of a study of Poplar Council from 1919–25, described how the new council 'for the first time ... looked like its electorate. It included railworkers, dockers, labourers, postmen, a road engineer, a toolmaker, a leadworker and a farrier'.[20] At its inaugural meeting, the Labour council elected a mayor, who accepted the nomination but refused the pageantry of robes and chain that would set him apart from other councillors. Mayor George Lansbury described the new council as

20 J. Booth, *Guilty and Proud of It*, London: Merlin, 2009.

'class-conscious socialists working together', to change people's lives. They drafted schemes for slum clearance to build municipal housing, invested heavily in health programmes, especially maternity and child welfare, which reduced infant mortality significantly, provided a range of free services to unemployed workers, brought in a minimum wage for council employees, and equalised the wages of men and women employed by the council. Male council employees enjoyed a 25 per cent pay increase, on average; the wages of female council employees rose by 75 per cent.

The new council worked closely with local trade unionists, and organised public meetings to share its polices with the community. It set what it considered a fair rate to pay for these new and increased services, but the rates that local residents paid included a 'precept' paid to the London County Council (LCC) for cross-London services, such as drains, sewage, parks and police. When Poplar Council examined the formula for this precept, it discovered that the burden fell disproportionately on the poorest boroughs. Poplar's Labour councillors were newcomers to office, but they had a local rebel tradition to draw on. In March 1921, George Lansbury proposed that the council stop collecting the rates for cross-London bodies. They set a rate of four shillings and four pence instead of six shillings and ten pence, and thrust themselves on a collision course with the LCC and central government, who threatened to prosecute.

Poplar's councillors were summoned to court on 29 July and told that, if they did not levy the precept they would be sent to prison. Minnie Lansbury said: 'Poplar will pay its share of London's rates when Westminster, Kensington, and the City do the same.'

The councillors marched to court with thousands of supporters. Lansbury assured them: ' ... if we have to choose between contempt of the poor and contempt of court, it will be contempt of court.' The question, he said, was not whether their refusal was legal or illegal but whether it was 'right or wrong'.

John Scurr said the government was 'on the horns of a dilemma. If they send us to prison they will not get their money; and if they don't send us to prison they will bring the law into contempt. Poplar does not care on which horn they choose to impale themselves.'[21] The councillors' legal team included the Fabian Henry Slesser and W. H. Thompson, who had been jailed three times for conscientious objection during the First World War.

The council lost, and the judge told the councillors to prepare to stay in prison until their contempt was purged. The arrests took place at the beginning of September. Twenty-five male councillors were placed in Brixton prison; five women councillors, including Minnie Lansbury and another former ELFS activist, Nellie Cressall, were sent to Holloway Prison. Julia Scurr was also imprisoned there while her husband was locked up in Brixton. Very few councillors were left to run the administration in their absence. The night before the first arrests, the council met to plan how to continue functioning with such depleted numbers. Outside the Town Hall, 6,000 supporters gathered. As the meeting ended councillors sang 'The Red Flag', 'bringing particular passion', said Lansbury, to the lines 'Come dungeon dark or gallows grim, this song shall be our parting hymn'.

---

21 Booth, *Guilty and Proud of It*, p.50.

In prison they fought for their human rights. Lansbury recalls:

> We all refused to ... [wear] prison uniforms ... [and] to
> do any work and ... drink the tea or eat the food. In a
> few days the food was changed ... we all went on strike
> against being locked in our cells all day, and as a result
> we had them opened after breakfast until after supper.
> Then we went into the police commissioner's room and
> entertained ourselves with lectures and discussions ... we
> were entertained after 8 o'clock by public meetings and
> singing outside our windows. [22]

They won daily visits instead of two per week. Family members,
MPs, magistrates, churchmen, councillors and council employees,
including dustmen, roadsweepers, surveyors and engineers
visited them. They won the right to hold council meetings
in prison, the first one (of 32) held on 11 September. From 27
September, the women councillors in Holloway were bussed over
for these meetings.

Lansbury had been pleasantly surprised by a comment made
by a warder soon after the councillors arrived: 'He said "Don't
worry, you'll win. Every cause has to be fought for, and always
prison opens up the way to reform".' The government threatened other boroughs that if they followed Poplar's example they
would be imprisoned too. The threat backfired. Stepney Council
and Bethnal Green Council both voted to withhold the precept
too. With the rebellion spreading, the government and LCC
backed down. Poplar's rebels were released on 13 October. That
same week a conference was convened to equalise cross-London

22 Lansbury, *Looking Backwards and Forwards*.

rates. Poplar's rates were relieved by six shillings and sixpence in the pound, and one shilling in the pound was added to the rates of Westminster and the City of London.

For the Lansburys though, this incredible victory was soon overshadowed with great sadness. Minnie Lansbury had become ill in prison, and struggled with her health after being released. Over Christmas, a heavy bout of 'flu became pneumonia. She died, aged 32, on 1 January 1922. Thousands took to the streets to pay respects as her coffin was borne on the shoulders of four Poplar councillors, amid a procession led by hundreds of unemployed workers. At Bow Bridge the coffin was transferred to a motor hearse for a service at Ilford crematorium. Her ashes were later interred in East Ham Jewish Cemetery.

Mourners described her as a 'lover of justice' who dedicated 'a life of toil and labour in the relief of distress and the uplifting of her fellow men (sic)'. William Morris's poem, *Hear a Word*, was read:

Mourn not, therefore, nor lament it,
That the world outlives their life
Voice and vision yet they give us
Making strong our hands for strife.

The struggles for social justice that Minnie Lansbury gave her life for continued to flourish and, as the next chapter shows, they blossomed on both sides of the Thames.

Female Poplar councillors on their way to Holloway Prison.

Male Poplar councillors in Brixton Prison.

BROMLEY REC GROUND

FOWIS ROAD

BRUCE ROAD

OLYMPIC PARK

A12

MINNIE LANSBURY MEMORIAL

BOW ROAD

TREVITHICK WAY

BOW CHURCH

ARNOLD ROAD

A12

FAIRFIELD ROAD

TOMLINS GROVE

GEORGE LANSBURY

PARNELL ROAD

BOW ROAD

ALFRED STREET

WELLINGTON WAY

BOW ROAD

HARLEY GROVE

ROMAN ROAD

COBORN ROAD

ST STEPHEN'S ROAD

DANE PLACE

SELWYN ROAD

ANTILL ROAD

NORMAN GROVE

MILE END

THE WOMAN'S DREADNOUGHT

MILE END

GROVE ROAD

OLD FORD ROAD

MILLENNIUM PARK

VICTORIA PARK

GROVE ROAD

OLD FORD ROAD

WEST BOATING LAKE

100M

N

222

WALK

Start at Crown Gate, Victoria Park, E3 5SN.

1. Crown Gate
Enter the park and you will see the lake where the suffragettes did their umbrella stunt in 1913. This was a well-established 'speakers' corner' area. Across Old Ford Road, at number 288, lived the writer Israel Zangwill, a founder of the Men's League for Women's Suffrage. Walk east along Old Ford Road.

2. Old Ford Road (1)
Just before you reach the Lord Morpeth pub, a plaque on the side wall indicates the former site of the ELFS Women's Hall. Sylvia Pankhurst and Norah Smyth lived here with Mr and Mrs Payne. Until 2014, the pub's sign featured a suffragette and photos of ELFS activities were displayed inside the pub. Continue along Old Ford Road.

3. Old Ford Road (2)
On the corner with St Stephen's Road a plaque indicates the former site of a disused pub, the Gunmakers Arms, converted by the ELFS into the Mother's Arms mother and baby clinic and Montessori school.

4. St Stephen's Road
Opposite St Paul's Church a housing estate has replaced the earlier buildings that included, at number 103, the timber merchants/sawmill that belonged to Bessie Lansbury's father.

Several members of the Lansbury family were connected with this business. Wood from this mill furnished the Mother's Arms and also was made into a speakers' platform that the ELFS used outside their Bow Road premises. Continue to the junction then turn right into Roman Road

5. Roman Road

The ELFS office was at number 321 (before street renumbering). On the right-hand side looking west was Arber's, the company that printed the *Women's Dreadnought*. The paper was sold from a stall on Roman Road. Bow Baths stood on the eastern end of Roman Road. A police raid on a suffragettes meeting here in October 1913 caused serious injuries. The ELFS 'People's Army' trained there. Turn left into Dane Place then right into Norman Grove.

6. Norman Grove

At number 45, a plaque recalls the toy factory established by the ELFS that provided work to local women during the First World War. It closed in the 1930s. Cross into Selwyn Road, turn left into Antill Road then right into Coborn Road. Turn left into Malmesbury Road, past the school, then walk through the estate into Harley Grove.

7. Harley Grove

The Sikh Temple here replaced a synagogue opened in 1927, which in turn replaced a Methodist Chapel. Continue to the end of Harley Grove

8. Bow Road (1)

George Lansbury House is a small estate built on his former home at 39 Bow Road. Lansbury lived there for 23 years. A plaque mounted on a stone facing Bow Road recalls a 'great servant of the people'. Turn left along Bow Road.

9. Bow Road (2)

At Electric House, by the corner with Alfred Street, the Minnie Lansbury memorial clock mounted in the 1930s juts out. It fell into disrepair but was restored in 2008. Minnie lived on Wellington Road, across the road, now renamed Wellington Way. Walk past Bow police station, whose windows suffered attacks by suffragette stones. Turn right into Tomlin's Grove.

10. Tomlins Grove

In December 1913, a suffragette protest outside Councillor le Manquais' home at number 13 was violently attacked by police. Turn left into Arnold Road, follow round into Trevithick Way, walk up a few stairs and cross into Bruce Road. Turn right into Powis Road.

11. Powis Road

Kingsley Hall was a community centre established by socialist, pacifist Christians, Muriel and Doris Lester in 1915, providing educational and recreational facilities. From 1922–6 Muriel Lester was an alderman serving Poplar's radical Labour council. The centre served as a soup kitchen during the 1926 General Strike. That year Muriel Lester travelled to India to meet Gandhi. He stayed at Kingsley Hall during the round-table conference on India's future in 1931.

Women strikers outside Pink's jam factory, 1911.
TUC Library Collections, London Metropolitan University

9

PEOPLE'S POWER IN BERMONDSEY

Cross the Thames from the City over London Bridge and you come to Borough High Street – a Roman road boasting smart office blocks and increasingly up-market cafes. On Tooley Street, heading east, tourists queue for the London Dungeon. To the west, pungent smells emanate from a food market with international flavours and exorbitant prices. Beyond the market lies Southwark's cultural quarter, Tate Modern, the rebuilt Globe Theatre and swish restaurants. The sole cultural institution in these streets that testifies to harder times endured by nineteenth-century locals is the Clink Museum, which tells the grim story of London's prisons.

London gaols were filled with debtors, pickpockets, petty criminals and, intermittently, with political activists too. Clerk-enwell had the highest concentration of prisons but Southwark came a close second. Its accommodation for convicts included the notoriously harsh Marshalsea prison, which closed in 1842.[1]

When John Dickens, a naval clerk mired in financial difficulties, was caged up there in 1824, his family took lodgings nearby and his twelve-year-old son became the breadwinner. Slaving away in a boot-blacking factory by the Thames inspired young Charles

---

1 This replaced the medieval White Lion Prison.

Dickens' later searing descriptions of London's poverty, notably in *Little Dorrit* (1850s), a vivid novel centred on the Marshalsea. In *Oliver Twist* (1837), Dickens described Jacob's Island, near St Saviour's Dock, Bermondsey, east of London Bridge:

> ... rooms so small, so filthy, so confined, that the air would seem to be too tainted even for the dirt and squalor which they shelter ... every repulsive lineament of poverty, every loathsome indication of filth, rot, and garbage: all these ornament the banks of Jacob's Island.

When London was hit by a further cholera outbreak in 1849,[2] Henry Mayhew noted that more than half the capital's deaths over a three-month period occurred south of the Thames, especially in Lambeth, Southwark and Bermondsey:[3]

> ... anyone who has ventured to visit [Bermondsey] will not wonder at the ravages of the pestilence in this malarious quarter, for it is bounded on the north and east by filth and fever and on the south and west by want, squalor, rags and pestilence. Here stands ... the very capital of cholera ... Jacob's Island ... insulated by the common sewer.[4]

Several decades after Dickens and Mayhew had written about Jacob's Island, little had improved. Booth's 1903 poverty survey

---

2   See discussion of 1831 cholera outbreak in Chapter 2.

3   Since 1965 Bermondsey has been incorporated into the London Borough of Southwark. In the 1840s, 'Southwark' referred to the northwestern segment of that borough.

4   *Morning Chronicle*, 23 September 1849, quoted in D. Russell and M. Tichelar, *Class Struggles in South London 1850–1950*, London: Southwark-Lambeth History Workshop, 1981.

of Southwark and its environs described people in 'chronic want' or at best 'very poor'. Many were Irish immigrants from Cork engaged in casualised wharfside work. In St Saviour's, 68 per cent of the population lived on or below the poverty line, infant mortality was 28 per cent, and the average life expectancy, albeit skewed by the infant death rate, was 36.8 years. When Dickens was writing *Oliver Twist*, Bermondsey's population numbered roughly 65,000. Despite the high death rate, it doubled over 50 years, peaking at 136,660 in 1891, when it was regarded as one of the most insanitary, overcrowded and impoverished places in Britain.

George Orwell followed Dickens to Bermondsey 100 years later, basing himself in a decrepit Tooley Street dosshouse while he researched *Down and Out in Paris and London*. If Orwell had stayed, instead, in the heart of Bermondsey, he would have told a different story. Much of the area had been transformed during the 1920s and 1930s by the remarkable pioneering efforts of a socialist council rooted in the idealism of a handful of rebellious activists. Their rebellion was not against a particular political opponent or authority figure, but against the dire conditions and widespread hopelessness around them. They believed that the lives of people in the area *could* be transformed. They won the confidence of local residents and were themselves strengthened by the drive of Bermondsey's people, who grasped that hope and fought for their dignity, emancipation and rights.

On 5 May 1908, 16 people gathered in Yalding Road, Bermondsey, the home of Tom Briggs, a bookbinder, to discuss the creation of a new radical movement in the area. The only political choice for those lucky enough to vote was Liberal or Conservative, and the Conservatives usually won. Briggs's friends wanted to establish a socialist third force – a branch of the Independent Labour Party (ILP).

Local activists, such as Frederick Lessner, an immigrant German tailor and friend of Karl Marx, had made stuttering attempts to form a Bermondsey ILP in the 1890s. It held outdoor meetings in Southwark Park, and at Dockhead by Lee's Temperance Bar. Harry Quelch, who lived at 21 Southwark Park Road, edited the Social Democratic Federation (SDF) newspaper *Justice*. He met socialist and trade union colleagues at the General Garibaldi pub, close to his house, or at the Bricklayers Arms in Old Kent Road. During the 1887 agitation around unemployment, Bermondsey SDF held a very large meeting there, with William Morris chairing and John Burns speaking, but these initiatives remained fleeting and marginal.[5]

Two people opted out of this incipient group, so Bermondsey's first ILP branch was formed with 14 members. These included a remarkable, idealistic couple – Ada and Alfred Salter – who met at the Bermondsey Settlement, a centre for anti-poverty work in the local community established by John Scott Lidgett, a left-leaning Methodist.

Ada Salter came to the Settlement as Ada Brown, a committed Christian from rural Northamptonshire, whose convictions drew her to social activism amongst the urban poor. Alfred Salter grew up in Bermondsey's more prosperous neighbouring district, Greenwich. His aspirational lower-middle-class parents were Plymouth Brethren by conviction but by the time Alfred settled in Bermondsey, he had shed these religious beliefs, which he felt

---

5   See *South London Chronicle*, 19 March 1887. Quelch became the business manager of the radical publishers Twentieth Century Press, founded by William Morris, and was a close associate of Lenin during his time in London.

were excessively focused on a glorious afterlife. He wanted social justice for Bermondsey's people here and now.

Salter won a scholarship to study medicine at Guy's Hospital in Southwark. Every day, as he travelled between Greenwich and Guy's, he saw Bermondsey's deprivation and desolation. His professors thought they were grooming a very promising student for a Harley Street career, but Salter had already chosen the mean streets of Bermondsey. He found a crop of other idealistic young doctors, and they formed a cooperative medical practice where they shared approaches to community health and pooled their income. They offered medical consultations at minimal cost, sometimes free, to a desperately poor population frequently exposed to life-threatening illnesses and soon acquired several thousand patients.

Alfred married Ada in 1900 and they had a daughter, Joyce, in 1902. As a student Alfred had joined the Marxist SDF and then the Fabians, both of which shaped his philosophical outlook. Through these connections he engaged in occasional illicit activities at night by the Thames, helping to smuggle fugitive immigrant radicals into the country, but in general he considered the SDF too concerned with theory over practice.

Across London, the Labour Party was in its infancy. The SDF and Fabians were too small and aloof, so Alfred and Ada reluctantly looked at first to the Liberals as a possible vehicle for practical social activism. The local Liberals asked Alfred to be their parliamentary candidate but he rejected the offer. Meanwhile, he was converting Ada from liberalism to socialism, and she was converting him back to Christianity – its Quaker variety.

By March 1910 the fledgling ILP branch had broadened its support base and celebrated its first success. Ada Salter became London's second female borough councillor[6] – and the sole socialist among Bermondsey's 54 councillors. The night she was elected, Ada, Alfred and fellow activist Eveline Lowe,[7] fantasised about what a socialist local council could do. They would pull down slums and build a tree-lined garden city, with bathrooms in every house and nursery schools for all under-fives. Every hungry schoolchild would be fed; a community health centre would offer free diagnosis by specialists and send TB sufferers to Switzerland for treatment. Ada imagined the red flag flying over the Town Hall. Eveline Lowe added, 'and over the new County Hall'.[8] Alfred dreamt of it flying over Big Ben.

Three months later, their dreams turned into nightmares. Their daughter, Joyce, had suffered two very severe bouts of scarlet fever. The Salters' close friends thought they should have sent Joyce out of the borough to a boarding school or a Quaker school, rather than risk her sharing a local school environment where killer diseases were rife. But Alfred and Ada, on principle, refused to allow Joyce privileges inaccessible to other Bermondsey children. Very unusually, she contracted a third bout of scarlet fever, just after her eighth birthday. This time she didn't recover. But instead of destroying the Salters' idealism, this tragedy enhanced their determination to give every Bermondsey child a future.

---

6   Reina Lawrence was the first, winning a by-election on Hampstead Borough Council in December 1907.

7   Her husband, George Carter Lowe, was part of the doctors' cooperative.

8   County Hall was starting to be built, opening in 1922, with further blocks added in the 1930s. After Thatcher's government abolished the Greater London Council in 1986, the building was sold to private investors.

That night in 1910, when they dreamt of transforming Bermondsey, but had just one council seat, Alfred said that they would need twelve years to win the borough for socialism. In 1922 the Labour Party, in which the ILP was pivotal locally, won 38 out of the 54 seats on Bermondsey Council. Ada Salter became Mayor, and Alfred Salter won the parliamentary seat for Labour too. In the interim, a campaigning movement with a shared progressive vision was growing, but it needed a physical base.

Soon after the ILP branch was established in 1908, its members collectively rented a shop at 79 Grange Road, converted its main space into a small meeting hall and bought an old printing press, operated by Charlie Gamble, a compositor. Gamble shared his skills with other members, and they printed propaganda leaflets for open-air meetings and Thursday evening debates in the hall. They soon outgrew this space.

On Fort Road, an adult education facility had fallen into disrepair. The ILP rented it for twelve months with an option to buy. The veteran socialist James Keir Hardie officially opened the Fort Road Labour Institute on 8 July 1911. The building's original foundation stone, on one side of the entrance, bore the name of Lord Rosebery, a Liberal. Its new foundation stone on the opposite side, read: 'Socialism the hope of the world.'

The local branch had barely started to discuss how best to utilise this centre to promote socialism locally, when it was commandeered by a spontaneous movement that suddenly erupted among thousands of Bermondsey's unorganised and impoverished female workers.

Bermondsey's workplaces, like those of the East End, were largely demarcated by gender. Men were primarily engaged in dock work, transport, engineering and printing. Some worked within a declining leather industry, still recalled in local signs for Tanner Street, Morocco Street, Leathermarket Gardens and the Leather Exchange public house.

Bermondsey Street, which cuts through the former leatherwork area, was home to Christy's, the biggest hat factory in Europe, which employed large numbers of men and women. But women workers were mainly concentrated in a different industry. Raw food materials arrived in abundance at the docks, and a food processing and packaging industry grew in the nineteenth century. It began with tea packing, sugar refining, grain and spice milling, and later produced and packaged biscuits, cakes, confectionary, ice-cream, margarine, jam, sauces, pickles, meat and fish pastes, jellies and custards.

Hartley's Jam and Sarson's Vinegar had factories on Tower Bridge Road. Spillers dog biscuits were made at Jacob Street, while biscuits for human consumption were manufactured at Jacob's factory on Wolseley Street and at Peek Frean's site on Drummond Road, which employed 2,300 workers in 1911. Crosse & Blackwell's jam and pickles plant was in Crimscott Street and Pearce Duff's custard factory was on Spa Road.

At a time when most unskilled male workers generally earned at least 15–20 shillings a week, Bermondsey's female workers usually took home seven to nine shillings, and factory girls under 16, just three shillings a week. Some Bermondsey children, as young as six, did factory shifts after school.

In the summer of 1911, striking tramway workers met at the new Labour Institute. They were earning 25 shillings a week working a ten-hour day, six days a week, and were fighting for 30 shillings a week and an eight-hour day. When the women saw their brothers, husbands and uncles called out on strike by their unions and gaining improved conditions through collective action and solidarity between workplaces, they couldn't help reflecting on their own exploitation.

On 11 August, the local papers reported 'turbulent scenes in Tower Bridge Road and Old Kent Road' the previous evening, 'which resulted unfortunately in a baton charge by the police'. As the transport strike spread, lorries and vans were waved down and even attacked by militants determined to halt deliveries and persuade drivers to return their vehicles to their workplaces. Mounted and foot police tried to keep the road clear for delivery vehicles but a large body of strikers continued to block it. The police made many arrests.

The papers also reported an unexpected act of solidarity. Female employees of Benjamin Edgington's tent-makers at Duke Street, London Bridge, came out in solidarity with the men. They paraded through Tooley Street 'singing the socialist Marsellaise "Fall in and follow me!"'. Some of Pearce Duff's female workers did just that.[9]

These events dominated discussions locally over the following weekend. On the Monday morning, as the solid strikes among Bermondsey's male-dominated occupations continued, hundreds of women at a confectionery factory walked out, demanding a change to their conditions. They had no union but acted spontaneously and collectively. They marched to nearby factories calling their sisters out. Within a day, 14,000 women workers at 21 Bermondsey factories were on strike. One young worker at a chocolate factory told a reporter from the *Southwark and Bermondsey Recorder*: 'We are striking for more pay, mister, and we won't go in till we get it.' The amounts that the strikers demanded

9   *South London Press*, 11 August 1911.

varied depending on their existing pay. Not all the women came out – some felt strong bonds of loyalty to their employers, despite enduring long hours for low wages; others feared they might be victimised when the strike ended. But the majority of women struck, and even where production continued, it was severely disrupted. The local papers reported that: 'The women appeared to be in the highest of spirits when they came out on Monday. Armies of them paraded the streets of Bermondsey while the men who had also struck held meetings on the corners of the principal thoroughfares.'[10]

The newspapers' editorial columns, however, condemned the wildcat strikes, which imposed 'flagrant injustices' on decent local firms. Peek Frean's spokesperson, Mr Green, told the *South London Press* that the company ' ... had no reason whatever to suppose that there was any dissatisfaction whatever among our hands either with the rate of wages or the conditions of employment. While not confessing to be model philanthropists ... we have always been on excellent terms with our workpeople.'[11]

Initially, half the Peek Frean workforce came out, but striking car-men picketed the entrance so no goods could leave the factory. Peek Frean rewarded the loyalty of those who continued to work by giving them double wages during the action. Another Peek Frean representative described the women's tactic of moving as a troop from one factory to another to call women out, as a 'reign of terror'.[12]

Employers were surprised and very alarmed. Around 40

10 *South London Press*, 18 August 1911.

11 *South London Press*, 25 August 1911.

12 During the Dock Strike of 1889, women there and at other local workplaces – Spratts, Southwell Jam factory, Lloyd's tin-plate manufacturers – came out in solidarity with the southern side dockers, and joined striking dockers on protest marches.

per cent of jam and biscuits consumed throughout Britain were processed and packaged in Bermondsey's factories. Mary Macarthur, a Glasgow-born union organiser and ILP member, who had moved to London and founded a general women's union – the National Federation of Women Workers (NFWW) – was excited rather than alarmed. She sped down to Bermondsey to meet and support the strikers. From the sheer numbers that came out on the first day, and the enthusiasm and self-organisation they had already shown, Macarthur believed they could make significant gains. The difficulty would be sustaining the strike long enough to succeed.

Back in April she had been powerless to affect the outcome of a seemingly promising movement by women workers at the Idris soft drinks bottling plant in Camden. Initially, 50 women walked out over the sacking of Annie Lowin, a 25-year-old widowed mother of two, who had worked for the company for 13 years. The number striking quickly rose above 90. The company insisted that they were right to sack her because of 'persistent lateness' and 'incivility to a timekeeper'. On the day she was sacked, she had arrived three minutes late. Macarthur and Lowin's co-workers believed she was being victimised because she had started to take up union issues about poor sanitary arrangements in the factory: women sometimes worked up to their ankles in water; they also had to boil water for tea in the same pails used for washing the floor.

Her colleagues wrote songs for the picket line. One, written to the tune of 'Every Nice Girl Loves a Sailor', said:

Have you been to work at Idris?
No we won't go in today

For we're standing by a comrade
And we'll never run away
She stood bravely by the union
And she spoke up for us true
And if she gets the sack, we never will go back
Whatever they do, whatever they do.

The strikers stood firm and won support from well-unionised male workers at two nearby factories, who levied their members to help sustain the women while they were striking. The employer, though, recruited local unemployed men to fill the jobs the pickets left idle. Bermondsey, however, had closer-knit communities which resisted attempts to recruit scab labour. In Bermondsey many men were simultaneously striking against their employers. Women and men were supporting each other's struggles.

Macarthur, assisted by local ILP volunteers, turned the newly opened Labour Institute on Fort Road into a strike headquarters. She appealed through the *Daily News* for material support, requesting not money but food. Local shopkeepers and well-wishers donated bread, milk and barrels of herrings, and gave money too. Macarthur's ILP team distributed the food from Fort Road and Ada Salter set up additional food distribution points.

Despite local newspapers' editorial bias against the strikers, individual reporters empathised with the women's action and recognised the hardships they faced while striking:

> ... every day since Tuesday an immense crowd ... weary and with the pinch of hunger on their faces marched to the hall of the Independent Labour Party in Fort Road

where they were presented with loaves of bread. Clinging on to the skirts of the women were the children, piteously crying for food, and the bread as soon as it was received was split into small portions [for] the hungry children.[13]

Outside Pink's jam factory on Staple Street, women held placards stating: 'We are not white slaves. We are Pink's slaves' and 'More trouble at Pink's'.

Throughout the morning of Monday 14 August, striking Bermondsey women marched and chanted 'Are we downhearted?' answering in unison 'No!' They reached Southwark Park for a rally in the afternoon. Dockers' leader Ben Tillett, Poplar MP George Lansbury and Mary Macarthur, of the NFWW, greeted the strikers. Tillett, one of the organisers of the simultaneous strikes among dock and transport workers, promised that the men would not return to work until the women's demands were met.

In concert with the industrial action, women in Leroy Street and Wolseley Street, near Jacob's biscuit factory, began to organise rent strikes. By Friday, several factory bosses came to the negotiating table, and more than 4,000 women had joined the National Federation of Women Workers. By the end of the following week the dispute was mostly over. Strikes had taken place at 21 factories and in 18 of them the women had made considerable gains in pay, achieved agreements to end piecework, and established a union in most of them.[14] In the three factories where no gains were made, Macarthur believed the women might have won if they had held out longer.

---

13 *South London Press*, 18 August 1911.

14 Peek Frean (biscuits) and Southwell (jam) agreed pay rises but would not recognise a permanent union.

Alfred Salter and Mary Macarthur calculated that the pay increases, between one shilling and four shillings a week, would mean a redistribution of at least £7,000 from company profits to the pockets of local women workers over the coming year, probably considerably more. The women cherished that increase but just as importantly Macarthur believed they had acquired ' ... a new sense of self-reliance, solidarity and comradeship ... making it certain that, whatever the difficulties and dangers of the future, they will never again be ... without hope'.[15]

The ILP gained prestige for its prominent role during the strike. Salter told the press, 'I shall not rest satisfied until every working man, woman and girl in Bermondsey is a member of a trade union.' The response was immediate. In early September a National Union of Barmen, Barmaids and Potmen was launched at the Labour Institute. Leaflets inviting barworkers to join this union described bar staff earning 14 shillings for a 100-hour week. Publicans said they provided many barworkers with free board and lodgings but barworkers retorted that accommodation was overcrowded and they shared poor food.

The August strikes inspired women workers beyond Bermondsey. In September, the ILP journal, *Labour Leader*, reported that women workers had formed unions in Clapton, Hoxton, Shadwell and Woolwich. Three hundred women among a 1,000-strong workforce at Murray's confectioners in Turnmill Street, Farringdon, came out on strike in late August. The women there were known locally as 'Murray's white mice', because of the powder that clung to them. Some of them earned just four shillings and eight pence a week for a 56-hour week, with few

---

15 *Women's Trade Union Review*, October 1911.

breaks. They were subject to petty fines, while any bonuses for increased productivity went to the foremen. The women had started to form a union and, inspired by the Bermondsey strikers, they decided to take action.

At the end of their first week on strike, they ambushed a convoy of food intended for 'loyal workers' who had not come out. The strikers celebrated this moment in a picket-line song (to the tune of 'Three Blind Mice'):[16]

> Murray's white mice
> See how they fight
> They collared the fish and the cheese and the bread
> 'Twas meant for the blacklegs, they ate it instead
> And the boss was so wild that he stood on his head
> Murray's white mice.

The following week, the employers offered to cease fining employees and start a profit-sharing scheme for women who had worked in the factory for at least twelve months. But they made the women's return to work conditional on them giving up their trade union membership. The women stayed out. A few days later a settlement was reached which left the Board of Trade to establish fair wage rates; all the strikers were reinstated.

During the 1911 strikes, Bermondsey ILP engaged directly with large numbers of local workers on a daily basis. One of its members – an employer rather than an employee – proposed an initiative which would increase regular contact and support the party materially. John Dhonau, whose mother Margaret married

16   *Weekly Times and Echo*, 27 August 1911.

a German immigrant from Sobernheim in the Rhineland, ran a successful bakery in Keetons Road, near Peek Frean's factory. He proposed to Alfred Salter that the ILP should take over his private bakery and turn it into a cooperative venture. The profits would support the ILP's political activities.

Political groups frequently raised funds through sales of groceries, tea and tobacco, or through jumble sales, but this was a much bigger project. The ILP publicised the scheme and received a very enthusiastic response. They formed a bakery management committee, with Salter as secretary. Having acquired a number of loans through a friendly society connected with the party, they opened a new state-of-the-art bakery behind the Labour Institute in July 1914, and employed Dhonau as manager. In a trade notorious for long shifts at low pay, the ILP established exemplary trade union conditions. Customers joined the cooperative venture and shared its success, and the ILP became a regular feature in their lives.

The party's forward march in Bermondsey, which looked so promising, ran into the buffers that same year when Britain went to war. The war was enthusiastically supported in many working-class areas, including Bermondsey, as young men signed up. The ILP nationally had a proud record of anti-war activism in the Boer War, and promoted pacifist politics. Its leader, Keir Hardie, said in 1913: 'All forms of militarism belong to the past ... Militarism and democracy cannot be blended. The workers of the world have nothing to fight each other about ... Patriotism is for them a term of no meaning.'

Fenner Brockway, the editor of *Labour Leader*, had launched the 'No Conscription Fellowship', which enrolled men of military age pledging to resist conscription. Alfred Salter was a staunch pacifist, as much from Quaker convictions as socialist beliefs. He helped to found a Bermondsey branch of the Fellowship. Charles Ammon, a Postal Sorters' Union activist, who was elected chair of the fledgling Bermondsey ILP at its initial meeting, was another outspoken pacifist.

The ILP's work before the war had earned it respect, affection and support from the local community and practical involvement in campaigns. Suddenly, though, many members of that community were swept up in a wave of patriotic hysteria. Opponents of the war were portrayed as 'pro-German', or as 'traitors'. The Fort Road Institute, which epitomised unity and progress, became a place of conflict and violence. Anti-war meetings there were physically attacked. The cooperative bakery came under sustained vilification for giving donations to anti-war campaigns and hiring conscientious objectors as workers. When forced conscription legislation was passed in 1916, many ILP members locally resisted this measure. In July that year, 19 members of Bermondsey ILP were imprisoned for conscientious objection and anti-war campaigning, making it extremely difficult for the branch to function.

As the war dragged on, though, the initial zeal for it among Bermondsey's working class began to subside. But those who had supported the war were slow to restore their faith in the ILP. At the parliamentary election in December 1918, and with the franchise now extended to more working-class voters, Alfred Salter fought West Bermondsey for Labour. But, like other candidates associated with anti-war campaigning such as Charlotte Despard in Battersea, he lost. Gradually, though, war-supporting workers came to doubt the 'patriotic' parties' rhetoric about a 'peace dividend' and 'homes fit for heroes' and started to fall back into the Labour fold, regardless of the ILP's war-time positioning. The 1919 local election results were more promising for the ILP. Labour captured 24 of the 54 seats and 16 Labour councillors were from the ILP, including Jessie Stephen and Ada Broughton, who had both been very active in the suffragette movement.

During 1919, the Labour Institute resumed its role as an organising centre for striking trade unionists, a support centre for strikers' families, and a base for campaigns to improve everyday lives. The most significant strike that year involved railworkers whose powerful local branch participated in a bitter national dispute. Lloyd George denounced the strikers as an 'anarchist conspiracy' but ultimately had to accede to most of their demands. The railworkers had strong support locally, and the community witnessed the anti-war ILP solidly supporting working people's struggles.

At the next local election, in 1922, Labour won 38 of the 54 seats. Ada Salter was elected Mayor – but, like Lansbury in Poplar, refused to wear the mayoral robes and chain. That same year her husband was elected to Parliament in West Bermondsey. Labour, with the ILP as its beating heart, could finally implement real and sustainable changes to the lives of Bermondsey's residents, starting to turn dreams they articulated twelve years earlier into reality. Their manifesto promised

> to make Bermondsey a fit place to live in ... to promote health, to lower the death rate, and to increase the well-being ... of the 120,000 people who live here. We will not allow our district to continue to be ... vilified by the Daily Press as a horrible, evil-smelling, slum-ridden and unlovely place. We will ... cleanse, repair, rebuild

and beautify it, make it a city of which all citizens can be proud. Bermondsey is our home and your home.

During the Bermondsey Revolution the council embarked on a massive programme of slum clearance, developing model cottage-style council housing, improving residents' living structures and sanitation, and simultaneously rescuing many of them from the clutches of slum landlords. The Salters opposed high-rise flats, but the population density and the demand arising from slum clearance meant that new council housing necessarily included four- and five-storey blocks. Nevertheless, these were built to an excellent standard, and with adequate play spaces for children.

A promise to plant 10,000 trees in the first five years in power proved too ambitious, but they did plant more than 5,000. Disused green spaces, including graveyards, were reclaimed and redeveloped as gardens, and new spaces carved out where possible to make additional gardens and playgrounds. Flower-growing competitions were enthusiastically promoted and taken up by Bermondsey's families. In 1926, the council's Beautification Committee, initiated by Ada Salter, employed 36 workers.

Radical transformations in housing were accompanied by visionary investment in health provision creating an 'NHS before the NHS'. A community health centre which still stands on Grange Road brought a range of surgeries under one roof – maternity welfare, dental surgeries, a foot clinic, and Britain's first municipal solarium for treating the borough's many TB sufferers. The council developed garden tuberculosis shelters in some parks and gardens, allowing sufferers to sleep in the fresh air, and did send some children for treatment in Switzerland.

The innovative approach to health that Bermondsey Labour pioneered also provided information so that people could confront health hazards themselves. The council customised a set of 'cinemotors' – vans with screens on the back – which stopped at housing estates, near community centres and next to parks, and used power from adapted lamp-posts to show health films to crowds that sometimes reached 1,000 people. They also showed films indoors in schools, youth clubs and workingmen's clubs, and at the Town Hall. Bermondsey's Labour Council presided over one of London's most impoverished boroughs but drastically reduced death rates, including infant mortality rates, achieving similar successes to Poplar's radical Labour Council where the ILP was also very prominent.

Radical Labour councils were able to lead a rebellion against destitution and hopelessness because they had the political legitimacy and some of the powers and resources to do so, though they constantly battled with the London County Council and central government for more resources. But the 1911 women's uprising had shown that people at the grassroots could also effect change themselves by acting collectively, in solidarity with each other, rather than waiting for politicians to take the lead. That spirit revealed itself once again on Bermondsey's streets during the 1926 General Strike. Bermondsey and its neighbouring districts, Southwark and Camberwell, were strategically important for the strike in London – Bermondsey because it included the docks and many unionised factories, Camberwell because a major bus company, Tillings, founded in 1897, was located there, and Southwark because of the confluence of roads at Elephant and Castle, used by large numbers of buses and commercial vehicles.

Bermondsey's Trades Council, to which dozens of local

unions were affiliated, formed a local Council of Action (COA). Bermondsey's radical Labour Council set up an emergency committee on the first day of the strike to liaise with that COA, and provided municipal facilities for meetings and rallies, and as a distribution point for strike pay. It helped Bermondsey COA bring out a daily strike bulletin using Labour Party and council equipment and materials. Alfred Salter regularly phoned through information for this bulletin from Parliament or TUC headquarters. Seven bulletin distribution points were established, which handed out 6,000 copies a day throughout the strike.

Southwark COA did not have the same level of support from its local politicians, but one National Union of Railwaymen (NUR) activist and Communist Party member, Tommy Strudwick, had a typewriter and printer at his home in Swan Street near Old Kent Road. He produced a newssheet for Southwark district until police raided his home, arrested him and confiscated his equipment. He was sentenced to two months hard labour for 'spreading disaffection'. The authorities identified the NUR as a key player in the local COAs. On 6 May, police invaded an NUR meeting at the Bricklayers Arms pub on Old Kent Road, arresting many strike organisers.

At Bermondsey's Surrey Docks, which normally had a 2,000-strong workforce, just seven dockers came to work on the first strike day. The 'turbulent' scenes of 1911 on Tower Bridge Road were repeated as strikers attempted to block delivery vehicles. With government encouragement, dock companies recruited blackleg labour, including soldiers and several hundred students from Oxford and Cambridge universities, to unload ships. The *South London Press* reported that Guy's Hospital students also played a 'patriotic' role signing up as 'specials' to bolster police numbers. On Thursday 6 May, when police and strikers clashed near Hay's Wharf, there were 32 arrests. The most dramatic scenes were played out at Elephant and Castle, where mounted police fought large crowds blockading the streets leading to the roundabout and preventing goods traffic and buses from getting through. Some strikers climbed up buildings and rained missiles down on the police.

During the strike, Bermondsey Council twinned with the mining village of Blaenau in the South Wales valleys. Bermondsey continued making community collections and contributed over £7,000 to support the Welsh miners over the coming months, while they continued to strike.

In the early 1930s, the whole country was in the throes of a terrible economic depression and dramatically rising unemployment. Bermondsey was partly cushioned by the diversity of its industrial base, but unemployment was high enough locally to cause severe hardship to many families. The depression forced people to compete for scarce resources, and tested the resilience and bonds of solidarity between members of the community. It undermined ordinary people's faith that their local and national politicians could find a way out of the crisis. A fast-growing fascist movement, led by Sir Oswald Mosley, exploited the situation. Although his main focus in London was north of the Thames, in the East End, he established branches and supporters' groups south of the river in Battersea, Balham, Brixton, Camberwell, Lewisham, Peckham and Streatham. But he was never able to establish a branch in Bermondsey, where trade union organisation and identification with Labour's local achievements were strong. That did not stop Mosley from planning to march thousands of fascists through Bermondsey on 3 October 1937 in an attempt to establish a local base. The dramatic events of that day are described in the next chapter.

On Saturday, 7 September 1940, the London Blitz began, and Bermondsey, whose docks and factories handled crucial supplies, suffered terrible bombing. The very next evening, a bomb destroyed the Labour Institute and the cooperative bakery, killing four bakery workers. Alfred Salter was philosophical about the fate of these two institutions that, for nearly three decades, had played such a pivotal role in advancing the struggles of Bermondsey's people for better lives, truly providing them with 'bread and roses'. He wrote to a pacifist socialist friend, 'It is a terrible tragedy but even greater is the loss of life in Bermondsey'.

LONDON LEATHER, HIDE & WOOL EXCHANGE

CHRISTYS' LONDON

ST THOMAS STREET

BOROUGH HIGH STREET

BOROUGH

GREAT DOVER STREET

DEVERELL STREET

STAPLE STREET

LONG LANE

WESTON STREET

LEATHERMARKET STREET

MOROCCO STREET

BERMONDSEY STREET

TANNER STREET

TOWER BRIDGE ROAD

ABBEY STREET

NEW KENT ROAD

LOWER BRIDGE ROAD

MASON STREET

OLD KENT ROAD

THE GRANGE

GRANGE ROAD

SPA ROAD

ALSCOT ROAD

MANDELA WAY

DUNTON ROAD

SOUTHWARK PARK ROAD

ALMAR GROVE ROAD

FORT ROAD

200M

WALK

Start at the corner of Southwark Park Road and Alma Grove, opposite the Harris Academy, SE16 3T2.

1. Southwark Park Road

The roundel on the building that curves into Alma Grove indicates a former public house (the Rose and Crown), but no trace remains of the pub opposite, the General Garibaldi, where local socialists and trade unionists met in the 1890s. Regulars included Harry Quelch, an associate of Lenin, and editor of the socialist newspaper *Justice*. Walk down Alma Grove and turn right into Fort Road.

2. Fort Road

As you enter the estate at the end of the street, a sign on the left marks Alfred Salter House. The Labour Institute that stood near here was the hub of Bermondsey's progressive struggles until it was destroyed in the Blitz. Behind it stood Bermondsey Independent Labour Party's (ILP) cooperative bakery. Cross diagonally rightwards through the estate, towards Dunton Road.

3. Dunton Road

Exit the estate on to Dunton Road at Dhonau House, named after John Dhonau, a socialist baker of German heritage whose private bakery business was transformed into the ILP's cooperative bakery. Turn right then left into Southwark Park Road, which becomes Grange Road.

4. Grange Road (1)

The health centre on the corner with Alscott Road was the centrepiece of Bermondsey Labour Council's radical and pioneering healthcare initiatives. Notice the sculpture, by Allan Howes, of a mother and child, high above the entrance. A notice on the entrance refers to this 'historic' health centre. Continue along Grange Road.

5. Grange Road (2)

At number 79, Bermondsey ILP established its first meeting hall, and published propaganda leaflets on a printer it installed here.

6. Grange Road (3)

The Alaska Factory, which opened in 1869, made products from seal fur. Its exterior is still intact. An information board nearby describes the company's history. Opposite is Spa Road. The artist Thomas Keyse, whose house was at the spa entrance, established a pleasure garden here in the 1700s. Pearce and Duff's Custard factory, whose workers joined the 'Women's Uprising' in 1911, was on Spa Road. Continue to Tower Bridge Road and turn right.

7. Tower Bridge Road

The scene of confrontations between police and striking transport workers during 'the great unrest' of 1911 and during the General Strike of 1926, as strikers sought to prevent delivery lorries from transporting goods to destinations across the river. A busy Sunday morning street market was held at the southern end of Tower Bridge Road for many decades. Enter the garden/ graveyard on the corner of Abbey Street.

8. *Abbey Street*

The garden behind the seventeenth-century St Mary Magdalene Church has ornate gravestones and tombs, including one for the Rolls family – later of Rolls-Royce cars. Walk through the gardens, exit on Bermondsey Street and turn right.

9. *Bermondsey Street*

Wealthy West End volunteers supporting girl and women workers established the charitable Time and Talents settlement just past the church, in the early 1900s. Christy's – the biggest hat factory in Europe – was established in the 1840s at number 175, and occupied two large buildings opposite each other. The factory used beaver, bear, marten, minx, hare and rabbit skins to make hats. Stop at the park on the corner with Tanner Street.

10. *Tanner Street*

Tanner Street's name reflects Bermondsey's leather industry, developed in the fourteenth century. The park was opened in 1929 on the site of the former Tanner Street workhouse and St Olave's Church, as part of the environmental improvement and beautification of the borough. A plaque below the noticeboard credits Alfred Salter and Bermondsey's progressive Labour Council with the park's creation. Its fountain is made from a section of St Olave's tower. Cross Bermondsey Street into Morocco Street.

11. *Morocco Street*

There are further indications of the historical leather industry here and on Leathermarket Street, including the large Morocco Store sign on the left (Morocco leather is made from goatskin). This building was originally a spice warehouse. Continue into Leathermarket Street.

12. Leathermarket Street

A Leather, Hide and Wool Exchange was established here in the late 1870s, but has now been converted into a pub. A series of relief sculptures depict the different processes of leatherwork. Follow the road round into Weston Street, past the Leathermarket industrial estate, converted largely into studios. The Leather Market was established here in 1833. It suffered considerable bomb damage in the Blitz. Turn right into Long Lane.

13. Long Lane

Thousands of anti-fascists erected barricades here, to prevent Mosley's British Union of Fascists marching through Bermondsey. See Chapter 10.

14. Staple Street

Pink's jam factory was established here in the 1880s. Its workers were prominent in the women's strikes of 1911. The factory was closed in 1925 and demolished to make way for municipal housing in the 1930s. Continue on Long Lane and turn right into Borough High Street.

15. Borough High Street

The John Harvard Library celebrates a seventeenth-century local clergyman who went to America and left a bequest, with money he had inherited, to help establish an education facility – Harvard University! The local history library at the back of the building is on the site that was once Marshalsea prison, where Charles Dickens' father was held.

Bermondsey Labour Institute.

Middle section of Cable Street mural.

10

NO PASARAN!

Cable Street and Long Lane

Rebel movements of the 1830s, such as the Chartists, placed democracy at the heart of their agenda. But, 100 years later, London's fastest-growing rebel movement condemned democracy as the greatest evil and aimed to replace it with dictatorship. The British Union of Fascists (BUF) commandeered the language of freedom and redemption, but threatened every democratic gain and step towards equality achieved during decades of struggle. Leading this energetic new movement was a young, charismatic, aristocratic politician: Sir Oswald Mosley.

Mosley won a Conservative seat in Harrow, West London, at the age of 22, regaining the same seat twice, as an Independent, after falling out with the Tories over Ireland.[1] He flirted with the Liberals but joined Labour (gaining a reputation for extra-parliamentary flirting, too), and won a by-election for Labour in the West Midlands seat of Smethwick in 1926.[2] His first wife, Cynthia 'Cimmie' Curzon, daughter of India's former Viceroy, joined him on the Labour benches when she won Stoke-on-Trent in 1929.

---

1   Mosley supported self-determination for the Irish people in a united Ireland and was a harsh critic of the Black and Tans.

2   In 1964 this safe Labour seat achieved national notoriety when it unexpectedly returned a Tory majority as voters were swayed by a campaign crudely exploiting racial tensions.

By February 1931, the economic crash had neared its peak. Unemployment in Britain had almost doubled from an unprecedented 1.5 million in 1929. Mosley had proposed radical remedies influenced by his close associate, John Maynard Keynes, but a suspicious Labour hierarchy rejected them and thwarted Mosley's political ambitions.[3] That month, the Mosleys and several Labour activists, including a handful of MPs, left Labour to form the New Party. A party of 'action based on youth' mobilising 'energy, vitality and manhood to save and rebuild the nation', it combined left- and right-wing policies and unashamedly advocated dictatorship. It had a militaristic internal hierarchy, and its own physical defence force (the 'Biff Boys'), trained by Oxford-educated Peter Howard, who captained the English Rugby Union team, and the recently retired East End boxer, Ted 'Kid' Lewis, born Gershon Mendeloff to Jewish immigrants.

The New Party's trajectory became clearer after Mosley returned from a fact-finding mission to Europe, centred on Mussolini's fascist Italy, in early 1932. In October 1932 the New Party rebranded itself as an insurrectionary movement called the British Union of Fascists and dressed its members in jackboots and militaristic black uniforms with lightning flash armbands. It launched a weekly newspaper, the *Blackshirt*, in February 1933, with the slogan 'Britain First'. Issue 1 declared: 'On to Fascist Revolution!' Mosley's emphasis on young people featured powerfully in BUF propaganda. Other parties, he said, only called upon youth 'to immolate themselves on the battlefield'; his party offered young people 'the chance ... to serve the ... country in times of peace'. A powerful message for all who had lived through the First World War.

---

3   Nationalisation of key industries, public works programmes, higher pensions and protectionist trade and industry policies.

The fascists recruited a mini-army of 200 Blackshirts – largely unemployed youth – to live in its Chelsea barracks. A pair of boots, three meals a day and daily wages from three shillings and sixpence to ten shillings and sixpence were attractive bait. Food tickets were issued at a 7.30 a.m. roll call. Blackshirts worked until 5 p.m., though some had evening duties supporting public meetings. They needed a signed pass to leave the barracks, and at 11.15 p.m. it was 'lights out'.

Beyond this mini-army, Mosley's movement in London did not initially pursue the young or hungry.[4] Under the name January Club, it hosted wining and dining soirees at the Ritz and the Savoy for well-heeled potential recruits. They dined on fine food while Mosley whined about broken Britain. His biggest catch, in late 1933, was press baron Lord Rothermere whose *Daily Mail* outstripped all competitors. He also published the *Daily Mirror*, the *Sunday Pictorial* and London's *Evening News*.

Outside London, Mosley wooed miners in the Northeast and Wales, cotton workers in Lancashire, farmers in Dorset, and small business owners and unemployed ex-military in many towns. Having established 500 local branches, an unpredictable turn of events during 1934 forced the BUF leaders to drastically rethink, after which the movement focused primarily on east London where they had members but no branches.

On 14 January 1934 Mosley's movement received an extraordinary boost. Britain's widest-read newspaper published a double-page spread proclaiming 'Hurrah for the Blackshirts'. Rothermere's article rehashed Mosley's stock phrases: the 'tired old gang' of 'senile politicians'; the 'revival of national strength'; and the 'new age requires new methods'. Rothermere claimed

---

4   Battersea was an exception – see Chapter 6.

that young people wanted Britain 'to develop that spirit of patriotic pride ... which has transformed Germany and Italy'. He provided contact details so 'young men' could join up. Mosley, a suffragettes' supporter in the 1920s, wanted women recruits too; Rothermere was more old-school.[5]

With Rothermere's backing, though, Mosley planned an ambitious set of indoor rallies in London. The first filled the Albert Hall on 22 April. Rothermere's rival, Lord Beaverbrook, gushed: 'The peroration was perfect ... Suddenly Sir Oswald's voice ceased ... the cheers and the handclapping rose to a storm.'[6] The *Manchester Guardian*, allergic to Mosley's hyper-nationalist doctrines, noted several occasions where applause became 'almost rapturous', especially when Mosley told Britain's Jews to 'put Britain before Jewry'.

The second rally, at Olympia, attracted 15,000 people but was a public relations disaster for Mosley. Workers snapped up cheap tickets, while the most expensive ones were presented by captains of industry seeking decisive leadership in hazardous times, and couples arriving in Daimlers and Rolls-Royces. The political class was there too: 150 MPs searching for inspiration, while some peers wore black shirts – blending in with 2,000 others similarly attired, half of them stewards.

Two radical left-wing forces – the Communist Party (CP) and the Independent Labour Party (ILP) combined to confront Mosley's movement ideologically and on the streets. The CP, which launched the *Daily Worker* newspaper in 1930, had previously denounced more mainstream Labourites as 'social fascists',

---

5 Three prominent suffragettes – Mary Richardson, Norah Elam and Mary Mien – became very active within the BUF.

6 *Daily Express*, 23 April 1934.

but it was jolted by events in Germany in January 1933, where communists and socialists fought each other and the Nazis took power. In 1932 the ILP shed members when it freed itself from the discipline of a rightward-drifting Labour Party, but was committed to intensifying its grassroots campaigns.

The day before the rally, Mosley assured Police Commissioner Viscount Trenchard that BUF stewards would maintain order inside the hall since the BUF had trained stewards, and proposed that the police focus on anti-fascist demonstrators outside the building. Trenchard complied. However, dozens of anti-fascists surreptitiously ensconced themselves *inside*. Rothermere's papers had offered £1 and a free rally ticket to authors of published letters beginning 'Why I like the Blackshirts'. Anti-fascists wrote convincing spoof letters, obtained tickets, and forged more.

In the hall a spotlight illuminated Mosley, who believed his hour had come, but three minutes into his speech a heckler shouted 'Down with Mosley, down with Mussolini, down with Hitler. Fascism means hunger and war!' Three minutes later a similar interjection emanated elsewhere. The outbursts continued like clockwork. One protester climbed the rafters for an aerial heckle. On the leader's signal, stewards concealing knuckle-dusters under their gloves viciously beat up further hecklers inside the hall; a 21-year-old student, Jack Miller, was thrown over a balcony and received serious head injuries. Stewards inflicted further beatings in the gallery surrounding the hall before dumping bloodied hecklers outside.

Doctors treated 80 protesters that night. If Mosley imagined this display would impress business magnates who might require a force to combat militant workers, he misjudged them. Most were repelled by these methods and soon withdrew their backing.

His explicit anti-Semitism alienated others. At Olympia Mosley denounced Labour politicians 'inspired by the German Jew, Karl Marx', Tories who admired 'the Italian Jew Benjamin Disraeli', and Liberals led by that 'typical John Bull, Herbert Samuel'. Rothermere took several weeks to observe others' reactions then distanced himself through a public letter exchange, hypocritically citing Mosley's anti-Semitism, while continuing to idolise Hitler.[7]

Mosley's party went into free-fall. The White City rally pencilled in for August was replaced with a September gathering in Hyde Park, pre-empting the embarrassment of empty seats. The *Blackshirt* showed snapshots of saluting supporters; other newspapers, though, used panoramic images showing 5,000 fascists encircled by police and 100,000 anti-fascist protesters, who drowned out Mosley's speech.

The growing anti-fascist movement could not foresee the consequences of its success. After the Olympia and Hyde Park fiascos, they expected Mosley's movement to melt away. Instead it reinvented itself, focusing on east London – an area known for militant industrial struggles and home to London's largest Jewish community, many of whom came to Hyde Park in response to CP leaflets printed in Yiddish. Two young Jewish communists, Max Levitas and Jack Clifford, eager to mobilise others, were arrested at 4 a.m. near Nelson's Column. The plinth bore a slogan: 'All out on September 9 to fight fascism.' Levitas had a wet paint-brush in his pocket. He failed to convince Magistrate Barker that, although he intended to paint slogans, he hadn't. Levitas

---

7   Rothermere continued to avidly support Adolf Hitler until just before the Second World War broke out.

was fined £5.[8] The *Jewish Chronicle* urged Jews concerned about fascism to stay indoors and avoid adding to the police's troubles; the first of several times that East End Jews would ignore *meyvins* (self-appointed experts) commenting from a distance.

The BUF opened its first east London branch, in Bow, in October 1934, signalling its intent to build a populist, working-class, fascist movement especially in Irish-Catholic areas bordering Jewish communities. Mosley thought he was pushing an open door, encouraging anti-Semitism there. His emergent movement would have visible targets on which to vent their growing frustration about their own circumstances. One year later, *Blackshirt* writer Clement Bruning celebrated the movement's 'great popular support in East London'. The BUF, he said, had brought 'hope and sunlight into lives darkened by long years of hunger, squalor and despair', and shown how 'to cast off the foreign yoke of a domineering, all pervading Yiddish culture, which strives to make East London take on the character of Odessa or Warsaw'.[9]

Mosley still relished his central London showpieces. At the Albert Hall in late October 1934, he announced a 'new battle in British history', in which the 'great cleansing spirit of fascism' was pitted against the 'unclean, alien influence in our national and imperial life' – Jews. In March 1935, he returned to the Albert Hall, to condemn the Jewish community as the 'nameless, homeless and all-powerful force which stretches its greedy fingers from the shelter of England ... grasping the puppets of

---

8   Report in the *Blackshirt*, 14 September 1934, entitled 'Jews desecrate Nelson's Column'. On Max Levitas's 99th birthday in June 2014 the author presented him with an enlarged copy of this report.

9   *Blackshirt*, 4 October 1935.

Westminster, dominating every party of the state'.[10] But East End Jews, too busy looking for work to grasp puppets, were more worried by local speakers on soapboxes, inciting their non-Jewish neighbours against them, than Mosley's theatrical antics in glitzy venues. The fascists built vibrant branches in Bow, Bethnal Green, Limehouse and Shoreditch. At first they parachuted-in experienced street orators but gradually developed a cadre of well-known local speakers including Mick Clarke and Owen Burke, who drew support especially among Catholics.

The physical threat to East End Jews grew as the fascists introduced new strains of anti-Semitic propaganda. In February 1936, Mosley's movement became the British Union of Fascists *and National Socialists*, a shift from Mussolini's fascism towards Hitler's more racially obsessed brand. Until then, most BUF anti-Semitism targeted Jewish *behaviour*, alleging that Jews were price-cutters, sweating employers, slum landlords, pedlars of criminality and vice, and physically violent against fascists. In 1936 fascist street-orators began to describe Jews as 'rats and vermin from the gutters of Whitechapel' and 'hook-nosed, yellow skinned dirty Jewish swine'. Speakers declared: 'It is gentiles versus Jews, white man versus black man.' Jews were 'a species of sub-humanity'.[11] By declaring Jews less than human, they legitimised brutality. Physical attacks, death threats, daubings and smashed windows became daily occurrences. East End Jews complained that the police failed to protect them.

Parliament debated anti-Semitic terror in east London in March and July that year. Local MPs detailed dozens of sickening

---

10 *Blackshirt*, 29 March 1935.

11 D. Rosenberg, *Battle for the East End*, Nottingham: Five Leaves, 2011, pp 100–1.

incidents. The Home Secretary denied police partiality and asked, pathetically, for 'everyone on all sides' to 'behave reasonably'. Beleaguered East End Jews sought help from their West End-based community leaders, but the Anglo-Jewish Association and Board of Deputies trivialised or dismissed their claims, while the *Jewish Chronicle* generally downplayed the threat.[12] Local Jewish activists concluded that they had to find solutions within the East End by mobilising and empowering the local Jewish community and gaining support from local non-Jews.

The *Arbeter Ring* (Workers' Circle) became the catalyst. Its Jewish Labour Council called a conference in July 1936 at ABSA House, 46 Commercial Road. Delegates came from 87 Jewish organisations and associations, including synagogues, youth groups, trade unions and friendly societies. This conference created the Jewish People's Council Against Fascism and Antisemitism (JPC), a united grassroots body ready to combat the fascists and make common cause with non-Jewish antifascists. The JPC took a sophisticated view of Mosley's endgame, understanding how he was using anti-Jewish violence and anti-Semitic rhetoric to gain power and overthrow democracy. The JPC argued that all who valued democracy had an interest in fighting both anti-Semitism and fascism. Mosley dismissed the JPC as a 'Communist front'. It was much broader, but several leading members were communists, and this contributed to its success. Within CP branches, the Jewish and Irish communities that the fascists tried to set against each other began to build cooperation.

---

12 The exception was a *Jewish Chronicle* special correspondent reporting from the East End in July/August 1936, who gave more realistic assessments of the problems Jews faced there.

British
Union of
Fascists
mobilising
leaflet.

The JPC organised public meetings with joint Jewish/non-Jewish platforms to attract mixed audiences. When Mosley announced plans to invade Jewish areas of the East End on 4 October, promising 'four marching columns and four great meetings' to celebrate the BUF's fourth anniversary, the JPC petitioned the Home Secretary to ban the march, collecting nearly 100,000 signatures of local Jews and Gentiles in two days. Home Secretary Sir John Simon said freedom of speech and movement was vital for democracy, and privileged the BUF's freedom over the local community's voice, so the JPC urged 'Citizens of London' to collectively ban the march themselves.

The ILP and CP both played crucial roles in the final mobilisations, as did the Labour League of Youth – a radical Labour

Party segment. The CP, though, had to overcome a severe wobble in the week preceding the event. When Mosley chose to march on 4 October he was deliberately disrupting the CP's plans. Its Young Communist League had booked Trafalgar Square that day for an anti-Franco rally aiming to raise £100 towards Spanish Medical Aid. Faced with Mosley's spoiler, the CP proposed to go to Trafalgar Square to rally for Spain, then march to the East End to show opposition to Mosley, and hold an evening meeting in Shoreditch, a Blackshirt stronghold. But with the march to Trafalgar Square commencing as Mosley would be entering the East End, the march back east could only be a token gesture. Local CP branches rebelled, continuing their work to prevent Mosley's march. Halfway through the week the Party's London District Committee cancelled the Trafalgar Square rally and printed over its leaflets, 'Alteration: Rally to Aldgate 2pm'. Gardiners Corner clock tower at Aldgate overlooked the streets which Mosley's troops intended to pass through.

On Thursday morning, CP branch secretaries received a revised plan and embarked on 72 hours non-stop activity to maximise numbers demonstrating and make tactical preparations. They set up ad hoc medical points where anti-fascists could receive treatment arising from expected confrontations, without lying in hospital waiting to be arrested; identified places where youngsters could roll marbles under police horses to halt charges; appointed a network of runners to carry information and direct crowds to maximum effect; and gathered materials to erect barricades in Cable Street and surrounding streets (assuming correctly that fascists would be redirected there if Gardiners Corner was blockaded). Walls were whitewashed and pavements chalked with anti-fascist slogans and mobilising calls. The *Daily Worker*'s special London Supplement published on the Saturday directed protesters to strategic points.

Trade union militants mobilised Jewish sweatshop workers, and dock and railway workers – many of Irish heritage. The Irish community's role would be pivotal, since Mosley's project of cementing an East End base depended on exploiting antagonisms between Irish and Jewish communities. Beyond the East End, unions with a record of anti-fascist activism mobilised members too.

While grassroots bodies prepared for defiance, the leaders of the main political parties, and the TUC, and editors of mainstream newspapers advised people to stay indoors. The *Jewish Chronicle* published an 'urgent warning', instructing Jews to 'keep away'. It declared: 'Jews who ... become involved in ... disorders, will be actively helping antisemitism.' Rabbis read similar messages from the Board of Deputies to their congregants 24 hours before the demonstration.

East End Jews voted with their feet. Tens of thousands, supported by local non-Jews, completely blockaded Gardiners Corner. Anti-fascist transport workers parked trams in front of Gardiners as a barricade. Mounted police swung long truncheons and broke heads but the wall of people stood firm.

Five-year-old Binnie Yankovitch had a bird's eye view of the action from her Sunday morning dance class on the top floor of Gardiners. Binnie's parents knew that an anti-fascist demonstration would take place that afternoon but assumed she would be safely home before then. However, Binnie and her friends were still dancing when the conflagration began:

there was this incredible noise ... [we] kids rushed to the window ... The people were fighting the police ... horses neighing and ... rearing up ... police hitting men with their truncheons ... people shouting, running, throwing things, holding their heads with blood pouring down their faces. I never went back to dance class again.[13]

Unable to clear a path through Gardiners Corner the police considered an alternative march route further south, closer to Royal Mint Street where the fascists were waiting. Directly opposite them was Cable Street – a narrow artery leading from the city towards the docks. The street was lined with shops beneath tenement flats. The name plates – Feldman's buttonholes, Feigenbaum's provisions, Wonofsky's boot repairers, Lefcovitch's stationers – typified Cable Street's first half mile.[14] The shopkeepers and most residents on this stretch were Jewish. There were fewer Jewish businesses at the Limehouse end. Names such as Kelly, O'Brien, Higgins and Sullivan adorned shop-fronts there. Fascists and anti-fascists had battled for the allegiance of the Irish community, and Cable Street was a barometer of this struggle.

At the City end shopkeepers pulled down their shutters. Anti-fascists built barricades. An overturned lorry filled the width of the street, buttressed by bedding and furniture. Members of Cable Street's Irish community and their local friends came to the Jewish end to help repel fascist interlopers. Dockers and railway workers carried crowbars to lift paving stones and reinforce the barricades. Labour League of Youth activist, Aubrey Morris,

---

13 Interview with Binnie Yeates (née Yankovitch) by the author, in 2011, for the film, *From Cable Street to Brick Lane*, by Hazuan Hashim and Phil Maxwell.

14 Olive Lefcovitch who ran the stationery shop was the cousin of the author's grandfather.

whose grandmother owned a bagel bakery in Cable Street, recalled the first wave of mounted police attempting to clear Cable Street being 'pelted from ground level with broken paving and cobble stones and from every window with missiles ranging from filled piss-pots to lumps of wood, rotten fruit and old bedding'. Women kept up this aerial barrage. 'As more police entered the fray,' Morris recalls, 'a large number of dockworkers ... helped sustain the resistance.'[15]

By late afternoon the police conceded defeat. They ordered Mosley to turn round and disperse his followers. Mosley accused the government of surrendering to 'red and Jewish terror', but complied. Exuberant anti-fascists marched to Victoria Park Square, occupying a platform that local fascists had been protecting for their leader. At a meeting on the 75th anniversary of the battle, Cable Street veteran, Ubby Cowan, commented, 'The Home secretary had said there could be a march, so we gave him one!'[16]

The words, 'They shall not pass!' (borrowed from the Spanish Republicans simultaneously resisting Franco's forces) were chalked on pavements and barricades, whitewashed on walls, and chanted by anti-fascist demonstrators. Twenty-one-year-old Charlie Goodman was one of 79 anti-fascists arrested on 4 October, and received a custodial sentence. One of his prison experiences highlighted the clash between the conservative Jewish establishment and rebellious East End Jews. Goodman recalled:

15 A. Morris, *Unfinished Journey*, London: Artery, 2006, pp.54–5.

16 Talk by Ubby Cowan at a Cable Street commemorative meeting at the Jewish Museum, London, October 2011.

I was visited by a Mr Prince from the Jewish Discharged Prisoners Aid society ... an arm of the Board of Deputies [who] called all the Jewish prisoners together and asked 'What are you here for?' ... one chap said: ' ... I've been out of work, things have been bad ... I went and did a bust (robbery).' Prince replied, 'Don't worry, we'll look after you.' The next five or six received the same response and then he came to me. 'What are you here for?' he asked. 'Fighting fascism,' I said. 'You!' said Prince. 'You are the kind of Jew who gives us a bad name ... it is people like you that are causing all the aggravation to the Jewish people.'

Goodman became one of approximately 200 Eastenders whose experience in Cable Street impelled them to volunteer for the International Brigades to fight Spanish fascism. He returned from Spain wounded. At least 36 Eastenders never returned. In 1939, as the Second World War started, Goodman enlisted in the British army, but like other *brigadistas*, who had actually used weapons against fascists, he was given a menial role. He confided that his first 'action' in the war was punching his own superior officer for making an anti-Semitic remark.[17]

Despite their massive setback at Cable Street, the fascists saw the local elections of March 1937 as the opportunity to make their east London political breakthrough. They concentrated on their three strongest areas, Bethnal Green, Limehouse and Shoreditch, standing two candidates in each. They paired high profile party ideologues with well-known local activists. The *Blackshirt*

---

17 C. Goodman, 'The East End Battles On', *Jewish Socialist*, Spring 1985; and informal conversations with the author, mid-1980s to early 1990s.

confidently announced: 'The March to Victory Begins'. They failed to win any seats. In Bethnal Green they took 23 per cent of the vote but, on average, across the three areas, four out of five voters rejected the fascists. Mosley accused Jews of block-voting Labour to defeat his candidates. But Jewish voters were concentrated in Whitechapel, and were relatively insignificant in the districts the BUF contested. Certainly the Jewish People's Council campaigned vigorously and influenced voters during the election, but it was overwhelmingly non-Jewish East Enders who defeated Mosley at the ballot box.

In July 1937 the BUF applied for permission to march through Limehouse but the Home Office refused. When the fascists sought permission to march through the East End in October 1937, exactly a year after the Battle of Cable Street, they were again stymied after local organisations lobbied the new Home Secretary, Samuel Hoare. Undeterred, the *Blackshirt*'s newly appointed editor, A. K. Chesterton (a cousin of the writer G. K. Chesterton) promised to invade 'unconquered' areas with propaganda, insisting that 'On October 3rd we shall march again.'

Still smarting with disbelief that East End Irish dockers had supported the Jews, Mosley selected another dockers' area – this time south of the Thames. The fascists announced a route from Parliament Square to New Kent Road, then through Tooley Street and Dockhead to an open-air rally at Mill Pool in West Lane, Bermondsey. Bermondsey's Communist Party immediately proposed a counter-march and won instant support from the local ILP. Bermondsey and Rotherhithe Trades Council, representing 60 local trade union branches, came on board and issued a belligerent anti-fascist statement:

> Mosley has no branch in Bermondsey – he represents
> no mass movement ... This spot ... is surrounded by the
> new flats erected by the Labour Council ... a monument
> to Labour's magnificent record of social progress in the
> borough. It was as if he came to demolish these buildings
> brick by brick before the very eyes of the people who put
> them up.

Local political figures lobbied the Home Office to ban the march but the Home Secretary argued that, since very few Jews lived there, the threat to individuals was negligible. Local radicals, including the Trades Council, favoured a militant response but there were divisions on tactics. London's Labour Party Executive suggested a boycott, allowing the march to pass, ignored, through empty streets. A respected local churchman, Revd Leslie Davidson, Rotherhithe Labour MP, Ben Smith, and the left-leaning *News Chronicle* supported this strategy. Smith told a large public meeting that Mosley's procession would happen anyway, but 'If we leave the route empty we will have achieved our object. We can have unity for a boycott but not for force.' His audience rebelled. The majority favoured direct confrontation to block Mosley's march. Over the next few days several local Labour Party branches defied the London Labour Party Executive, declaring their support for a militant counter-protest.

The day before the march, the *Blackshirt* reserved its front page for Mosley's florid anniversary message:

> ... five years of advance in the face of money power, press
> power, party power and Jewish power ... during which
> the flame of the faith has grown within us until the blaze

of our belief and of our determination lights the dark places of our land and summons our people as a beacon of hope and of rebirth.

The bombshell was tucked away inside the paper. The march route had been altered: the starting and finishing points were unchanged, but it would now pass through Marshalsea Road, Long Lane and Abbey Street, taking it through the heart of working-class Bermondsey. This development gave added impetus to those planning to physically prevent the fascists entering the area.

Mosley's supporters assembled near Millbank. Banned by the 1937 Public Order Act from wearing a political uniform, Mosley wore a grey jacket over his black shirt. Some 3,000 marchers formed up three abreast in a procession, convoyed by 30 mounted police at the front, and busloads of foot police bringing up the rear; 'one policeman for every fascist marcher', the *Daily Mirror* remarked.

Just as at Cable Street, thousands of anti-fascists constructed their own barricades with locally available materials. In Long Lane, protesters 'borrowed' a huge water tank from a nearby factory, which became the centre of a 30-foot wide barricade. The *News Chronicle* reported: 'Iron ovens, cisterns and wheelbarrows were chained together and strung across roads.' The *Daily Herald* described how

Barricades of costers' barrows, fences with barbed wire, with red flags flying at the top, were flung up at incredible speed; when police tore them down, others were erected a few yards further on ... Mounted and foot police, with lashing batons, swept ... into the crowds of anti-fascist demonstrators ... Missiles were hurled from roofs: eggs, stones and fireworks were flung at the marchers and at police horses.

The *News Chronicle* described how mounted police 'charged down Staple Street into the crowd in Long Lane ... One man who was being taken away by the police after being struck on the head with a baton was rescued by a crowd of about 40 dockers.'

Faced with angry crowds and improvised barricades, the police diverted Mosley's troops from their chosen route and led them instead around the rim of the borough. The *Daily Worker* reported that, when they finally returned to their planned path and reached Jamaica Road, they 'met another barricade ... of men, women and children from the great flats that Labour has built in Bermondsey'. Banners hanging from these blocks proclaimed: 'Socialism builds. Fascism destroys. Bermondsey against fascism.'

Mosley never reached Mill Pool where he planned to address local people at an open-air rally. The police funnelled his marchers into Southwark Park Road, cordoned off local side streets, leaving Mosley speaking only to his marchers. Meanwhile, anti-fascists occupied Mill Pool, where a Communist Party speaker, Ted Bramley, said: 'The 100 per cent cockney borough of Bermondsey has given the same answer to Mosley as the Jewish lads and girls did in Stepney just twelve months ago.'

Bermondsey's protest involved smaller numbers than the East End in 1936, but the authorities' response was harsher. Several East End Jews were among 111 people arrested. Magistrate Campion commented, 'It is extraordinary how many of the population of Whitechapel and the East End seemed to choose Bermondsey for a Sunday afternoon walk.' Campion condemned the anti-fascist demonstrators, for causing disorder and threatened to punish them 'vigorously'. At least 23 custodial sentences were imposed. Former dock union secretary, Frederick Thompson, aged 60, received three months after being identified at the centre of a 'violent crowd'; John Morton received five months for assault and three months for insulting behaviour after he tried to rescue another man who had been arrested. Betsy Malone, 23, was treated more lightly – fined a pound for taking a running kick at a policeman and telling him to arrest someone his own size!

The *Blackshirt* put its best gloss on a frustrating day, insisting that their marchers *did* pass despite the 'violence of the apes'. But the defeat at Bermondsey represented the last of the major street confrontations between the two rival rebel movements of 1930s London. After Bermondsey, Mosley's movement struggled to maintain its working-class base or make further inroads in the capital's poorer districts.

It is tempting to attribute the BUF's defeat in London to the superior street tactics used by the anti-fascists. Each major public show of fascist strength had been countered, especially in Hyde Park, Cable Street and Bermondsey. Mosley himself made many errors, starting with the Olympia fiasco. But an additional strategy cementing these street victories and preventing the fascists from dividing Londoners along ethnic lines was enacted in the housing sphere, especially in the East End where people lived in overcrowded, damp, dilapidated accommodation, at the mercy of private slum landlords, who evaded demands for rent controls, put off making repairs, but moved swiftly to evict families in arrears. Mosley's movement tried to convince non-Jewish tenants, especially those living in compact Irish communities, that Jews monopolised the best housing and best jobs locally, when, in truth, both peoples suffered. But impoverished communities rarely encountering each other directly were vulnerable to messages harnessing fear and envy.

The Stepney Tenants Defence League (STDL) was a broad-based, grassroots organisation, started by communist activists, which began working on estates where Jews and non-Jews lived side by side. The STDL drew tenants together in joint campaigns to reduce rents, improve their estates, and defend those at risk of evictions. The movement mushroomed between 1937 and 1939, spreading to other East End districts. Two people from different backgrounds but sharing common values, who played key roles in the STDL, were Father John Groser and Phil Piratin.

Groser came from Australia but studied theology in Yorkshire. He worked in a slum parish of Newcastle, and then as an army chaplain during the First World War, during which he expressed the view that the war was caused by capitalism. He then spent two years working in Cornwall before taking a post at St Michael's Church, Poplar, in 1922. By then he had familiarised himself with Conrad Noel's Catholic Crusade for Social Justice, which aimed to create heaven on earth rather than painting heaven as the reward for a good life.[18] Groser, a Labour Party supporter, moved to Christ Church, in Watney Street, Stepney in 1929, as the economic depression was rendering life hell on earth for the poorest Eastenders. He helped congregants with their daily

---

18 Noel was known as the 'Red Vicar' of Thaxted where he lived from 1910 until his death in 1942.

problems and encouraged them to fight for their rights. In 1932 he organised a conference on unemployment locally, and spoke of how unemployment caused physical depression, ill health, 'frustration of personality, the loss of proper self-respect' and created 'an embittered and hopeless section of the community'. People devoid of hope were ripe for receiving fascist messages that promised to restore their self-esteem.

Phil Piratin was born on Coke Street, Whitechapel, to Ukrainian Jewish immigrants. He focused on the same pressing problems as an atheist and materialist. Piratin demonstrated outside Mosley's Olympia meeting in 1934, joining the Communist Party a week later. He struggled to understand how an aristocratic interloper such as Mosley got a hearing among poor Eastenders, but was convinced it was not simply by pushing anti-Semitism. He surreptitiously attended local fascist meetings and observed:

> There were certain latent antisemitic prejudices ... but above all these people ... [lived] miserable squalid lives. Their homes were slums. Many were unemployed. Those at work were often in low-paid jobs. We urged that the Communist Party should help the people to improve their conditions of life [so] we could show them who was really responsible for their conditions and get them organised to fight their real exploiters.[19]

Groser and Piratin encountered each other through the STDL. Groser was its president in the late 1930s. The STDL's main

---

19 P. Piratin, *Our Flag Stays Red*, London: Thames,1948.

strategy was to hold meetings enabling tenants to identify their problems – usually hygiene and health issues, vermin, lighting, urgently needed repairs – then encourage collective campaigning. Where landlords would not respond to reasonable demands, the STDL initiated rent strikes. Tenants placed their rent in the hands of a third party. The STDL informed the landlord that the rent was available to be collected when the repairs were done, hygiene was improved and so on. Several slum landlords refused to negotiate and tried to enforce evictions, but they met united resistance from their tenants. The STDL won a spate of victories, including a landmark case in June 1937 on Paragon Mansions estate near Stepney Green, where STDL action prevented the eviction of

Barricades in Cable Street, 4 October 1936.

two large families of BUF members who had fallen behind with their rent.[20] In the aftermath, those families tore up their BUF membership cards. As Jewish and non-Jewish neighbours built friendship and solidarity in the course of fighting for housing rights, it made fascist messages scapegoating Jews less credible.

Halfway along Cable Street there is a remarkable artwork covering one side of a large building. The Cable Street mural, commissioned in 1976, and completed in the early 1980s, depicts the dramatic events of 4 October 1936 when Eastenders united against Mosley's fascist invaders. The location is very apt. West of the mural was the Jewish section of Cable Street; the east leads to the Irish end. On the day of the battle, people walked past this building from the Irish end, not to attack the Jews but to support them. The building was St George's Town Hall. In March 1939, it hosted a large conference addressed by Michael Shapiro and Ella Donovan, leading STDL activists of Jewish and Irish heritage respectively. Communities that could have been at each other's throats were discussing 'Better Housing for the East End' and planning a common future.

Shortly before this conference, two East End estates began simultaneous rent strikes through the STDL. One was Brady Street Mansions, an overwhelmingly Jewish estate in Whitechapel; the other, Langdale Mansions, a more mixed estate closer to Cable Street. Hampstead-based landlords, rejoicing in the names Craps and Gold, owned both estates. This became the STDL's longest running dispute, eventually resolved on 30 June 1939 after 21 weeks, during which the estates were barricaded with barbed wire and a constant rota of pickets guarded

---

20 In Hayfield Passage. A gated community stands on the site today.

against incursions by bailiffs or police. Only residents could enter. Regular tradesmen and milkmen carried a special pass. The tenants won rent reductions; £10,000 of arrears was written off; the landlords agreed to spend £2,500 on repairs immediately and £1,500 annually in subsequent years.[21]

By then the BUF had become irrelevant in the East End. The 'people's victories' in Cable Street and Bermondsey in 1937 and the crucial work of the STDL had stopped Mosley from consolidating the populist movement he had tried to build among London's disadvantaged and disempowered. But he was recovering a middle-class following. Six weeks before war broke out, the BUF held an anti-war rally in Earls Court attended by 20,000 supporters. When an audience member asked Mosley what his party would do if Britain was attacked by fascist Germany, Mosley replied that if Britain was attacked by *anyone*, every BUF member would defend Britain, but, he added, 'a million Britons shall not die in your Jews' quarrel'. During the war Mosley was among nearly 1,800 individuals imprisoned as potential fifth columnists. His nemesis, the communist movement, continued to grow, despite wartime restrictions. A radical, reforming, Labour government elected in 1945 brought real material gains for working-class Londoners, proving, as Bermondsey's banners proclaimed, that while fascism destroys, socialism builds.

---

21 £2,500 then is equivalent to nearly £150,000 today.

ALDGATE EAST

ALIE STREET

LEMAN STREET

WHITECHAPEL HIGH STREET

COMMERCIAL ROAD

ALTAB ALI PARK

MULBERRY STREET

ADLER STREET

COKE STREET

PLUMBERS ROW

FIELDGATE STREET

GREENFIELD ROAD

TOWER HAMLETS INTERNATIONAL BRIGADE
— in honour of the residents and the Tower Hamlets
to fight in the International Brigade Spain 1936 – 1938
They fought alongside the Spanish people to
stop fascism and save sports and peace for all.
They went because their eyes eyes could see no other way
"No Pasaran"

CHRISTIAN STREET

BURSLEM STREET

HESSEL STREET

HESSEL STREET

HESSEL ST E1

PONLER STREET

LANGDALE STREET

CANNON STREET ROAD

COMMERCIAL ROAD

CABLE STREET

CABLE STREET

ST GEORGE'S
GARDENS

100M

282

WALK

Start at Whitechapel Art Gallery (Aldgate East Station), E1 7QX.

1. *Whitechapel High Street/Gardiners Corner*

The redbrick building diagonally opposite with a pointed silver roof replaced Gardiners department store, which closed in 1971 and collapsed in a fire a year later. Here the City and East End thoroughfares meet. This was completely blockaded on 4 October 1936, preventing the police clearing a path for Mosley's fascists. Turn left and cross over to Altab Ali Park.

2. *Altab Ali Park*

St Mary's Gardens was renamed Altab Ali Park in 1998, to commemorate a 25-year-old Bengali clothing worker killed in a racist attack in May 1978 by youngsters influenced by the political descendants of Mosley's Blackshirts. Walk through the park and turn right to St Boniface's Church.

3. *Mulberry Street*

The original German church standing here was bombed by the Nazis and rebuilt in the 1960s. Germans were one of several minorities living in the East End. Walk down Mulberry Street, turn left, then right into Fieldgate Street.

4. Fieldgate Street

The synagogue on the left began as a *shtibel* (prayer room in a house), one of dozens in the area through which Mosley wanted to march. It closed in 2013. Three Ashkenazi Synagogues still function in the East End plus one Sephardi synagogue on the East End/City Border.[22] At 15 Fieldgate Street, the Communist Party had local headquarters. Rowton House on the left (luxury apartments) was a former doss-house in which Stalin and Maxim Litvinov stayed during the 1907 Congress of the Russian revolutionary movement. Turn into Greenfield Street. Walk to the junction with Coke Street.

5. Greenfield Street

Phil Piratin, who joined the Communist Party after demonstrating outside the fascists' Olympia meeting, grew up on Coke Street then Greenfield Road (Street). Chief architect of the communists' anti-fascist strategy, he was a key figure in the Stepney Tenants Defence League. Turn left at Commercial Road.

6. Commercial Road

The Jewish People's Council Against Fascism and Antisemitism (JPC) was created at a conference in July 1936 at 46 Commercial Road. The JPC opened an office at 164 Commercial Road. The building with a decorative arch above the door at 133 was formerly the Grand Palais Yiddish Theatre, which closed in 1961. Turn right into Hessel Street.

---

22 Ashkenazi refers to Jewish communities from western, central and eastern Europe, Sephardi, to communities that were established over several centuries in Spain and Portugal before being expelled in 1492.

7. Hessel Street

Named after Phoebe Hessel, born Phoebe Smith in Stepney in 1713. She disguised herself as a man to serve in the army. This was one of the main Jewish market streets of the East End. Continue to the junction with Ponler Street.

8. Ponler Street

Just to the right was Langdale Mansions where Jewish and non-Jewish tenants united in a successful rent strike in 1939. Turn left along Ponler Street then right into Cannon Street Road. Continue to the junction with Cable Street.

9. Cable Street

Look rightwards. Between this junction and Leman Street, three sets of barricades blocked the fascists from marching through Cable Street. Turn left and cross to the Cable Street mural, depicting the events of 4 October1936, on the side of St George's Town Hall. The mural designed by Dave Binnington was adapted and completed by three artists including Paul Butler who restored it in 2011.

10. St George's Town Hall

This building hosted the Better Housing conference in March 1939. A plaque commemorates East End volunteers who went to fight against fascism in Spain. Cecil Day-Lewis penned the unattributed quote, 'They went because their open eyes could see no other way.'

Detail from Cable Street mural.

CONCLUSION

In March 2011, I stood in front of the Cable Street mural interviewing Paul Butler, one of the three artists who completed it in 1983. He was looking forward to spending the summer restoring the mural in time for the Battle's 75th anniversary celebrations in October that year.

The mural is a startling, disturbing and exciting piece of work which shows missiles, bottles and fists flying, truncheons drawn, marbles ready to be rolled under the hooves of police horses, while the fascists wait for their opportunity to march. Butler assured me 'it is not a celebration of violence'. It 'celebrates the barricade, the slogan from the Spanish civil war, "they shall not pass" ... [and] the left's solidarity – the mix of Irish dockers and Jewish workers and all the other groups involved in the Battle ... it was painted for the local community to celebrate this place', but it was also 'a monument that transcended ... [the] local aspect'. Anti-fascists from far and wide continue to visit it.

Compared with several of the rebellious campaigns recorded in this book, the community uprising against the police, who were facilitating Mosley's fascists that day, is privileged by having a large, permanent, public reminder of what took place, as well as a local committee which organises commemorative events every five years, including meetings, marches and community festivals.

Murals celebrating London's radical history are few and far between. The walk accompanying Chapter 6 includes the 'Battersea in Perspective' mural, which celebrates local heroes, of whom four are intimately connected with its radical history.

In Copenhagen Street, Islington, a mural alongside the Mitre pub commemorates the huge 1834 march that started nearby, demanding freedom for the Tolpuddle Martyrs. Two Poplar radicals, George Lansbury and the suffragette activist and rebel councillor Minnie Lansbury (Glassman), are commemorated through large rectangular plaques at separate locations on Bow Road, which detail their political involvements. Some other rebels featured in this book, though, have small circular plaques, which in most cases obscure or dilute their political radicalism.

Several local authorities in London now have plaques commemorating events. At the Highbury Barn pub in Islington in 2011, the late Tony Benn unveiled a plaque marking the Peasants' Revolt of 1381, during which they burnt down Highbury Manor House. It would seem fitting to mount a plaque at the former site of Gardiners Corner in Aldgate, where a mass blockade prevented the fascists from entering the East End in 1936 and forced the police to try, unsuccessfully, to reroute the march via Cable Street. But where could such a plaque be meaningfully mounted when the corner itself is monopolised by glass towers providing luxury flats and plush City offices?

Those who seek to illuminate the city's rebellious past and put it into a conversation with the present, so that the rebels of today and tomorrow can draw encouragement and inspiration from earlier struggles on these streets, are challenged by how quickly areas of London are being transformed, made more exclusive, and severed from their past. I hope that this book will help that conversation to take place.

The campaigns this book highlights reflect rebellions in London between the 1830s and the 1930s against different targets: political and economic elites ring-fencing democratic rights;

traditional sources of authority and moral leadership such as the churches; large employers of labour in gasworks and on the docks, as well as smaller employers exploiting sweatshop labour; and those who have sought to divide workers on racist lines. We can detect similarities in the tactics adopted to wage these struggles, recognise how one struggle influenced another, and attempt to identify common qualities among those outstanding individuals so prominent within these campaigns.

Several of these individuals had to struggle to overcome personal challenges before thrusting themselves into radical politics. Will Thorne and Ben Tillett, leading figures in industrial struggles of the1880s, both knew the hardship of long hours of work when they were six and seven years old respectively. Their colleague Tom Mann at least had the benefit of three years education from the age of six but was down a pit at ten. Rudolf Rocker, the anarchist/libertarian agitator and champion of the East End's immigrant sweatshop workers, had fought against an authoritarian regime that pervaded the orphanage in which he was confined after his parents died young. The suffragette Rosa May Billinghurst and the Chartist William Cuffay both fought against disability from their earliest years. George Lansbury endured a torrid time in his early 20s in Australia where he had been lured with promises of economic advancement. Long stretches of unemployment were interrupted by periods of work on the land where he said he felt treated like a serf.

Each of these individuals displayed great personal resilience that supported their efforts to effect change for the many among whom they organised. They were 'dreadnoughts' in the sense that the East London Federation of Suffragettes identified – people who feared nothing. They were prepared to take risks for what they considered to be right, and face the consequences, including imprisonment. And some paid the ultimate price for their activism. Minnie Lansbury died at 32, within months of having a torrid time in prison. Emily Wilding Davison was just 40 in 1913, when she never regained consciousness after her Derby Day protest. Mary Macarthur, a hugely energetic organiser of women workers who, according to her colleagues, had 'the heart of a lion', died at 40, two years after her husband and eight years after her stillborn son.

Several individuals featured in this book supported multiple struggles during years of campaigning. Charlotte Despard fought against poverty in Battersea, supported women strikers, and led campaigns for women's votes and equal opportunities through the Women's Freedom League. George Lansbury helped mobilise support for the dock strike, promoted the suffragette cause, and fought as a councillor against discriminatory rates policies imposed by the London County Council. Nellie Cressall and Minnie Lansbury were both active campaigners in the east London suffragettes before they ended up imprisoned as rebel Poplar councillors. Ben Tillett was a key organiser in the dock strike and later played an active role in establishing the *Daily Herald* newspaper. Israel Zangwill was active in the Men's League for Women's Suffrage and later in the pacifist Union of Democratic Control. However, that probably tells us as much about the linked nature of the struggles themselves as it does about the individuals who participated in them.

Campaigns linked thematically over gaps of several decades honoured the influences of previous generations of fighters. The Chartists of the 1830s, the Reform League of the 1860s and 1870s and the suffragettes in the first two decades of the twentieth century led London's assault on the exclusivity maintained by political elites. When the suffragettes adopted the purple, green and white tricolour, they consciously adopted a symbol previously used by the Chartists. At the gigantic suffragette rally in Hyde Park in 1908, speakers recalled the dramatic Reform League demonstrations of the 1860s in the very same park.

Peter Kropotkin, a Russian political exile who settled in London in 1886, argued that, 'Without mutual confidence no struggle is possible.'[1] His observation was borne out by the rebellious campaigns that have been recorded in this book. Although grassroots movements threw up extraordinary leaders, it was these movements' shared sense that change could be won, and their ability to engage in united collective actions, based on mutual confidence, especially in workplace struggles, that enabled them to sustain their campaigns and win important victories. The methods they shared – leaflets, petitions, newspapers, strikes, mass demonstrations and rallies and, where it was felt necessary, physical force – were geared towards collective rather than individual actions.

The suffragettes were one of London's most successful rebel movements but pose the biggest challenge to our understanding of how change is brought about. Their movement did not pass Kropotkin's 'mutual confidence' test. It was far from united. The Women's Freedom League (WFL) split from the dominant Women's Social and Political Union (WSPU), and the East London Federation of Suffragettes (ELFS) were forced out. The more longstanding campaigners of the National Union of Women's Suffrage Societies (NUWSS) disagreed with WSPU tactics and remained aloof from them.

---

1   P. Kropotkin, *Anarchist Morality*, Edmonton: Black Cat Press, 2005 (1897).

The WSPU can claim to be fearless and courageous tactical innovators – adding hunger strikes, stone throwing and arson attacks to the range of militant activities adopted by London's rebel campaigns – although these tactics also symbolised a move away from collective action. Other sectors of the suffrage movement maintained collective approaches and introduced their own non-violent forms of civil disobedience such as the refusal to pay taxes, the deliberate disruption of the census, and rallies on the doorsteps of government ministers' homes. Paradoxically, the divided and devolved nature of the movement meant that the suffragettes' opponents were continually challenged from many different angles. But, more pertinently, dominant suffragette histories need to give more credit to those who adopted less flamboyant, less sensational, but more sustained collective actions.

The poet and writer Anthony Anaxagorou, born in north London in 1983, has said: 'Rebellion is when you look society in the face and say I understand who you want me to be, but I'm going to show you who I actually am.'[2] He captures the spirit of defiance, the refusal to accept second-class status, and the drive for change that has animated movements for better lives in London over the last 200 years. Throughout that period, London has continued to nurture rebels and agitators, visionaries and dreamers. Their impact has been felt in every decade. Dreams have been crushed, hopes have been dashed, campaigns were won and lost and fought for all over again, and new activists have emerged.

But Anaxagorou, as the son of Cypriot migrants to London, also embodies a crucial element that dominant narratives have pushed

2   www.anthonyanaxagorou.com.

to the margins. Migrants have played a key role in several of the movements that have shaped London's rebel history, from William Cuffay, the black leader of London's Chartist movement in the 1840s, who was the son of a Caribbean slave, to the women and men of Irish heritage whose strikes at Bryant & May's match factory and on the docks ignited the new unionism. From the early Indian MPs, Dadabhai Naoroji and Shapurji Saklatvala, and Battersea's first black mayor, John Archer, who overcame entrenched racist attitudes to win popular support across communities, to the Jewish workers who fought for their rights in sweatshops and battled against Mosley's fascists, immigrants have been vital in the struggle to improve conditions for all Londoners.

A vignette in Chapter 2 described those sweatshop workers marching from the East End to Hyde Park singing a Yiddish anthem, *In Kamf*. Its closing stanza includes the line: '*Nayer kemfer vet brengen di tsayt*', which means 'new fighters/activists will be brought by the [new] times'. In 1983 and 1984, activity in London's financial district was brought to a halt by Stop the City blockades. In 1991, Trafalgar Square, location of the Bloody Sunday protests and of many political rallies since, was filled with gay and lesbian activists who staged a mass Queer Wedding ceremony. A few years later the authorities, who kept a tight rein on protests around government buildings, were outwitted by guerrilla gardeners who mounted Winston Churchill's statue and gave him a bright green mohican. In June 2011, as the Occupy movement made its presence felt in cities around the world, activists pitched a tent city outside St Paul's Cathedral that was finally evicted in February 2012.

Away from the centre, young people in black communities led uprisings against the police and set shops and cars on fire in Brixton and Broadwater Farm, Tottenham in the 1980s, and again in Tottenham in 2011, following the police shooting of Mark Duggan. The participants in 2011 were a more ethnically diverse group of impoverished lower classes in the locality including white people. Back in the heart of the City, in 2013, migrant cleaners at the Barbican, Guildhall and across Corporation of London buildings won the Living Wage after a two-year battle involving strike action organised through the radical Independent Workers Union of Great Britain (IWGB).

London remains a vibrant and rebellious city and we should honour those who had the courage, conviction and determination to blaze the trail.

BIBLIOGRAPHY

Ahmed, R. and S. Mukherjee (eds), *South Asian Resistances in Britain*, London: Continuum, 2012

Beames, T., *The Rookeries of London*, London: Thomas Bosworth, 1850

Besant, A., *Annie Besant: An Autobiography*, London: Theosophical Society, 1893

Booth, J., *Guilty and Proud of It*, London: Merlin, 2009

Branson, N., *Poplarism 1919–1925*, London: Lawrence & Wishart, 1979

Brockway, F., *Bermondsey Story: The Life of Alfred Salter*, London: ILP, 1995 (1949)

Brust, H., *I Guarded Kings: Memoirs of a Political Police Officer*, New York: Hillman-Curl, 1936

Charlton, J., *It Went Just Like Tinder*, London: Redwords, 1999

Connelly, K., *Sylvia Pankhurst*, London: Pluto Press, 2013

Davis, M., *Sylvia Pankhurst: A Life in Radical Politics*, London: Pluto Press, 1999

Despard, C., *Women in the New Era*, London: Suffrage Shop, 1910

Fishman, W., *East End Jewish Radicals 1875–1914*, London: Duckworth, 1975

—— *East End 1888*, London: Duckworth, 1988

Fryer, P., *Staying Power: The History of Black People in Britain*, London: Pluto Press, 1984

German, L. and J. Rees, *A People's History of London*, London: Verso, 2012

Gissing, G., *The Nether World*, London: Smith, Elder & Co., 1889

Goldman, E., *Living My Life, Vol. 1*, London: Pluto Press, 1988 (1931)

Goodway, D., *London Chartism 1838–1848*, Cambridge: Cambridge University Press, 1982

Jacobs, J., *Out of the Ghetto*, London: J. Simon, 1978

James, C.L.R., *Letters from London*, Oxford: Signal Books, 2006

Kapp, Y., *Eleanor Marx: The Crowded Years 1884–1898*, London: Virago, 1979 (1976)

Laity, P., *The British Peace Movement 1870–1914*, Oxford: Clarendon Press, 2002

Lansbury, G., *My Life*, London: Constable and Co., 1928

Lansbury, G., *Looking Backwards and Forwards*, London: Blackie, 1935

Linehan, T., *East London for Mosley*, London: Frank Cass, 1996

Lovett, W., *Life and Struggles of William Lovett in His Pursuit of Bread, Knowledge, and Freedom*, New York: A. A. Knopf, 1920 (1877)

Mackay, J. H., *The Anarchists*, Boston: Benj R. Tucker, 1891

Marcus, J., *Suffrage and the Pankhursts*, London: Routledge & Kegan Paul, 2005

McCarthy, T., *The Great Dock Strike 1889*, London: Weidenfeld and Nicholson, 1988

Montefiore, D., *From a Victorian to a Modern*, London: Archer, 1927

Morris, A., *Unfinished Journey*, London: Artery, 2006

Mulvihill, M., *Charlotte Despard: A Biography*, London: Pandora, 1989

Pankhurst, S., *The Suffragette Movement*, London: Virago, 1977 (1931)

Piratin, P., *Our Flag Stays Red*, London: Thames, 1948

Pugh, M., *The Pankhursts*, London: Penguin, 2002

Radice, E.A. & G.H., *Will Thorne: Constructive Militant*, London: Allen & Unwin, 1974

Raw, L., *Striking a Light: The Bryant and May Matchwomen and Their Place in History*, London: Continuum, 2009

Rocker, R., *The London Years*, Nottingham: Five Leaves/AK Press, 2005 (1956)

Rosen, A., *Rise Up Women!*, London: Routledge & Kegan Paul, 1974

Rosenberg, D., *Battle for the East End*, Nottingham: Five Leaves, 2011

Rudder, B., *Builders of the Borough*, London: Battersea & Wandsworth TUC, 1994

Russell, D. and M. Tichelar, *Class Struggles in South London 1850–1950*, London: Southwark-Lambeth History Workshop, 1981

Saklatvala, S. (Sheri), *The Fifth Commandment*, Manchester: Miranda

Press, 1991

Srebrnik, H., *London Jews and British Communism 1935–45*, London: Vallentine Mitchell, 1995

Sugden, K. (ed.), *Criminal Islington*, London: Islington Archaeology & History Society, 1989

Taylor, R., *In Letters of Gold*, London: Stepney Books, 1993

Thompson, D., *The Early Chartists*, London: Macmillan, 1971

Thorne, W., *My Life's Battles*, London: G. Newnes, 1925

Visram, R., *Ayahs, Lascars and Princes*, London: Pluto Press, 1986

Wadsworth, M., *Comrade Sak: A Political Biography*, Leeds: Peepal Tree, 1998

Wayne, L., *Union Bread*, London: Jewish Socialists' Group and Socialist History Society, 2009

White, J., *The Rothschild Buildings*, London: Routledge & Kegan Paul, 1980

—— *London in the Nineteenth Century*, London: Jonathan Cape, 2007

Wise, S., *The Blackest Streets*, London: Bodley Head, 2008

INDEX